Beyond Segregation

Multiracial and Multiethnic Neighborhoods in the United States

Michael T. Maly is Associate Professor of Sociology at Roosevelt University in Chicago.

Beyond Segregation

Multiracial and Multiethnic Neighborhoods in the United States

MICHAEL T. MALY

TEMPLE UNIVERSITY PRESS
Philadelphia

To Thais Belle Rulich-Maly —

may you inherit a more just and tolerant world

Temple University Press
1601 North Broad Street
Philadelphia PA 19122
www.temple.edu/tempress

⊗ The paper used in this publication meets the requirements of the American National Standard for Information Sciences—Permanence of Paper for Printed Library Materials, ANSI Z39.48-1992

Library of Congress Cataloging-in-Publication Data
Maly, Michael T., 1968–
    Beyond segregation : multiracial and multiethnic neighborhoods in the United States / Michael T. Maly.
        p. cm.
    Includes bibliographical references and index.
    ISBN 1-59213-134-4 (cl. : alk. paper) — ISBN 1-59213-135-2 (pbk. : alk. paper)
    1. Pluralism (Social sciences)—United States. 2. Multiculturalism—United States. 3. Ethnic neighborhoods—United States.
    4. Discrimination in housing—United States. 5. United States—Race relations. 6. United States—Ethnic relations. I. Title.

HT221.M35 2005
305.8'00973—dc22

                                                                    2004051696

2   4   6   8   9   7   5   3   1

Contents

Preface

METHODS OF STUDY

I CHOSE TO STUDY neighborhoods because they are the essential place to understand the local processes involved in the maintenance (or demise) of stable racial integration. While numerous studies on residential settlement focus on the impact of economic and demographic conditions and changes on how urban neighborhoods are formed, maintained, and reformulated along racial lines, they do not provide adequate information on microlevel actions that promote or discourage racial separateness. As Richard Taub, Garth Taylor, and Jan Dunham note in their book *Paths of Neighborhood Change:* "If ecological factors are overwhelming [to local residents], it is because of the effect of these facts on the perceptions and actions" of local residents (1984: 186). In other words, this statement has two related implications. First, integration and segregation are experienced by individuals in local communities. Second, while larger social forces (e.g., biased real estate and banking practices) influence local communities, individual action (or inaction) make these outcomes real.

Beyond Segregation is the story of the emergence, existence, and maintenance of three racially integrated communities. Using qualitative methods, I examine the vital role leaders and community groups play in neighborhood outcomes. Exploring the microlevel decisions by local leaders, as well as the conflict and negotiations of community groups working to stabilize racially changing neighborhoods, provides insight into the historical context of neighborhoods, the fluidity of neighborhood life, and the role of individual agency. By highlighting the broader lessons that can be learned and the limitations that become apparent as leaders and community groups intervene to stabilize racial change, I seek to advance our understanding of the complexity of racial integration in the increasingly multicultural world of the post–civil rights era and of the relationship between local decisions, collective action, and structural forces.

I set out to identify multiracial and multiethnic communities in New York, Chicago, and Oakland. While the cities differ in terms of region, population size, and political culture, they are all multiracial and multiethnic, given their racial and ethnic compositions and role as port-of-entry cities for immigrants. Employing a quantitative measure of neighborhood diversity (discussed in Chapter Two), I located neighborhoods that had maintained a multiethnic and multiracial mix for more than a decade and selected three communities for analysis: Uptown in Chicago, Jackson Heights in the borough of Queens, and San Antonio and Fruitvale, adjacent areas of Oakland. These communities make for some interesting comparisons and contrasts. They were all once predominantly non-Hispanic white, experienced racial change over the course of four decades, and yet were able to slow racial transition and stabilize racial integration. The unique history, racial mix, and economic character of each community allowed me to analyze efforts to maintain integration in disparate contexts.

I conducted field research between 1996 and 1999. To paint a complete picture of each community, I collected data from as many sources as possible. First, I conducted more than seventy-five open-ended interviews with leaders in the three neighborhoods to obtain the fullest picture of community life.[1] Community leaders were selected as appropriate informants based on the size of each community and their roles as representatives of organizations and interests that significantly impact community life. They also maintain positions of authority, act as intermediaries when conflict occurs, and can shape and determine the flow of resources available in a community. Although the leaders were not selected at random, care was given to interview leaders from a range of groups—elected officials, political organizations, schools, lending institutions, housing providers, real estate agents and developers, youth-oriented groups, social service agencies, religious organizations, and local advocacy organizations.

Second, I made use of whatever printed data were available. News media accounts, community group reports and newsletters, flyers, and published accounts by scholars and journalists proved excellent sources of community history and reinforced the interview data. Finally, I conducted participant observation by attending community meetings and events, and by exploring the culture of each community.[2] To increase the validity of the study, I tested the information from each source of data against that provided by the others. Each contributed to the overall goal of understanding local responses to multiethnic and multiracial integration, as well as the complex motivations of groups working toward stabilizing racially changing neighborhoods. The use of these methods offers significant insight into the responses of individuals and groups to the influence of larger social forces.

PLAN OF THE BOOK

Chapter One outlines the reality of racial segregation and the historical legacy of the prointegration movement's efforts to maintain racial integration across the metropolitan United States. Chapter Two examines residential settlement patterns by race at the neighborhood level over the past two decades. I focus on newly engendered neighborhoods with different forms of racial and ethnic integration marked by a multiethnic and multiracial character, and expanding without the conscious efforts of the prointegration movement. Chapters Three, Four, and Five present the case studies of Uptown, Jackson Heights, and San Antonio–Fruitvale as representatives of the changing form of racial and ethnic integration, including the story of how each community reacted to racial change and how contextual differences led to varied social dynamics, community debates, and organizational approaches.

Acknowledgments

THIS BOOK WOULD NOT have been possible without the efforts, openness, and patience of many. I would first like to thank all the respondents who gave of their time to share not only the details of their communities, but also their words, ideas, and various understandings of the world. I thank the many people who welcomed me into their homes and offices to share their stories. From them, I learned a great deal about community life, urban dynamics, and the importance of human agency in creating change. I specifically thank John Nicholson, Andy Lowry, Rosalinda Palacios, Rudy Greco, and Sylvia Fava.

Thanks to the U.S. Department of Housing and Urban Development for sponsoring a nine-city, fourteen-neighborhood study conducted by the Policy Research Action Group and the Leadership Council for Metropolitan Open Communities in 1995. This work, directed by Philip Nyden and John Lukehart, paved the way for my own research. Additional thanks go to HUD for awarding me one of fifteen HUD Dissertation Fellowships. This fellowship allowed me to spend significant amounts of time in New York City and Oakland. Thanks also to Roosevelt University for providing me a research leave and the Mansfield Institute for Social Justice for funds to complete the manuscript.

Many thanks to friends and colleagues who have helped me along the way. I am forever indebted to Stan Pollock not only for introducing me to the intellectual life and sociology, but for showing me that it is okay to enjoy both. Ken Johnson taught me the rigor required to do social science research properly (all the way to the end). Philip Nyden introduced me to the field of urban studies and provided me numerous opportunities to expand my research and intellectual faculties. Harvey Choldin gets credit for the title. Larry Bennett walked me through the writing process, reading every draft chapter and providing detailed comments, insight, and reassurance. At Roosevelt University, I thank the following people for providing valuable criticism and assistance: Michael Bryson, Heather Dalmage, Jeffrey Edwards, Michael Ensdorf, Douglas Knerr, and Jack Metzgar. I also thank B&P, Steve Serio, and Tony Tlougan for their unwavering support.

At Temple University Press, I thank my editor, Peter Wissoker, for his encouragement, reassurance, and humor. I also thank Jennifer French and Bobbe Needham for production assistance.

Thanks to family, particularly my parents and brothers, for their support, love, and encouragement. Most importantly I thank Amelia Rulich for entering my life and making it infinitely better. Her love, encouragement, selflessness, and sense of humor are gifts that I cherish every day. Finally, thanks to our daughter, Thais, for reminding me to enjoy each moment and focus on what truly matters.

Introduction

As I began this research, ten years ago, a chorus of scholarly and political voices proclaimed the inevitable decline of the city. The cries rang out about the plethora of problems that threatened urban centers. Claims of cities in the midst of crisis and collapse have continued. The consensus, at least among some scholars, is that older cities, beset by a myriad of social problems, have lost their luster and no longer serve their function as areas of entry for newcomers who seek economic opportunity. Indeed, while there is substantial evidence that the death knell has not rung for cities, a variety of trends in the last decades of the twentieth century painted a disturbing portrait of their health. The movement of manufacturing jobs away from cities and the departure of middle-class taxpayers led to growing numbers of poor residents in need of expensive services just as city revenues were declining. Many cities experienced fiscal crises. They lost federal dollars to fund education, infrastructure, and mass transit. Cities became more polarized between the affluent and the poor, highlighted by the rise and concentration of poverty, homelessness, and crime. In short, cities became symbols of many of our country's larger social problems.

Within this context, one aspect of concern among scholars has been the sharp division in residential settlement by race. A cadre of scholars turned its focus toward understanding the lines of racial and ethnic separation that mark housing in the metropolitan United States. A brief analysis of the literature leads to a fairly direct conclusion: urban space bears a racial stamp. The racial separateness that characterizes urban areas has been a physical, social, and symbolic indication of inequality and reflects the country's failed promise of accommodation and integration. Segregation between whites and nonwhites has reached shockingly high levels; one racial group or another dominates the majority of metropolitan neighborhoods. For example, the average white person in the United States lives in a neighborhood that is more than 80 percent white, while the average black person lives in one that is mostly black. Segregation of blacks and whites has remained at high levels for more than a century. And while Latinos and Asians are less segregated from whites in

U.S. cities and suburbs, they now live in more isolated settings than they did two decades ago.

Such racial division might not be of such concern if it were the simple result of self-segregating attitudes. The dark side of the story of urban growth and development is that high levels of racial segregation have been constructed through institutional discrimination in the real estate and banking industries, and supported by many acts of private prejudice and discrimination. Housing discrimination originated with the Federal Housing Administration (FHA) and antecedent agencies. FHA policies institutionalized a method of assessing mortgage-lending risk that systematically undervalued minority and racially mixed neighborhoods. As a result, segregation has undermined the strength of minority communities by concentrating poverty in them and by amplifying the effects of economic restructuring or change. Compared to residents of many integrated or white neighborhoods, minorities who live in segregated and isolated neighborhoods receive lower-quality education and municipal services and fewer amenities; their job access is more restricted; they are more exposed to crime and violence. This book, akin to a study of the causes of urban decline, focuses on unpacking the institutional mechanisms that perpetuate inequality and urban problems.

The volume of research on the extent of segregation and on the powerful institutional forces that maintain its boundaries makes it difficult to believe that integrated neighborhoods even exist. And, until recently, most scholars have paid scant attention to integrated spaces. The conventional wisdom of racial change has held that the inevitable results of nonwhites moving into all-white neighborhoods are racial transition and resegregation. In fact, many scholars have viewed or characterized efforts to stabilize integrated neighborhoods as fragile, if not doomed. Douglas Massey and Nancy Denton, in their popular book *American Apartheid*, take an even more cynical view, claiming that local efforts that attempt to maintain integration are "schemes" that treat merely the symptoms rather than the causes of segregation (1993: 227). From this perspective, efforts to maintain integration do not challenge the larger discriminatory system of housing allocation but only preserve a few islands of integration in a sea of segregation. This view might lead readers unfamiliar with the literature on successful efforts to maintain integration to believe that individuals are powerless to effect change and work toward breaking down the color line.

In reality, a dialectic exists between individual agency and social structures, often overlooked in examinations of race and housing. In this context, I look at local responses to racial change, focusing on the efforts to mitigate structural forces and maintain racial integration. Rather than produce more documentation of the extent and the structural underpinnings of racial divisions, I examine the agency of individuals to effect change (or maintain the status quo) and the social processes that occur in racially mixed neighborhoods.

The thesis of this book is twofold. First, racially and ethnically integrated neighborhoods not only exist but also can be maintained, stabilized, and even promoted through direct and indirect local strategies. Empirical work indicates that racially integrated neighborhoods are not as rare or as unstable as people might think. In fact, racially mixed neighborhoods are not only increasing in number but also becoming more stable (Ellen 2000). Further, qualitative analyses of racially mixed communities reveal that local agents can successfully intervene to prevent racial transition and stabilize integration in the face of racially biased housing markets. Hundreds of communities across the country—in a progressive movement to sustain integrated spaces—have produced effective strategies (not schemes) that challenge the stereotype of integrated neighborhoods as temporary and unstable. These communities illustrate that resegregation is not the inevitable result of structural forces; individual agency plays an important role in shaping the nature of residential settlement patterns.

Second, in our post–civil rights era, there is the emergence of a different "type" of integrated community that challenges many of our assumptions about racial settlement patterns and race relations. Across the country, we are witnessing the emergence of unplanned stable integration that involves multiethnic and multiracial populations. The United States is experiencing one of the most dramatic demographic shifts in its racial and ethnic composition since the early 1900s. Traditionally, the term "race relations" meant social relations between whites and blacks. Today, however, over a fourth of all Americans are nonwhite. In three decades the nonwhite population will double (due largely to increasing Latino and Asian immigration), while the white population will remain relative stable. The increase in racial, ethnic, and cultural diversity has differentially impacted metropolitan areas and cities. The result is not only the growth of multiethnic and multiracial metropolitan areas, but also an increase in the number of multiethnic and multiracial neighborhoods.

The shifts that produce these multiracial and multiethnic communities are related to global economic and demographic changes that affect not only the United States, but also its urban landscapes. For example, the effect of a tremendous influx of immigrants to cities has recast the social, cultural, and economic character of many communities. One noticeable result is the emergence of a new form of integrated community, a microcosm of the larger U.S. demographic and social changes. Many of these fail to resemble the old models—"ethnic enclaves" or "urban villages" where residents share a common culture and pursue a relatively unified set of interests. Residents of these new integrated communities comprise numerous subgroups with assorted lifestyles, class interests, goals, and ideologies. These subgroups struggle not only against external forces (e.g., developers, City Hall), but also among themselves. These communities differ from well-known models of racial integration such as Oak Park, Illinois, or Shaker Heights, Ohio, in that the established residents and the racially and culturally different incoming groups never intended to be neighbors, and what residents have in common are their differences. What makes these communities fascinating is that, while we might predict that such differences would make integration difficult, many have been able to remain stably integrated.

What follows is a critical look at integrated neighborhoods in the United States that moves beyond segregation and the seemingly intractable social problems that plague urban areas. While some scholars and the public have viewed integrated communities in the United States and efforts to maintain them as temporary, recent research has begun to highlight these places and the strategies used to preserve black-white integrated residential spaces. My goal, however, is to move not only beyond segregation, but also beyond the common story of integrated residential communities to examine integrated areas where residents did not make conscious efforts early in the process of racial change to sustain integration. Such integrated spaces, fast emerging in our nation's urban centers (particularly port-of-entry metropolitan areas), require us to rethink traditional conceptions of race and neighborhood, racial change, and integration. They also provide insight into the prospects and challenges for interracial and interethnic understanding, cooperation, and coexistence in the twenty-first century.

DESEGRATION DOES NOT EQUAL INTEGRATION

This book is about racial integration and race relations. Persistent racial inequality in the United States has been a key justification for endorsing integration; that is, integrated settings should improve the life chances of people of color. Yet there has been debate over the relative success or desirability of integration as a tool for improving racial justice.[1] Scholars and the U.S. public are divided on both issues. Some authors suggest that race relations have improved to the point that blacks, in particular, have been fully integrated into the nation's political and cultural life, as well as its moral community (Thernstrom and Thernstrom 1997; Patterson 1997). Others argue that integration has failed, but for differing reasons (Wicker 1996; Jacoby 2000). Still others argue that integration is an illusion and searching for it prevents us from a real "reckoning" with racism (Steinhorn and Diggs-Brown 1999). It is beyond the scope of this book to provide a nuanced discussion of the feasibility of racial integration writ large. Such a discussion would involve examining the integration of people of color into the nation's social, political, cultural, and economic life. With that said, it seems clear that integrated housing is one avenue toward achieving racial justice. Indeed, integrated neighborhoods, as the case-study communities in this book attest, represent positive alternatives to the historic patterns of racial segregation and separation. I do not wish to be a Pollyanna, however, so this book's intent is to examine the prospects and limits that this model of integration has for moving our society toward greater equality.

Before moving on, I want to address some definitional and procedural issues. Most studies of residential settlement patterns by race include a call by scholars and policy analysts for federal and state involvement in guaranteeing open housing markets and eliminating discrimination from public life. Such calls are clearly valid, given that antidiscrimination policy is a necessary starting point in reducing segregation. As Ingrid Ellen points out: "Discrimination powerfully limits the ability of minorities to move into predominantly white areas and maintains white areas as an option to which whites can escape" (2000: 174). In other words, housing discrimination limits freedom of choice for minorities and thus perpetuates segregation and white separation from integrated neighborhoods. Freedom of choice in housing is obviously a basic civil right, and securing it for all citizens is a basic requirement.

The question then becomes: where do we go from there? Not everyone agrees about what comes after securing freedom of choice. An important distinction needs to be made at this point between "desegregation" and "integration," terms often used interchangeably and viewed as opposites of segregation. Desegregation is the opposite of segregation; integration is not. For many people, the fight for freedom of choice in housing is really a fight to desegregate the country's neighborhoods and cities. Desegregation, in theory, seeks to make blacks and other people of color full recipients of the American dream (i.e., quality housing and education, equal access to jobs, and full participation in the polity) through formal efforts to eliminate policies or practices that effectively (intentionally or otherwise) promote segregation, regardless of outcome. The goal of desegregation is not necessarily to achieve integration. Thus, while desegregation efforts can result in an increase in racially and ethnically integrated neighborhoods, it does not necessarily follow that this will occur (as is evident in school desegregation cases). For example, strong homogenous black or Latino communities could emerge. And all minority neighborhoods are not necessarily problematic. In fact, if there is a problem with all-black or all-Latino communities, it is not that they are homogenous; it is that under a discriminatory system such communities have unequal access to jobs, good schools, and quality housing.

Integration in neighborhoods implies creating or sustaining interracial mixing in residential settings and, it is hoped, greater interracial interaction. Integration is more complex and controversial than desegregation, given that it is impossible to legislate. Like desegregation, integration seeks to break down discriminatory barriers and give nonwhites greater access to safe, amenity-rich neighborhoods that contain quality housing and good schools. But integration is more creative than desegregation; it is, in the words of Martin Luther King, Jr., "a genuine intergroup, interpersonal doing" (Washington 1986: 118). This distinction is important, given the potential of interracial or interethnic contact to expand freedom of choice in the housing market.

Two important and related issues need to be touched on here. First, racially integrated neighborhoods provide the type of interracial contact that can reduce prejudicial attitudes (Jackman and Crane 1986; Ellison and Powers 1994; T. C. Wilson 1996).[2] The more contact people have with members of different racial groups, the greater the chance of minimizing mistrust, fear, or suspicion among groups. This "contact hypothesis" is tied to the prospect of greater freedom of choice, in that prejudice is a root motivator for discriminatory acts in the housing market. Interracial contact can reduce the prejudices of white real estate agents and their clientele, thus promoting freedom of choice (DeMarco and Galster 1993).

Second, it seems obvious that an increase in integrated residential spaces in a metropolitan area will reduce overall rates of segregation. Reducing segregation also seems to expand freedom of choice, as empirical evidence suggests that, after controlling for other factors, metropolitan areas with less segregation have lower rates of housing discrimination (Galster and Keeney 1988). Working toward stable racially integrated spaces is thus a tool to eliminate segregation by getting at discrimination, which obviously limits freedom of choice. I would also argue that if freedom of choice and open housing are to truly exist, a full range of housing choices must be available, including stably integrated neighborhoods. Such neighborhoods have not been a viable option for people of color and whites, given entrenched racial prejudice and discrimination in housing and lending markets. In other words, for freedom of choice "to be more than a hollow prospect presumes that there are actually such [stable racially diverse] neighborhoods from which to choose" (DeMarco and Galster 1993: 147). Racially integrated neighborhoods have long been stereotyped as temporary, of poor quality (with high crime, inferior housing, poor schools, etc.), and likely to resegregate (Taub, Taylor, and Dunham 1984; Ellen 2000). If freedom of choice in housing is to be fully achieved, these stereotypes have to be challenged and stable racially integrated neighborhoods have to be viewed as a policy goal.

1 Racial and Ethnic Segregation and Integration in Urban America

"SEGREGATION THEN, segregation tomorrow, and segregation forever," shouted George Wallace on a chilly Inauguration Day in 1963 in Montgomery, Alabama. While Wallace's insistent cry was a broad rejection of integration in general, he may as well have been talking about how Americans organize residential space. Even after the Fair Housing Act of 1968, U.S. urban areas remain tremendously segregated. This should come as no surprise; a look around any metropolitan area in the United States reveals the familiar pattern—a sizable number of blacks concentrated in central cities (usually impoverished) and whites living in the suburbs or, as George Clinton of Parliament Funkadelic put it, "chocolate cities and vanilla suburbs." Most of us seem to accept this pattern as inevitable, even natural. For many Americans, residential diversity and integration may sound appealing but seem unworkable in practice, as scholars and the media highlight segregated and homogenous environments and ignore integrated ones. In our current urban landscapes, the presence of gated communities, fortresslike building developments, private security forces, racial ghettos, and a patchwork of isolated, racially homogeneous sprawling suburbs suggests that Wallace was right.

While the weight of evidence indicates that residential segregation has been a predominant feature of modern urban life, it is neither inevitable nor even universal. Racially integrated neighborhoods do exist and can remain stable. Places like Chicago's Uptown, Queens's Jackson Heights, and Oakland's San Antonio–Fruitvale exemplify this reality. And while the focus of this book is not to revisit the existence, causes, and consequences of residential segregation by race highlighted in many scholarly accounts (see Massey and Denton 1993), a brief recounting of the historical and cultural context that supports segregation as a normative, if not valued, feature of modern urban growth and development will set the stage for the story of these three racially integrated communities.

This historical and cultural context is part of what makes it difficult for us to consider integrated neighborhoods as viable and sustainable. Organizer Saul Alinsky echoed a common misperception when he characterized racial integration as merely the time between "the entrance of the first black family and the exit of the last white family" (Sanders 1970: 86). Yet there have been numerous efforts to create and promote racially and ethnically integrated communities in the United States during the last half century. Hundreds of interracial organizations in both urban and suburban communities have actively pursued and achieved stable racially integrated residential environments. The focus of this chapter is the "open housing" movement, which has largely been ignored, given the severity of segregation and its accompanying virulent effects. Communities involved in this movement have proven that despite formidable institutional and individual forces, segregation does not have to be inevitable or "forever"—integration is possible.

The Legacy of Racial Residential Segregation

Segregation in U.S. urban areas did not just happen; there was nothing "natural" about the way urban residential settlement became racially homogenous. Persistent patterns of segregation and the always tenuous possibility of integration evolved over the last century. Before World War I, urban neighborhoods were not as segregated as they are today. Blacks were only slightly residentially segregated from whites and European immigrant groups of similar economic circumstances, as there were few institutional structures to concentrate residents and workers in densely populated areas (Spear 1967; Yancey, Ericksen, and Juliani 1976; Hershberg 1981; Binder and Reimers 1995). Industrialization altered this arrangement, creating densely clustered worker housing and a segregated workforce (Drake and Cayton 1945; Greenberg 1981).[1] The availability of jobs drew both European immigrants and southern black migrants to northern cities. European immigrants initially lived in isolated neighborhoods, but this isolation was short-lived and enclaves were rarely homogenous (Lieberson 1963, 1980; Binder and Reimers 1995). The story was quite different for the large number of southern black migrants recruited to resolve worker shortages and serve as naïve strikebreakers (Grossman 1989; Trotter 1985).[2] Most whites in this period viewed the increasing numbers of blacks with fear, animosity, and hostility. Whites maintained the residential color line through a variety of violent acts, ranging from personal harassment to mob attacks to bombing (Rudwick

1964; Osofsky 1968; Kusmer 1976; Philpott 1978; Hirsch 1983). After the 1920s, more subtle methods such as neighborhood "improvement associations" sprang up to maintain racial boundaries by implementing restrictive covenants and restrictions on interracial sales (Helper 1969; Connolly 1977; Bauman 1987).[3] By 1940, all the major industrial centers in the North had substantially segregated zones and maintained significant levels of segregation between whites and blacks (Cutler, Glaeser, and Vigdor 1999).

These strict racial lines in residential patterns would solidify between 1940 and 1970, as the percentage of blacks in northern cities grew dramatically after World War II.[4] Newly arriving blacks found their housing choices circumscribed to select and narrowly bounded neighborhoods. White attitudes continued to support racial discrimination in housing and the systematic exclusion of blacks from white neighborhoods (Helper 1969).[5] These attitudes translated into action; if blacks did move into the neighborhood, incumbent whites moved out and most white home seekers simply avoided the neighborhood, guaranteeing resegregation (Molotch 1972). Even before restrictive covenants were declared unenforceable in 1948, some real estate agents "eagerly exploited whites' fears by blockbusting likely areas—selling to a black family, spreading fear among whites that the neighborhood was about to change; buying property from the panicked whites at bargain basement prices; then selling it to middle-class blacks looking for a nice neighborhood at higher prices" (Judd and Swanstrom 1998: 194).[6] In addition, until the 1970s realtors were obligated to steer potential home seekers to neighborhoods whose residents shared their race or nationality (Helper 1969). These private efforts made it less necessary for prejudiced whites to use personal or communal violence to defend their neighborhoods from integration or racial change.

Federal policies institutionalized many of these discriminatory acts and exacerbated racial tensions and color lines in cities. From the 1930s through much of the 1960s, the federal government provided financial support for a housing boom that was effectively put off-limits for blacks. For example, between 1930 and 1960, the Federal Housing Administration (FHA) and Veteran's Administration (VA) provided loan guarantees that accelerated suburban development by insuring loans and easing the task of purchasing a home (Jackson 1985).[7] And while FHA and VA programs provided tremendous housing and social opportunities to households in the postwar period, they were open only to white home seekers desiring suburban locales.[8] Federal administrators of insured financing programs promoted segregated housing and neighborhoods by favoring segregation over integration, suburbs over cities, and redlining of racially mixed or minority areas (Bradburn, Sudman, and Gockel 1971).[9]

In addition, government-backed urban renewal and public housing policies sharply limited the housing supply for black home buyers and renters, contributing to racial tensions and sharp lines of racial segregation (Judd and Swanstrom 1998). The housing acts of 1949 and 1954 gave local authorities federal funds to check blight and ghetto expansion by clearing "slum" properties for redevelopment, while turning to the construction of public housing to guarantee replacement housing (Bauman 1987). During the 1950s and 1960s, local public officials with tremendous private sector pressure used urban renewal and public housing, largely in black neighborhoods, to clear and rebuild on land in growing black areas that threatened white business districts and elite institutions (Rainwater 1970; Hirsch 1983). Thus, whites had more opportunities and great incentives to leave their communities, while blacks had fewer options as urban renewal, public housing, and discrimination narrowly defined the communities open to them. Combined with discriminatory institutional practices, racial transition became a striking urban process. The ghetto expanded as a "rolling tide" or "wave" over neighborhoods as a cumulative pattern of invasion and succession took place in U.S. cities (Goodwin 1979). In a relatively short time, the population of various northern cities became virtually all black.[10] Data indicated that in the thirty largest metropolitan areas from 1940 through 1970, segregation levels peaked in northern cities in 1950, edging downward slightly by 1970. In sum, by the end of the 1960s, the average black and white lived in a residential area where the vast majority of his or her neighbors were of the same race, making meaningful contact between whites and blacks outside the workforce extremely unlikely. As a result, integrated neighborhoods were deemed temporary and unstable, bound to resegregate regardless of local efforts to alter the outcome.

Since 1970, there has been some progress toward more integrated cities and regions. For example, from 1970 to 2000, the number of metropolitan areas with exceedingly high segregation indices decreased significantly, and the number of moderately segregated metropolitan areas increased (Glaeser and Vigdor 2001; Farley and Frey 1994). Also, the percentage of whites living in homogeneous white neighborhoods decreased dramatically in both cities and suburbs over this same period (Ellen 1998; Alba et al. 1995). However, racial segregation, particularly for blacks, remains a continuing and significant factor for understanding the spatial patterns of metropolitan areas and cities. For example, the greatest declines in segregation have come in places where fewer blacks reside and where a long history of segregation does not exist (e.g., fast-growing cities in the South and West), while segregation remains high in metropolitan areas with the largest black populations (Denton 1999; Glaeser and Vigdor 2001). Also, black suburbanization did little to desegregate metropolitan areas or eliminate black-white differences in residential quality.[11] While the movement of blacks to the suburbs did signal the lifting of the suburban-urban barrier for blacks, any optimism about greater residential integration between whites and blacks was short-lived.

Finally, there remains alarming evidence that minorities (particularly African Americans) experience continued and systematic discrimination in the real estate, lending, and insurance industries. Over the last three decades, real estate markets have continued to discriminate (e.g., steering minorities away from particular areas) by excluding minorities from certain neighborhoods, particularly in racially mixed (or potentially mixed) neighborhoods (Galster 1990; Turner, Struyk, and Yinger 1991; Urban Institute 1991; Yinger 1996). Financial institutions have extended far less private credit, fewer federally insured loans, and less total mortgage money to blacks and racially mixed areas than to socioeconomically advantaged white areas (Bradbury, Case, and Dunham 1989; Shlay 1989; Squires 1994). The practice of redlining certain neighborhoods continued between the 1970s and 1990s.[12] More than thirty years after the passage of Title VIII of the 1968 Civil Rights Act, which made it illegal to discriminate based on race, racial and ethnic discrimination in the real estate and lending industries has not abated. Discriminatory practices maintain significant levels of isolation and segregation, stack the deck against racially mixed communities, and perpetuate the assumption that mixed communities are not viable.

What accounts for these variable trends? We can look to two post–civil rights changes: shifts in individual attitudes regarding integrated neighborhoods and the enactment of legal barriers to discrimination. First, as noted, attitude surveys indicated that whites largely endorsed racial segregation in the 1950s and 1960s. However, by 1990, only 20 percent of white respondents agreed with the statement that "white people have a right to keep blacks out of their neighborhoods if they want to, and blacks should respect that right," down from 60 percent in 1964 (Schuman, Steeh, and Bobo 1985). Also, several studies indicate that whites' tolerance of black neighbors has increased over time and they have expressed less desire to move as the percentage of black in-migrants increased (Farley, Schuman et al. 1978; Farley, Steeh et al. 1994). White tolerance for black neighbors, however, drops substantially when blacks represent a sizable proportion of the population (Clark 1986; Schuman, Steeh, and Bobo 1985). Whites appear to accept racially mixed neighborhoods as long as whites are the clear majority, while blacks are more likely to accept an equal proportion of blacks and whites. This gap between white and black attitudes toward integration is central to understanding the persistence of segregation.

Second, since the 1960s, the federal government has passed legislation that was meant, at least in spirit, to "dismantle systems of discrimination" that maintain racial segregation (Squires 1996: 224). The Federal Fair Housing Act of 1968 and the Equal Credit Opportunity Act of 1974 prohibited discrimination in housing and housing finance markets. The passage of the Home Mortgage Disclosure Act in 1975 and the Community Reinvestment Act in 1977 provided communities greater access to information on the location of mortgages and required depository institutions to affirmatively ascertain and be responsive to the credit needs of their entire service areas. These statutes have not eliminated discrimination in mortgage lending and real estate practices, largely because the acts put the onus on individuals and communities to recognize and fight discriminatory behavior. However, at a minimum, these acts have provided community groups tools to successfully fight discrimination and disinvestment. Though it is impossible to measure, the law and the publicity surrounding successful lawsuits arguably have served to liberalize attitudes (Farley and Frey 1994) and to deter some lenders and realtors from discriminatory practices. However, such legislation seems unlikely to unravel decades of federal and local policies that mandated segregation.

DIRECTING DIVERSITY: THE PRO-INTEGRATION MOVEMENT

It should be obvious that the racial environment in which residential areas have existed over the last century has been one of tremendous segregation. Scholars and researchers have suggested that integrated neighborhoods are the exception, temporary, fragile, and doomed to eventual resegregation. Harvey Molotch, in his study of Chicago's South Shore neighborhood, went so far as to say that no amount of intervention is likely to reverse the process of racial transition (1972). This view, however, neglects the complexity of an important part of U.S. urban history. Urban and suburban communities over the last half century have organized and struggled to maintain a stable integrated racial composition.

Although these communities have been largely ignored or discounted by scholars as anomalies, no discussion of residential segregation and integration is complete without examining their experience. The efforts to promote stable integration, like the reality of pervasive racial segregation, are part of the sociopolitical context in which neighborhoods and residents existed during the second half of the twentieth century. These communities emerged out of the distinctive social conditions of the 1950s and 1960s, particularly the last wave of southern black migrants to northern cities, neighborhood racial transition, and the civil rights movement. Taken collectively, their efforts formed a social movement that has been referred to as the "open housing," "neighborhood stabilization," or "pro-integrative" movement. Regardless of the label, the movement centers on local reaction to racial change, reaction that includes organized and active intervention to prevent racial transition and to preserve racial integration.

These communities emerged from the civil rights movement and involved interracial coalitions working to promote the benefits of integration by developing an array of organizations, social networks, and institutions that focused directly on fostering stable integration (Nyden et al. 1998). Although these communities differ from the diverse communities that have emerged in the last two to three decades (outlined in Chapters Three, Four, and Five), there is much to be learned from them, as they provide a counterpoint to studies of racial segregation. The movement to maintain racially integrated communities provides invaluable lessons for those wishing to break down the barriers of segregation and its harsh effects. These communities show that segregation was not as universal as many scholars or common perceptions might suggest. However, their experience also reveals the depth and strength of the forces that encourage segregation.

Neighborhood Stabilization/Pro-integration

In the early 1950s and 1960s, the last wave of the Great Migration and overcrowded conditions in the established ghettos increased the number of black home seekers in northern cities. Urban renewal, public housing policies, and discriminatory practices reduced the available supply of quality housing open to blacks and as a result forced (or lured) many blacks to look for housing in older white neighborhoods. As blacks entered previously all-white neighborhoods, a variety of factors encouraged racial transition and what scholars have referred to as "invasion and succession."[13] The pattern typically went like this: a few middle-class black families, seeking to escape overcrowded conditions in the segregated zones and to gain better housing, would move into a predominantly white neighborhood. As blacks moved in, many whites took their presence as a harbinger of "change" and "decline." White fear of blacks, unscrupulous acts by the real estate community (e.g., blockbusting, racial steering), discriminatory bank policies in newly integrated areas, and other local factors (e.g., media coverage) quickened the pace of racial transition.[14] A common understanding of racial transition that emerged from this period suggests that when the size or composition of a relatively homogenous area is altered, racial transition occurs. For example, Carole Goodwin, in her book *The Oak Park Strategy*, demonstrates the link between increased black in-migration and racial change in Chicago's Austin neighborhood. As Austin's black population increased from less than 1 percent in 1960 to 32.5 percent in 1970, so did racial transition. Goodwin reports that between 1966 and 1973, 148 blocks changed from white to black, with most of this transition occurring between 1970 and 1973 as 113 blocks changed racial occupancy (1979: 48). This process occurred in city after city across the country and contributed to the notion that racially integrated neighborhoods were temporary and unstable.

In the light of rapid transitions of formerly all-white neighborhoods, a "tipping point" hypothesis emerged. This hypothesis assumes that racial transition moves gradually until the proportion of blacks reaches a threshold, the point (obviously variable) when whites no longer feel comfortable with integration or the presence of blacks in the neighborhood. Once this threshold is crossed, whites move out (often rapidly) and fewer whites are interested in moving in; the result is resegregation. A cycle is created that predictably leads to conditions that accelerate racial turnover, assures resegregation, and maintains a perception that segregation is the "natural" and inevitable outcome of city life (Keating and Smith 1996; Ottensmann 1995). The expectation is that as "other" groups "invade," the neighborhood is deemed vulnerable, making resegregation seem inevitable and integration temporary.

The tipping point, however, was not the result simply of individual preferences or comfort levels. A variety of mediating institutions and groups were influential in hastening the process of racial transition. Consider the following four: real estate brokers, lending agents, schools, and the media. The real estate community has a long history of blockbusting newly integrated areas and reaping hefty profits from the workings of the dual housing market while steering white home seekers away from black or integrated areas. Banks and other lending institutions continue to withdraw credit from commercial and residential areas experiencing racial change. Schools, a major factor in housing choices, can also work against integration. The reality is, regardless of objective standards, that predominantly white schools are perceived as superior and predominantly black schools as inferior. School officials who ignore racial imbalance in schools can prompt resegregation by fueling negative perceptions of the quality of the schools. The media has a substantial influence on individual opinion and perception, and, by and large, mass media accounts of integrated neighborhoods have been unfavorable. Terms like "open housing" or "equal-opportunity housing" are code words for housing for minorities. In sum, since larger social forces always influence individual housing and investment choices, to understand the nature of neighborhood racial change we must consider how these and other mediating institutions can (though they do not always) accelerate the process and pace of racial change. By devaluing integrated neighborhoods as attractive and inviting places to reside, these institutions have contributed to neighborhood racial change and segregated residential spaces.

Fortunately, these mediating institutions do not have complete control over the fate of a neighborhood. Residents in neighborhoods experiencing racial change do not live and move at the whim of discriminatory market forces; not all neighborhoods "tip." External factors favoring segregation cannot be downplayed, but a neighborhood's internal reactions to change also require careful consideration. In any area experiencing racial change there is always some "combination of interests, motives, and concrete acts by individuals and groups" that shapes the fate of the community (Goodwin 1979: 4). Existing residents and incoming residents react to change and thus set in motion processes that alter how communities perceive, define, and experience themselves. These processes, along with external factors, have significant impacts on the likelihood of resegregation.

A good example of this syndrome began to occur in communities experiencing racial change between 1950 and the mid-1970s. Neighborhood groups committed to integration maintenance emerged in almost every U.S. city where black in-migration and neighborhood racial change and transition occurred. For example, during the 1950s, neighborhood groups surfaced in the Boston-Edison section of Detroit, Park Hill in Denver, Shaker Heights in Ohio, Shepard Park in Washington, D.C., West Mount Airy in Philadelphia, South Shore in Chicago, and Teaneck, New Jersey.[15] Scores of other groups came to life in the 1960s and 1970s as "the knowledge and experience of earlier groups spread, as civil rights gained increasing national sympathy, and as the dynamic of racial transition reached into a greater number of neighborhoods and suburbs" (Wiese 1995: 114).[16] Although groups formed independently, in most cases the patterns of resisting resegregation were strikingly similar. Organizations began interracially and demonstrated a mixture of postwar liberalism, sympathy to civil rights, and enlightened self-interest (Wiese 1995). Group members attempted to prevent racial transition in the hope of stabilizing their community, maintaining racial integration, and avoiding resegregation (Saltman 1990). While many community members held liberal attitudes toward racial integration and civil rights, they also valued their homes, wanting neither to move nor to have their housing values plummet. As these groups became aware of each other, a national movement or umbrella organization called National Neighbors was formed in 1969. By the mid-1970s, National Neighbors represented more than two hundred such groups (Saltman 1990).

In many communities, initial organizing efforts did not center solely on racial integration, but on broad concerns of neighborhood stabilization. For example, the Sherman Park Community Association, representing a west-side Milwaukee neighborhood, was initially formed "not in response to an outside threat, but to improve the quality of life" in the area (Valent and Squires 1998). Also, it has been suggested that religious leaders in the West Mount Airy section of north Philadelphia became actively involved in efforts to prevent resegregation so members of their congregations and synagogues would not move to the suburbs (Ferman, Singleton, and DeMarco 1998). These early efforts to "defend" the community from destabilizing forces (Suttles 1972) quickly led to more "conscious communities" (Hunter 1978) and a stronger promotion of racial integration. These conscious communities reacted to racial change by adopting an interventionist approach.

The interventionist approach suggests that residents can achieve neighborhood stabilization and racial integration if they mobilize sufficient resources and institutional networks for collective action early on in the process of change (Galster 1987; Helper 1986; Saltman 1990; Taub, Taylor, and Dunham 1984). This approach puts a premium on organized community efforts to effect change. Richard Taub and colleagues expressed this view after reviewing racial change in various Chicago neighborhoods in the 1970s: "Ecological facts do not, in fact, unidirectionally determine neighborhood outcomes. Corporate and individual decisions always intervene and sometimes modify the connection between ecological circumstances and neighborhood outcomes. . . . What is clear is that interventions can and do work, and that they sometimes do in situations that might be considered unpromising on the basis of historical understandings" (Taub, Taylor, and Dunham 1984: 187).

While it is often assumed that individual or community-level group action gives way in the face of brute economic forces or embedded racist institutional practices, the effect of local interventions on neighborhood outcomes requires us to factor in grassroots involvement in neighborhood development. Decades of community studies have shown that local organized efforts can intervene to shape the outcome of a neighborhood (R. Fisher 1994). And researchers have shown that community groups faced with racial change and the institutional factors that promote racial transition can intervene through an array of local (and regional) organizations, social networks, and institutions. I refer to these communities as "diverse by direction" because local groups intentionally focused on integration. Groups attempt to direct the future of their neighborhood toward stable integration by ensuring that existing white households do not panic and that the overall stability and racial balance of the neighborhood is maintained.

Pro-integration Strategies

Over the last four decades, as part of the neighborhood stabilization movement or pro-integrative efforts, numerous communities have employed intervention strategies to promote neighborhood stability and racial integration. Diverse-by-direction communities face common struggles, including proposed zoning changes that threaten existing land use (e.g., urban renewal or highway construction), the workings of mediating institutions (noted earlier), and commercial and residential deterioration—all of which encourage racial transition and segregation. In all cases, local groups shape or direct their community toward stable racial integration by managing perceptions through a specific set of responses or interventions.

General Aim of Pro-integrative Efforts

In urban America, the identities of residential areas result from comparisons to other neighborhoods (Suttles 1972). This means that residential areas are symbolic as well as physical entities that maintain a general identity and are shaped by perceptions, real or imagined. Any neighborhood's "desirability" and the related demand for housing are strongly linked to the image of the community (Goetze 1979). Communities undergoing racial transition establish new identities, particularly in contrast to nearby or similar communities. Given the normative nature of segregation in the United States, it is no surprise that integrated neighborhoods are usually perceived as changing and unstable. Change is perceived negatively and assumed to bring lower property values, increased criminal activity, fewer municipal services, and deteriorating schools, businesses, and housing.

To promote positive views of a neighborhood's "type" and "future," communities attempting to sustain racial integration must challenge and change perceptions. Although image is not everything in a community, in the context of white racism, pervasive discrimination, and segregation, it is a key element in maintaining integrated communities. Communities experiencing racial change have taken notice of the importance of image, working to challenge the perception of instability as well as to promote positive images of racial integration. Indeed, communities experiencing success in maintaining racial integration make conscious efforts to change the social and cultural character of the community and to redefine its values and norms through private and public support for integration (Goodwin 1979; Saltman 1990; Nyden, Maly, and Lukehart 1997). This has meant making integration a stated goal, promoting it as a community strength and a part of all organizing efforts.

Communities challenging perceptions have employed a variety and combination of intervention strategies or models. One model relies on "pro-integrative" policies in area housing. Pro-integrative housing efforts involve everything from the promotion of fair and open housing to rehabilitation of existing housing stock to "affirmative marketing" strategies. These intervention strategies take aim at the dual housing market. Another general model has been referred to as community development or community building. Efforts conforming to this model deal primarily with quality-of-life and neighborhood-quality issues (e.g., crime, schools, economic development) as well as strengthening neighborhood networks and organizations to encourage greater interaction across racial lines. Underlying both intervention models is an awareness that challenging negative perceptions of racially integrated neighborhoods is a necessary step to maintain the racial balance.

Pro-integration Housing Interventions

Communities working toward maintaining racial integration must attend to the fear that racial integration will bring neighborhood decline, particularly through a lowering of housing quality and property values. Real estate agents who practice blockbusting and racial steering, owners who do not maintain their properties, lending institutions that redline the neighborhood, and interest groups who seek to alter the zoning of the neighborhood from residential to other uses—all are common enemies of integrated neighborhoods (Saltman 1990: 373). In diverse-by-direction communities, local organizations intervene in the local housing market to challenge the forces promoting segregation and pushing neighborhoods toward resegregation. Their interventions can be divided into those that seek to manage or maintain the racial integration and those that aim to encourage racial diversity (commonly referred to as "affirmative marketing") (Chandler 1992).

Interventions aimed at managing or maintaining racial integration work to replace the dual housing market with a unitary market in which all can participate (Lauber 1991). Initially, pro-integration groups focus on improving the quality of the housing stock by seeking rehabilitation funds for deteriorating properties. For example, in the late 1970s, the Sherman Park Community Association (SPCA) employed yearly windshield surveys to identify building-code violations and building deterioration. SPCA then worked with other agencies to secure block-grant funds to help low-income homeowners make home repairs (Valent and Squires 1998). Other communities have set up similar housing committees to preserve their housing stock. Given that integrated neighborhoods are typically older neighborhoods, housing maintenance and repair are vital to maintain the quality of life in a community.

However, while rehabilitating housing is initially important, the larger challenge for racially changing or integrated neighborhoods lies with the workings of the discriminatory housing market. Diverse-by-direction communities must commit significant time and energy to fair and open housing efforts if they wish to combat the forces supporting segregation. Direct pro-integration efforts use a variety of strategies to take aim at local real estate and lending institutions to maintain integration. For the most part, such groups implement anti-solicitation regulations to discourage panic peddling and blockbusting, ban For Sale signs to avoid perceptions of racial transition, lobby to prevent an overconcentration of public housing in the community, and offer equity insurance programs to protect property values of incumbent residents (Keating 1994; Lauber 1991; Saltman 1990; R. Smith 1993). For example, in the early 1970s, leaders in suburban Park Forest, Illinois, adopted several integration-maintenance ordinances. The ordinances prohibited racial steering of prospective home buyers and redlining by lenders, established a fair-housing review board to regulate real estate brokers, and empowered the village manager and the human relations committee to review complaints of racially discriminatory housing practices (Helper 1986; Berry et al. 1976).

Another strategy involves monitoring and testing for housing discrimination. Integrated communities across the United States have combated illegally discriminatory housing practices by documenting them through fair-housing audits.[17] In the 1970s, community groups worked with National Neighbors to conduct local and regional tests for real estate discrimination (Saltman 1990). Communities often team up with city- and regionwide fair-housing centers to conduct testing. In many cases, such efforts uncover discriminatory action, and these centers assist communities and individuals in obtaining legal recourse. These efforts allow pro-integration communities to face head-on actions detrimental to the maintenance of diversity.

A final and most controversial strategy employed by pro-integration groups is affirmative marketing. Pro-integration groups quickly realized that if there was demand for housing from just one racial group in a racially changing area, resegregation would quickly result. Thus, communities, particularly suburban ones, saw that the only way to maintain long-term racial integration was to attract white buyers to the market through affirmative marketing strategies. These strategies are designed to initiate and maintain racial integration, while expanding freedom of choice in housing (DeMarco and Galster 1993). Affirmative marketing strategies are considered choice expanding because they encourage "people of the race least likely to consider moving to an area to do so" (i.e., blacks to white areas, whites to integrated ones) (Saltman 1990: 402). The techniques communities use to encourage racial groups to make nontraditional and choice-expanding moves include the use of financial incentives for prodiversity moves, promotion of mixed-race rental or owner properties, and use of Federal Section 8 rental assistance to promote prodiversity moves (Chandler 1992).[18]

Affirmative marketing strategies are race-conscious attempts to counteract hundreds of years of racial steering and denial of housing opportunity. Usually this means trying to "fix" the problem of diminishing white demand for housing in racially changing neighborhoods (Richie 1990; Wiese 1995). For communities working toward stable integration, the reality is that, without whites moving into an integrated area, resegregation is a likely result. This has been true for the groups founded in the 1950s as well as for current efforts. For example, in 1995, local officials in Matteson, Illinois (a southern suburb of Chicago), employed affirmative marketing practices in an attempt to attract more white residents to protect the community's racial balance. Officials suggested that while the effort to maintain racial diversity might be painful, it was a necessary remedy for many residents who did not want to appear racist but were also concerned about property values (Lifson 1995).

Affirmative marketing strategies to attract whites have met with substantial criticism that emanates from different interpretations of the goal of the Fair Housing Act of 1968. One position holds that the act was meant to eliminate discrimination, not necessarily to ensure stably integrated neighborhoods. Thus, affirmative marketing limits freedom of choice, stigmatizes blacks, denies the viability of an all-black neighborhood, limits the ability of blacks to improve their own housing conditions, and ignores the reality that obtaining good housing is a higher priority than integration (Woodson 1988; Kearney-King and Marquis 1989; Leigh and McGhee 1986). The other position, shared by those implementing affirmative marketing strategies, argues that the ultimate purpose of the Fair Housing Act is to promote stable integration. It is argued that even without overt housing discrimination, housing markets would continue to behave in ways that produce and maintain racially separate communities, because institutionally embedded practices ensure that individuals do not have full knowledge of available housing options (DeMarco and Galster 1993; Galster 1992; Polikoff 1985, 1986). Affirmative marketing strategies differ fundamentally from the discriminatory practice of racial steering in that they are intended to expand housing choices, not limit them. A legal note titled "Benign Steering and Benign Quotas" (1980: 938) in the *Harvard Law Review* suggests that pro-diversity incentives are critical because "every time a community resegregates, the pattern of racial separation and hostility is reinforced . . . [and thus] the movement toward racial equality will continue to languish until some communities break out of the cycle of resegregation by creating a stable interracial environment that demonstrates racial harmony that is not only desirable but attainable."

These efforts to initiate and maintain racial integration over the long term through intervention in the housing market are critical to the success of stable integration. Such race-conscious policies would be unnecessary if U.S. culture did not discriminate. Since this is not the case, the interventions by local organizations to eliminate housing discrimination and lending continue to challenge images of racially integrated neighborhoods as unstable. They demonstrate that residents in racially changing areas are not helpless to prevent racial transition. Affirmative marketing efforts, however, cannot stand alone; interventions in the housing market are not sufficient to challenge the common perception of racially integrated communities as unstable. This is not lost on community leaders who are intervening in community processes to promote and maintain integration, as they have focused enormous time and energy on what I refer to as community-building efforts, mostly to improve neighborhood quality.

Community Building

To improve neighborhood quality, intervening communities require a well-organized community-based group. This is one factor that all diverse-by-direction communities share—community organizations actively involved in motivating grassroots awareness and involvement in neighborhood concerns (Saltman 1990). Key leaders have emerged to form these organizations and provide the impetus to maintain them. Usually all it took was a handful of people to start the process. For example, in the Sherman Park neighborhood, organizing efforts to promote diversity can be traced back to 1970, when seven families established a local organization to address neighborhood concerns (Valent and Squires 1998). In Indianapolis, four families (two white, two black) are considered the founders of the Butler-Tarkington Neighborhood Association, formed to "achieve an ideal racially integrated, beautiful neighborhood" (Saltman 1990: 38). A similar pattern emerged in other communities. Often religious congregations and ecumenical groups played a lead role in directing and sustaining efforts to maintain integration. These groups, drawing on decades of race dialogue, were situated in prominent positions of leadership (Nyden et al. 1998). As the fight for integration continued, successful communities had organizations that presented "unified, strong, stubborn images and succeeded in influencing key decision makers on local and state levels" (Saltman 1990: 374).

The primary concern of community-building activities is improving or maintaining the quality of life of the community. However, quality of life means different things to different people. In diverse-by-direction communities it means improving the overall image of the area by strengthening social networks, promoting the community, and balancing schools. Community-building efforts usually strike a balance between strengthening social ties and upgrading the neighborhood's physical quality. Indeed, all communities face this task. Where racially heterogeneous neighborhoods differ from racially homogeneous ones is in the priority given to maintaining racial integration. In the former, community building is that much more important. Leadership is required to direct local groups to improve neighborhood quality and to do so with the intent of stable integration.

Community leaders attend to neighborhood quality by working to sustain positive intergroup relations and networks through the formation of parent-teacher associations, religious groups, interfaith groups, Chambers of Commerce, youth recreational leagues, political parties, and block clubs. These groups create an environment that promotes more positive associations among individuals and communal groups, especially across racial lines (Saltman 1990; Nyden et al. 1998). When these efforts were labeled multicultural, the emphasis in the community shifted from black and white to the idea of a mingling of all races and ethnic backgrounds (Goodwin 1979). These social networks strengthen the sense of community in an area, and when their emphasis shifts toward interracial alliances, it creates a positive perception of racial integration and the changes taking place. In integrated areas, such efforts go a long way toward strengthening a community's social and cultural character.

Strong community associations, however, are just part of the picture. In racially integrated neighborhoods, residents often fear that economic development will flounder and crime will increase. Community organizations, realizing that these issues must be dealt with to reverse the perceived link between racial change and neighborhood decline, have begun to work with other organizations to pump life into sagging commercial strips. Although commercial marketing and maintenance largely has been left to the private sector, community organizations realize the importance of economic development in fostering a positive community image. Local organizations may leverage funds for façade and landscaping improvement, for example, to ensure the physical quality of the community.

More importantly, however, it is the efforts by groups to improve the social quality of the community, particularly in the areas of safety and crime, which are most important to changing perceptions. Studies indicate that racially integrated neighborhoods are perceived to have higher crime rates than racially homogeneous ones (Taub, Taylor, and Dunham 1984; Bratt 1983). Local groups, taking concerns over safety into account, have developed specific safety or crime-prevention programs. In Denver's Greater Park Hill neighborhood, for example, concerns over increased violence and gang activity spurred local volunteers to begin a block- and sector-organizing program that encouraged residents to meet one another, confer about crime problems, and be trained to respond to the needs of their neighbors in terms of safety and crime (K. Woods 1998:

98). Similarly, Milwaukee's Sherman Park neighborhood established a "watch" program that includes block-club organizing, graffiti cleanup, and crime-watch patrols (Valent and Squires 1998). These physical and social maintenance programs are necessary for racially integrated neighborhoods to alter perceptions that such areas are unstable and undesirable.

The racial mix of a neighborhood and its public school population are also intertwined. Schools tend to resegregate before housing markets do. If there are no efforts to ensure integration in the schools, white households will likely perceive the neighborhood as undesirable and resegregation can quickly follow (Saltman 1990). Various communities have recognized this by working with local school districts to get involved with citywide desegregation efforts. This was the case in Sherman Park, where citywide desegregation reduced fears that neighborhood children would be denied educational resources if minorities moved into the neighborhood (Valent and Squires 1998). In some communities, efforts were made to establish in the neighborhood a citywide magnet school with a special curriculum. In other cases, especially in suburbs, communities and school boards worked together to ensure desegregation. For example, in 1967 and 1968, the Shaker Heights (a suburb of Cleveland) Board of Education addressed racial imbalance in the school system by voluntarily instituting busing and magnet schools (Keating 1994: 102). In fact, school administrators in Shaker Heights helped fund pro-integrative efforts. These desegregation strategies are crucial for improving the perception of the neighborhood and maintaining integration.

A final element in maintaining the quality of life in a racially integrated neighborhood involves direct promotion of the community. Diverse-by-direction communities have realized the necessity of creating a positive identity, both internally and externally, through the telling of positive stories of the community (from crime reduction to festivals to the diversity itself). Using various media outlets, local groups have promoted their community through shaping how the community is represented. Communities have intervened through "direct marketing and promotional efforts touting the positive aspects of the community, pressuring local media to report positively on the community, and monitoring media and public officials' statements or comments about the neighborhood and responding to such statements when they appear damaging to the community" (Nyden, Maly, and Lukehart 1997: 516). Many communities publish local newspapers to create an internal sense of neighborhood identification. Memphis's Vollintine-Evergreen neighborhood, for example, established the *VE News*, which announces meeting dates, publishes articles about neighborhood residents and businesses, and features stories that celebrate the success of the neighborhood and its diversity. In terms of fostering a positive image of the neighborhood, some claim that the *VE News* is the "single most important institution in Vollintine-Evergreen" (Kirby 1998: 70).

In sum, community-building efforts are aimed at improving or maintaining the quality of life of the community. While some of these efforts are no different from those in racially homogeneous neighborhoods, they are even more vital in integrated ones. These efforts help deflect negative perceptions and promote integration as a positive community quality. Key to understanding the importance of such efforts is the realization that organizations in integrated communities undertook these efforts to improve neighborhood conditions *in order to* maintain stable racial integration.

Diverse-by-direction communities are unique. In them, leaders and organizations direct their efforts toward maintaining stable racial integration. Whether through intervening in the housing market or improving the quality of life in the neighborhood, these efforts intentionally seek to break the cycle of segregation-change-resegregation. These laudable efforts have proven successful in many communities. It is important to keep in mind, however, that neither affirmative marketing strategies nor other interventions guarantee stable integration. Affirmative marketing has generated controversy and has had difficulty attracting support from blacks, many of whom view such efforts as placing a negative value on black residents. Moreover, not all diverse-by-direction communities are successful. Juliet Saltman chronicles the failure of some communities to maintain their mobilizing organization and leadership, and ultimately their racial balance. In other communities, intervention efforts have served only to hold resegregation at bay, slowing down the process of racial transition by a decade or so. Some leaders, like Bobbie Raymond, former director of the Oak Park Housing Center, claim that pro-integration efforts are costly, impeding long-term success. The facts back Raymond's experience—it is estimated that Oak Park spends over $300,000 annually on integration efforts (Wiese 1995).

There is little doubt that the movement to maintain stable integration has been fragile. However, it is important to remember that one of the reasons these interventions and the communities they are trying to maintain are fragile is the sociohistorical legacy of racism. I agree with Saltman's suggestion that when neighborhoods become racially integrated in this country, they initially assume the "same status that the incoming minority group has in the society at large. As such they . . . are subject to the same levels of domination, discrimination, and segregation in the local community as the minority group experiences in the larger society" (1990: 394). This is what produces resegregation. Local interventions are vital, though sometimes insufficient, in breaking the cycle that produces resegregation. Despite the fragility and costs, such efforts are instrumental in maintaining racial integration and proving that segregation is not inevitable.

The Pro-integration Movement: Then and Now

The neighborhood stabilization movement has waxed and waned since the 1950s. Some observers have rung the death knell for the pro-integration movement, claiming that with the end of the Great Migration, fewer whites vigorously support open housing or racial integration, and the mainstream of middle-class African America has become increasingly weary of integration as an overt social goal. It has been suggested that pro-integrative groups have had a hard time attracting a new base of support, particularly among whites, who have always been its base constituency. This is visible in the support for pro-integration within the fair-housing coalition during the 1980s. Among the 460 fair-housing agencies and organizations surveyed by National Neighbors in 1994, just 68 (15 percent) included any kind of pro-integrative program (Wiese 1995: 117). Of these sixty-eight, half represented communities or neighborhoods working toward stable racial integration. Andrew Wiese sums up one perspective on the pro-integrative movement: "As the neighborhood diversity movement entered its fifth decade, changing social and demographic forces had conspired to produce a movement with proven tools but dwindling resources and an ever narrowing constituency" (1995: 17).

While there is evidence to support this rather dour outlook, there are signs of hope. In the 1990s, the movement received attention as several communities new to the pro-integration movement began employing its "proven tools" to promote neighborhood stability and racial integration. The cases presented in this book—while not necessarily part of the pro-integration movement—are examples of such communities. Also, Matteson, Illinois, for example, a middle-class-to-affluent community in south suburban Chicago, took on an ambitious affirmative marketing campaign in an effort to improve perceptions and maintain integration. Matteson achieved a good deal of media coverage, including an hour-long *Dateline* special, "Why Can't We Live Together?" broadcast by NBC on June 27,

1997, and hosted by Tom Brokaw. Finally, the Fund for an Open Society, founded in 1973 to promote integration in the Philadelphia area, emerged in the 1990s as "America's only national nonprofit working to promote thriving racially and ethnically inclusive communities" (Fund for an Open Society 2003). This organization moved to the forefront of the movement, attracting a national audience to its annual conferences. These conferences are the organization's most obvious attempts to fulfill its mission by equipping communities that seek to become racially inclusive with the skills and resources necessary, and by promoting the benefits of living in integrated communities to a wide range of audiences. While the overall movement may have declined, these examples suggest that reports of the movement's death are exaggerated.

WAS GEORGE WALLACE correct in his implication that racial segregation will (and should) persist in U.S. urban neighborhoods? Indeed, the evidence confirms that segregation has become a prominent feature of urban America. Any discussion of residential settlement patterns by race in the United States must acknowledge that segregation is the norm and that it is maintained through a series of institutionally embedded practices that continue regardless of federal legislation declaring them illegal. However, this same discussion must also consider that local communities can act to promote and maintain racially integrated communities. While such efforts may not be widespread enough to effect immediate meaningful change in the pattern of racial separation that occurs at the neighborhood level, they do call into question the assumption that segregation must or will remain forever. Indeed, the color line can never be discounted as a meaningful force in shaping where people live, what type of services they receive, and what the quality of their lives is. Nevertheless, it can be and has been challenged. Although segregation is perceived as normal in the United States, it is not normal in any inevitable sense. Such a mindset takes residents, activists, policy analysts, and scholars away from examining ways in which to support communities working to maintain their racial and ethnic mix.

2 Changing Demographics, Multiethnic and Multiracial Neighborhoods, and Unplanned Diversity

IN 1968, the National Advisory Commission on Civil Disorders, headed by Illinois Governor Otto Kerner, studied the race riots that had scorched U.S. cities the previous summer and reached a powerful conclusion. "Our nation is moving toward two societies, one black, one white—separate and unequal" (National Advisory Commission on Civil Disorders 1968). Segregation by race had persisted and intensified in urban residential areas over the decade. The Kerner Commission's report succinctly summarized what scholars had known for some time: racial segregation was extensive in U.S. urban areas and it was maintained by white racism. Pro-integrative leaders and groups had begun to acknowledge this reality and attempted—through a variety of strategies—to alter the entrenched institutional and attitudinal forces promoting segregation. Ultimately, the portrait of urban America reflected in these trends was one of separation and isolation of African Americans (and to a lesser extent, Latinos and Asians) from white residential areas and white mainstream culture—despite valiant community efforts to encourage integration.[1]

We are witnessing, however, the emergence of a new urban America that the nation lacks a ready vocabulary to describe. With the surge of immigration and economic restructuring in the 1980s and 1990s, urban areas began moving toward a more complex structure. Black-white conflicts remain the deep-seated, unresolved core of group relations in the United States; however, after the Hart-Cellar Immigration Act of 1965, the largest wave of immigrants since the early 1900s entered U.S. cities, largely from Latin America and Asia.[2] The presence of these newcomers has irrevocably altered the dynamics of race relations in cities. Race relations no longer concern only blacks and whites; individuals are no longer separate and unequal simply because of race, but also because of ancestry, language, immigrant status, and economic achievement. As Roberto

Suro, journalist and author of *Strangers among Us*, suggests: "After Rodney King, nothing could be so simple as black and white" (1998: 221).

The deepening complexity of race relations in the United States is visible in our cities and neighborhoods. In our post–civil rights landscape, demographic and economic shifts have greatly impacted the structure of cities and altered residential development. Cities and regions have taken on a multiethnic and multiracial character, shifting away from the more traditional black-white composition. And while overall rates of segregation remain high in most metropolitan areas, immigration and other social dynamics have altered the racial composition of cities and neighborhoods. While these shifts are not always noticeable through traditional or general indicators, they are increasing the likelihood of racially mixed neighborhoods, even when these are not planned.

This chapter closely examines residential settlement patterns by race at the neighborhood level over the past two decades. The data illustrate that metropolitan areas and cities are becoming more diverse, and that a significant number of stably integrated neighborhoods had emerged by the 1980s. These changes are blurring once sharp racially segregated lines, forcing us to reexamine the perceived inevitability of racially homogeneous neighborhoods.

CHANGING DEMOGRAPHICS AND NEIGHBORHOOD RACIAL MIXING

If the next decade mirrors the last, as it most likely will, immigration will annually contribute an estimated one million newcomers, largely from Asian and Latin America, to the United States. The 2000 census shows that at least three out of ten U.S. residents are not white and Latinos outnumber African Americans. By the year 2030, demographers estimate that one out of four Americans will be either Latino or Asian (Frey and DeVol 2000). Moreover, twenty-five metropolitan areas already fit the "year 2030" national profile: a quarter of the population of Los Angeles, San Francisco, Miami, Houston, and San Diego is already either Latino or Asian, and less than 60 percent is white. Indeed, the racial and ethnic composition of U.S. cities has undergone significant diversification in recent years. In 1997, for example, minorities accounted for at least one-third of all residents of the seven largest metropolitan areas; in none of the seven did a single group dominate (Pollard and O'Hare 1999). The new heterogeneity of cities bears attention as Asians and Latinos have joined blacks and whites as the main racial and ethnic groups. For example, between 1980 and 1998, the minority share of the population in central cities increased from 35 to 47 percent (U.S. Department of Housing and Urban Development 2000). As a result, the minority-majority split in U.S. cities no longer constitutes a black-white affair; a large number of cities are multiethnic and multiracial.

Immigration has a lot to do with this diversity increase in cities and metropolitan areas. Cities, usually a select few, have historically been home to immigrant newcomers and minorities (Fix and Passel 1994). Although recent census data provide some evidence of immigration to suburban locales, central cities continue to be the main entry points for immigrants. While the largest metropolitan areas in the country contain over half (54 percent) of the nation's foreign-born population (twenty-six million in 1997), the foreign-born proportion of the population was highest in central cities of metropolitan areas with five million or more population (Schmidley and Gibson 1999: 17). Some argue that the growth of multiethnic and multiracial metropolitan areas in parts of the country that already contain most of the minority population "balkanizes" these areas as socially and demographically distinct from other parts of the country (Frey 1991). This remains a possibility, but little evidence suggests that the same did not apply in earlier decades of heavy immigration. The crucial fact is that these areas do exist; they impart a new multicultural character to some our nation's most densely populated areas and thus deserve close attention.

Immigration has been beneficial for many central cities. Newly arriving immigrants diversify the racial and ethnic compositions of cities and metropolitan areas and stem population decline in many central cities.[3] Cities and metropolitan areas across the country are faced with population loss due to the flight of large numbers of native-born whites and blacks to less dense, faster-growing, more entrepreneurial metropolitan areas in the Southeast and in western states surrounding California. Yet within the last ten years new immigrants have kept the population balance sheet positive in many regions losing native-born residents. William Frey and Ross DeVol estimate that while New York lost 1,753,600 domestic migrants between 1990 and 1998, it gained 1,306,675 immigrants (2000: 19). Similarly, Orange County, California, lost 187,666 domestic migrants between 1990 and 1999 but gained 227,159 immigrants from abroad (U.S. Department of Housing and Urban Development 2000).

Increased Neighborhood Racial and Ethic Integration since 1970

The trend toward greater racial and ethnic diversity in U.S. metropolitan areas and cities has contributed to new and more complex neighborhood dynamics. Most importantly, the racial and ethnic composition of neighborhoods in immigrant gateways has become more racially mixed and, in some cases, multiethnic and multiracial. This change has contributed to lower segregation in metropolitan areas in nearly half a century. In part, this decrease is related to the drop in overall black population in many metropolitan areas, and the rise in Latino and Asian populations (Ottensmann 1995; Denton and Massey 1991). Numerous scholars have noted that the presence of Latinos and Asians serves as a "buffer" between whites and blacks, putting a hold on rapid racial transition (Santiago 1991; Maly 1998). The presence of multiethnic and multiracial metropolitan areas appears to be key to the decrease of segregated neighborhoods and the increase of integrated ones. William Frey and Reynolds Farley (1996), for example, demonstrate that the segregation and isolation levels of blacks, and to a lesser extent of Latinos and Asians, were lower and decreased more rapidly between 1970 and 1990 in multiethnic metropolitan areas compared to nonmultiethnic metropolitan areas.

I do not intend to downplay the continued severity of racial segregation in urban areas but to underline the reality that changing urban demographics and dynamics—particularly immigration—increase the possibility of racial and ethnic neighborhood diversity (Myers 1999). Such diversity impacts the context that neighborhoods find themselves in and will most likely reduce the number of completely segregated neighborhoods and increase the likelihood of mixed ones. Overall demographic and social change translates into "an increasing level of racial and ethnic diversity within urban neighborhoods in the nation's largest metropolitan areas," particularly multiethnic and multiracial neighborhoods (Denton and Massey 1991: 46). These neighborhoods or communities are microcosms of the larger demographic and social changes.

Recent evidence lends credence to this claim, as a near majority of neighborhoods in metropolitan areas across the nation are to some extent multiethnic or multiracial (Ellen 1998; Denton and Massey 1991). Richard Alba and his colleagues (1995), who examined the racial patterns in the New York City region between 1970 and 1990, found that by 1990, about 50 percent of all neighborhoods contained significant numbers of three or even four groups (whites, Latinos, and Asians; or whites, blacks, Latinos, and Asians). Three-fourths of the population lived in neighborhoods containing significant numbers of three or more groups, compared to just 10 percent in 1970.

In central cities of large metropolitan areas, all-white neighborhoods are significantly declining; most neighborhoods are composed of at least a few members of more than one minority group.[4] An Oakland community activist noted in our interview on October 17, 1996, that "you really do have ethnic groups living in the closest of proximities of one another. You don't go to an Italian section of Oakland. You can to some degree in parts of East Oakland . . . find a black section of Oakland, but even in that section you find white people, Portuguese people, Asian and Latino people on the block or around the corner. It is not likely that you get that community that is just corded off. And I grew up in a community where certain parts of town you needed to be ready to fight. And that is not the case here." These "corded off" sections, or segregated zones, are beginning to lose some of their strength in our nation's largest cities, as the number of completely homogeneous neighborhoods declines.

These findings challenge long-standing assumptions that the presence of multiple racial and ethnic groups in a neighborhood leads to quick resegregation or racial homogeneity. Since 1970, the existence of multiple racial groups has not pushed all neighborhoods toward segregation, and some racially mixed communities were more stable than suggested by traditional understandings of city growth and development. While the intense segregation characteristic of U.S. urban areas makes it easy to be skeptical of any claim of stably integrated neighborhoods, several factors help explain this apparent disparity, notably the manner in which scholars have studied segregation and integration. First, few scholars conducted systematic and generalizable examinations of the existence of integrated neighborhoods before 1970. Among these, the early studies indicate that racially integrated neighborhoods, though limited in number, existed before 1970 and that in some cases a substantial number of whites continued to move into racially mixed areas (Taeuber and Taeuber 1965; Rapkin and Grigsby 1960). Second, scholars examining the validity of the tipping point in the 1950s and 1960s did not find overwhelming support for a tipping point in urban neighborhoods (Goering 1978). If the racial tipping point was not triggering rapid racial transition at the rate suggested, it seems reasonable to suppose that more stable racially integrated neighborhoods existed than was commonly thought. Finally, the story of the pro-integration movement and the individual neighborhoods struggling for integration offers strong evidence that racially homogenous neighborhoods were not always the norm.

If racially and ethnically integrated neighborhoods were more common before 1970 than research and popular perception tell us, why do we know little about them? In part, the way scholars conceptualize integration and measure segregation masked the presence—and thus the importance—of integrated areas. Until recently, scholars focused on the existence, expansion, and maintenance of racially segregated living spaces; racial segregation, not integration, was the main concern. This made sense, given the extent of residential separation and its harsh economic consequences for low-income minorities. However, not all neighborhoods were segregated, and it was assumed that nonsegregated neighborhoods were integrated (at least temporarily). This assumption, however, misses an important point: lack of segregation is not the same as integration, nor is it the opposite of segregation (Ellen 2000). The tools used to measure segregation give us little information on whether a given neighborhood is integrated. Measures of segregation are commonly used to indicate how evenly or unevenly different racial groups are distributed across an entire geographic area or to estimate the proportion of blacks who would have to move into different neighborhoods to produce perfect integration in a city. The measure most frequently applied, the index of dissimilarity, provides an overall score for a larger metropolitan area, informing scholars of the distance an *average* neighborhood in a metropolitan area is from perfect racial evenness.[5] The measure provides information about the city or metropolitan area, not the neighborhood. This is why most of us talk about segregated cities or suburban areas, rarely noting the racial homogeneity of our neighborhoods or blocks.

Racial integration, on the other hand, is a more local phenomenon. Many of us speak glowingly of the racial integration of our neighborhoods, communities, and schools. Thus, to understand integration, measures need to be applied at the neighborhood level. In addition, while segregation is fairly easy to define (the absence of other groups), integration is more problematic, because it means different things to different people (Maly 2000). This makes measuring such a concept difficult and scholars have employed different measures based on the varying definitions of integration. Nonetheless, the various studies reach similar conclusions: over the last three decades cities have been repopulated on a more integrated basis. While racial segregation remains significant, old patterns are beginning to give way to more complicated neighborhood-level racial and ethnic mosaics.

Recent Studies of Integration

Residential integration has increased despite relatively stable indices of dissimilarity for majority racial and ethnic groups. When a group of scholars began to examine the presence and stability of racial integration in neighborhoods during the last three decades, using different samples, they noted the presence and relative stability of racially integrated neighborhoods (Denton and Massey 1991; Ellen 2000; Lee and Wood 1990; Ottensmann 1995). Remember that if we follow the assumptions of the racial tipping hypothesis, racially mixed neighborhoods should resegregate. Instead, these studies indicate that over the last two decades resegregation or racial transition is just one path that mixed neighborhoods take; mixed neighborhoods can also maintain stable integration. In fact, the studies suggest that the probability and pace of white population loss is no longer affected by the mere presence of minorities moving into a neighborhood. Three studies led by John Ottensmann revealed that the percentages of white households moving into racially mixed tracts were sufficient to maintain racial stability (Ottensmann, Good, and Gleason 1990; Ottensmann and Gleason 1991, 1992). In the most ambitious study of racial integration at the neighborhood level to date, Ingrid Ellen examined the extent, stability, and dynamics of racially integrated neighborhoods—defined as those with racial compositions 10–50 percent black—in thirty-four metropolitan areas (2000).[6] Ellen presents several important findings concerning racial integration in U.S. residential areas. First, she confirms an overall diversification of neighborhoods and an increase in the number of racially integrated neighborhoods. In thirty-four metropolitan areas, fewer white neighborhoods completely shut out minorities: the proportion of whites living in areas in which less than 1 percent of the population is black declined from 63 percent in 1970 to 36 percent in 1990. Second, and more importantly, the data reveal a steady growth in integrated neighborhoods between 1970 and 1990, where nearly one-fifth of all tracts were integrated by 1990. Third, the percentage of whites and blacks living in integrated communities increased: in 1990, 15 percent of the non-Latino white population in metropolitan areas lived in integrated communities compared to nearly one-third of the black population. While these percentages are not overwhelming, the share of whites living in integrated areas increased 14 percent between 1970 and 1980, and by 30 percent between 1980 and 1990. Meanwhile, the proportion of blacks living in majority black tracts decreased from over two-thirds to around 54 percent, while the proportion living in integrated neighborhoods rose from 26 percent to 32 percent (Ellen 2000).

Although Ellen's study suggests a more hopeful prognosis for racially integrated neighborhoods, Ellen found that segregated neighborhoods remain more stable than integrated ones. She reports that over 80 percent of predominantly white and black communities remained stable between 1980 and 1990, compared to less than half of racially integrated tracts. The institutional forces favoring segregation continue to make the prospect of stable racial integration less likely than segregation.

By using different analytical and conceptual tools from those used to monitor segregation, the research of these scholars uncovers the distribution of people in integrated neighborhoods in cities across the country and how they change over time. It provides a different picture of residential settlement patterns in U.S. metropolitan areas. Segregation is clearly present, but an increasing number of stably integrated neighborhoods exist. The data confirm that not only have the number of integrated neighborhoods increased since 1970, but also they are remaining stably integrated.

Chicago, New York, and Oakland

Most systematic studies of racial mixing use the percentage of blacks in a neighborhood to indicate the extent of its integration or segregation. This is not inherently problematic, as it provides a view of the racial composition of an area. However, this approach provides only a partial view of neighborhood racial dynamics. With the changing racial and ethnic character of the nation and its cities, it is important to move beyond black-white examination. Two-group models of racial integration can tell us little about how our nation's increasing racial and ethnic diversity is being played out at the neighborhood level. To accomplish this, we need tools to examine residential settlement patterns that focus on the extent and nature of multiracial and multiethnic neighborhood integration.

I offer such an examination, focusing on the central city neighborhoods of Chicago, New York, and Oakland between 1980 and 2000. The Neighborhood Diversity (ND) index is employed to measure racial and ethnic integration at the neighborhood level. The ND index defines an integrated neighborhood as one that closely compares to or resembles a given city's average for four principal racial and ethnic groups.[7] An ND index score was calculated for neighborhoods in Chicago, New York, and Oakland.[8] The score represents how close or far a neighborhood was from the city average of whites, blacks, Latinos, and Asians.[9] Using the median ND score for the city in a given year, raw scores were divided into three categories: integrated, moderately integrated, and segregated.

Another variable was constructed to further categorize neighborhoods based upon their stability or transition from 1980 to 1990. Based on their ND scores in 1980 and 1990, neighborhoods were categorized into five groups. For example, neighborhoods that were labeled integrated in both 1980 and 1990 are considered stably integrated (the same holds for moderately integrated or segregated). Neighborhoods that switched categories between decades were categorized as either "moving toward integration" or "moving away from integration." Thus, if a tract labeled "moderately integrated" in 1990 became integrated in 2000, it was categorized as moving toward integration.

Table 2.1 reports the extent and relative stability of neighborhoods over the decade, based on the ND index scores. The data are displayed by year and stability-transition category (presented in the fourth and fifth row for each city). The table indicates that almost half the neighborhoods in each city were segregated between 1980 and 2000. Yet each city also had a substantial percentage of integrated neighborhoods, albeit to varying degrees. In Chicago and New York, the percentage of racially integrated neighborhoods was small (less than 10 percent), increasing between 1980 and 1990, and then slightly declining in the 1990s. In Oakland, nearly one-fifth of all neighborhoods were integrated in 1980, although this decreased significantly over the next two decades. Oakland deviates from Chicago and New York in that it experienced a decline in the percentage of integrated neighborhoods between 1980 and 2000. This does not necessarily mean that Oakland is more segregated than Chicago or New York, as there are contextual and measurement factors that account for the rather steep drop in integrated neighborhoods.[10]

Looking at neighborhood stability in each city, Table 2.1 illustrates that over the twenty-year period less than 5 percent of neighborhoods were stably integrated, while 40 percent were stably segregated. Based on these percentages alone, it is easy to argue that stable integration is indeed rare and segregation the norm. I believe, however, that integrated neighborhoods are more common than the picture most studies of segregation portray. Certainly, the majority of neighborhoods in each city were either segregated or becoming less integrated in both decades. However, a significant percentage of neighborhoods in each city were either integrated or moving toward integration during the 1980s and 1990s. For example, in the 1990s, 13 percent of Chicago, 18 percent of New York, and 10 percent of Oakland neighborhoods were either integrated or become more integrated. And importantly, these neighborhoods accounted for a large number of residents in each city (in Chicago, 393,663; in New York,

TABLE 2.1. Neighborhood Diversity Index by City, 1980–2000

City	Year	Integrated	Moving toward integration	Moderately integrated	Moving away from integration	Segregated
Chicago	1980	5.0%	—	44.9%	—	50.1%
	1990	6.8%	—	43.2%	—	49.9%
	2000	6.1%	—	43.8%	—	50.1%
	1980–1990*	3.2%	9.1%	35.9%	7.4%	44.3%
	1990–2000*	4.2%	8.3%	34.9%	9.0%	43.6%
New York	1980	8.8%	—	42.9%	—	48.3%
	1990	9.2%	—	41.8%	—	49.0%
	2000	7.4%	—	44.4%	—	48.2%
	1980–1990*	4.1%	12.3%	30.4%	12.4%	40.8%
	1990–2000*	3.3%	14.8%	26.5%	17.2%	38.3%
Oakland	1980	19.6%	—	30.4%	—	50.4%
	1990	11.8%	—	37.3%	—	51.0%
	2000	4.9%	—	48.0%	—	47.1%
	1980–1990*	4.1%	12.3%	30.4%	12.4%	40.8%
	1990–2000*	4.9%	4.9%	36.3%	7.8%	46.1%

*These categories represent the movement or stability of tracts beginning in 1980.
Source: U.S. Bureau of the Census, 1980, 1990, 2000.

1,120,713; in Oakland, 81,284). Racially integrated neighborhoods are not anomalies.

Remember, too, that integrated neighborhoods in these three cities were defined as such because of their proximity to the average of four racial and ethnic groups, implying a multiethnic and multiracial composition. For example, the average each neighborhood was compared to in New York in 1990 was 43 percent white, 26 percent black, 24 percent Latino, and 7 percent Asian. Arguably, such a breakdown is extremely multiracial and multiethnic, so any neighborhood that comes close to that racial composition will be multiracial and multiethnic as well. A close look at the racial composition of neighborhoods labeled stably integrated reveals that they are indeed multiracial and multiethnic. In 100 percent of the stably integrated neighborhoods in Oakland, for example, no single racial or ethnic group exceeded 50 percent of the tract's population. In fact, 53 percent of the moderately integrated tracts in Oakland lacked a racial minority. In New York and Chicago the percentages were lower, but still significant (75 percent and 65 percent, respectively). Neighborhoods labeled integrated in this study were indeed multiethnic and multiracial.

The data from these three cities, however, do not indicate that integrated neighborhoods are immune from resegregation or racial transition.

My examination of neighborhoods in Chicago, New York, and Oakland confirms these findings. In the three cities, 85 percent of segregated neighborhoods in 1980 remained so in 1990, compared to 47 percent of integrated neighborhoods in 1980. These trends are similar between 1990 and 2000. Interpreting these data does not require an absolutist response. Undoubtedly, segregated neighborhoods remain the most stable of all. This has been true for almost a century. However, it is also significant that almost half of racially integrated neighborhoods remained stable over each decade, bucking the trend of racial transition and resegregation.

In sum, residential segregation by race in U.S. cities declined in the 1970s and 1980s, and racially and ethnically integrated neighborhoods became more prevalent and stable in each decade after 1970.[11] The rapid white-to-black succession appears less applicable than in earlier decades, as the overall trend for most neighborhoods is away from two-group structures and toward greater diversity. Applying varying definitions of integration to data from various samples reveals the presence of racially integrated neighborhoods in the post-1970 era, with the harsh lines of segregation beginning to blur. While the percentages are not overwhelming and such neighborhoods are not as stable as racially homogenous ones, stable racially integrated neighborhoods are more prevalent than most studies suggest. The data also reveal that integrated neighborhoods in some of our largest urban centers mirror the multiethnic and multiracial character of the metropolitan area and the nation. Many of these neighborhoods represent a new diversity emerging in urban areas, one that is changing the nature of race relations in cities.

SOCIAL FACTORS CONTRIBUTING TO THE NEW DIVERSITY

The social forces contributing to the emergence of this new diversity in the nation's largest cities are numerous. However, I believe two associated trends are key to producing multiethnic and multiracial urban spaces: the globalization of the economy and immigration. Many of America's largest cities and metropolitan areas are already, or are gradually evolving into, global centers of trade. This economic shift brings an expansion of the service economy, thus changing the social, economic, and spatial structure of our cities. The available jobs produced by this new economy also attract an incredible number of immigrants, primarily from Latin America and Asia, who are driving an increasingly multicultural mix of residents.

As Saskia Sassen notes: "Developments in cities cannot be understood in isolation from fundamental changes in the larger organization of advanced economies" (2000: 35). Cities have been economically transformed since the end of World War II. The traditional manufacturing base that spurred economic growth midcentury has given way to a complex postindustrial economy, as production shifted from goods to services. In the process, cities have become sites for advanced services and telecommunication facilities that are necessary to implement and manage advanced economic operations (Harrison and Bluestone 1988; Sassen 1992). Many large U.S. cities are reaching "global city" status, as their central cores and adjacent "edge city" growth corridors constitute command and control centers for the high-tech information economy. The economic markets of these cities, stretching beyond regional and national boundaries, attract firms involved in finance, investment, banking, consulting, accounting, and advertising.

How do changes in the organization of advanced economies contribute to more diverse racial and ethnic compositions in cities and neighborhoods? The nature of the economic changes creates new types of jobs and draws new people to fill the jobs. As growing global markets in cities bring in numerous new firms (e.g., corporate headquarters, financial institutions, start-up "new economy" businesses), the lines of inequality in cities are altered. The leading sectors of this new global economy attract highly qualified and educated employees, as well as low-wage, unskilled, and contingent service workers. The latter comprise the workforce of sweatshop and piece-rate labor operations. As global cities mature, they also require low-wage workers—such as retail clerks, cleaners, secretaries, maintenance and security personnel, and part-time and contingent labor—who provide services to this top sector of the global economy (Harrison and Bluestone 1988; Sassen 2000).

As cities have become major centers for financial and corporate headquarters, they have attracted highly qualified and trained employees to profitable and high-level technical and administrative jobs. These high-end workers (mostly non-Latino whites) earn large salaries and demand high-quality urban housing (as most prefer to live in the city) and services. And while these new workers may be a sign of prosperity for a city, they simultaneously drive an increase in low-wage, dead-end jobs. Immigrants and minorities are filling these low-wage, supportive, and conditional positions. Immigrants, in particular, represent a desirable labor supply because they are relatively cheap, reliable, flexible, and safe (Sassen 1988). They also lower the costs of keeping a highly skilled labor force in place (Waldinger 1996). Thus, the new economy is attracting new kinds of jobs and different workers, most of whom occupy different segments of contemporary urban space.

Recent economic changes affect cities in various ways. On the one hand, the influx of high-end workers, with their distinctive tastes, gives rise to commercial and residential gentrification. The demand for high-end housing has created a housing and homeownership boom throughout the country, driving up property values and rents while attracting high-priced commercial establishments. Private development, with the aid and approval of the city, stimulates much of the revitalization of older neighborhoods into gentrified districts, concentrating expensive housing, upscale dining and shopping, and entertainment (Bennett 1999). These districts cater to individuals at the top of the new economy and are largely disconnected from the rest of the city, except in their dependence on low-wage service workers that they draw from less-affluent areas.

On the other hand, gentrification has reduced the number of affordable housing units available to those at the bottom of the economic ladder. While both incomes and demand are increasing, the supply of affordable housing is not keeping pace (U.S. Department of Housing and Urban Development 2000). Nationally, the number of affordable housing units is shrinking when it should expand. Between 1991 and 1997, the number of rental units available to extremely low-income households dropped by 5 percent, a decline of more than 370,000 units (Nelson et al. 2000). In many cities, this trend puts substantial pressure on middle-income and low-income families who seek decent housing.

The growth of a well-paid labor force and gentrified districts rests on the availability and growth of a "population of others" (Sassen 2000). Cities or metropolitan areas with significant concentrations of corporate power tend to also have large numbers of "others," immigrants and the entire infrastructure of low-wage, nonprofessional jobs and activities crucial to maintaining corporate culture. Since immigrants constitute such a significant proportion of this "other" population, it should come as no surprise that immigrants continue to concentrate in the nation's largest metropolitan areas, those that are serving as the centers of the new economy. For example, a large proportion of newly arriving immigrants has clustered in New York, Los Angeles, San Francisco, Chicago, Houston, and Miami. In fact, two-thirds of all 1990–1998 immigrants are located in just ten of the nation's metropolitan areas (Frey and DeVol 2000). Roughly 40 percent have settled in the ten largest cities, which account for less than a tenth of the U.S. population.

That immigrants make up a significantly higher proportion of these cities' populations than they do in the U.S. population is a result of recent arrivals choosing to reside in the same metropolitan areas that immigrants did in the 1970s and 1980s. As a result, the share of Latinos and Asians in the metropolitan regions increases even more. The ten metropolitan areas with the largest Latino populations were also the ten largest gainers of Latino immigrants. They attracted more than half of new Latino residents between 1990 and 1996 and house 58 percent of the nation's Latino population (Frey 1998). The Asian population is similarly concentrated: a small number of metropolitan areas contain almost half of all U.S. Asian residents.[12] This concentration of immigrants creates an overall multiethnic and multiracial population that has slowly become visible at the neighborhood level.

Consider recent legal-immigration trends in the metropolitan areas of Chicago, New York, and Oakland between 1992 and 2000 (see Table 2.2), keeping in mind that in the 1990s the states of Illinois, New York, and California were among the top six in total number of admitted legal immigrants. Among the ten metropolitan areas most attractive to immigrants between 1992 and 2000, Chicago attracted over 325,000, New York nearly one million, and Oakland just over 128,000—together, over 20 percent of all immigrants. (While Oakland's share may appear rather small, the city's population in 1990 was around 370,000.)

Immigrants arriving in Chicago, New York, and Oakland in the 1990s

TABLE 2.2. Legal Immigration by Metropolitan Area—Chicago, New York, Oakland, 1992–2000

Year	Chicago #	Chicago %*	New York #	New York %*	Oakland #	Oakland %*
1992	38,157	4.70%	120,635	14.90%	14,629	1.60%
1993	44,121	4.90%	128,434	14.20%	16,087	1.80%
1994	40,081	5.00%	124,423	15.50%	13,701	1.70%
1995	31,730	4.40%	111,687	15.50%	12,011	1.70%
1996	39,989	4.40%	133,168	14.50%	15,759	1.70%
1997	35,386	4.40%	107,434	13.50%	15,723	2.00%
1998	30,355	4.60%	82,175	12.40%	13,437	2.00%
1999	33,754	5.20%	80,893	12.50%	10,794	1.70%
2000	32,300	3.80%	85,867	10.10%	16,150	1.90%
Total	325,873	4.60%	974,716	13.70%	128,291	1.80%

*This column represents the percentage of immigrants entering all U.S. metropolitan areas.
Source: U.S. Department of Justice, Immigration and Naturalization Service. 2000. "Legal Immigration, Fiscal Year 2000." Annual Report. May.

are contributing to net population growth, even as each city continues to experience white flight. In the 1980s, Chicago had the smallest percentage loss of whites (around 10 percent) and Oakland the largest (nearly 23 percent). Meanwhile, the percentage growth of Latinos and Asians in each city was substantial (in some cases doubling), undoubtedly influenced by immigration. Demographers suggest that the growth of Latinos and Asians in each city will not abate anytime soon. In Chicago, Latinos are the fastest-growing ethnic group and should become the largest population group by 2025 (Balu 1996). Immigration thus has stemmed population loss and significantly changed the racial, social, and political character of urban areas across the United States.

A quick tour through various neighborhoods in U.S. cities highlights the transformative effect of corporate expansion and immigration. The increase of wildly expensive condos and town homes in "hot" residential areas and the influx of upscale stores and restaurants illustrate the effects of corporate expansion. At the other end of the social spectrum, immigration and the low-wage infrastructure are equally evident—on storefront signs, which sometimes are displayed in numerous languages and do not conform to corporate franchising; on the faces of store owners, street vendors, servers and busboys, security personnel, and especially on the subways and buses; and in quickly diversifying schools. These shifts alter racial lines in cities and contribute to new and more complex neighborhood dynamics.

Unplanned Diversity

Traditionally, urban sociology has examined neighborhood change by focusing on neighborhoods that were supposedly "invaded" or "attacked" by outside forces (e.g., urban renewal, blockbusting) or people (e.g., racial change, displacement) and examining how communities sustain themselves through conscious community organizing. In Chapter One, we saw how neighborhoods across the country organized to maintain stable integration. Their approach represents the mainstream focus of urban sociologists. These communities articulated their desire for integration and tolerance early in the "invasion" of different racial groups and, while intervening in the process of racial change proved difficult, achieved some success in maintaining integration. As cities and regions change economically and racially, however, the traditional understanding of neighborhoods becomes less appropriate. As Janet Abu-Lughod notes in *From Urban Village to East Village*:

Increasingly, neighborhoods in the central zones of our largest cities no longer fit the old model of "ethnic enclaves" or "urban villages." Many no longer constitute—indeed if they ever did—natural communities where residents share a common culture and pursue a relatively unified set of interests vis-à-vis "outsiders." Rather, in addition to the major black ghettos and the barrios of the larger cities, which almost constitute cities in themselves, there are now numerous multi-ethnic, highly diversified districts containing subgroups with varying lifestyles, class interests, goals and ideologies. Such areas do not form unified or "natural" communities, but are indeed the arenas within which subgroups struggle, not only with "outside" interests, such as developers or city governments, but with one another. (1994: 5)

Abu-Lughod aptly captures how larger demographic and economic shifts are altering the structure of neighborhoods and challenging our traditional understandings of how cities develop. She also points to a new form of neighborhood diversity or integration.

In cities across the country, a "new diversity" is emerging in many neighborhoods that does not resemble the structure of pro-integrative neighborhoods. While such neighborhoods may have changed racially over time, complete "invasion" or "transition" did not occur, nor did a single type of diversity emerge (e.g., black-white). In fact, numerous communities, "at no one's request and by no one's design," are being transformed from racially homogeneous to multiethnic and multiracial neighborhoods (Sanjek 1998: 367). And by most accounts, the newcomers and established residents in these city neighborhoods (and some suburbs) "never intended to be neighbors" (Horton 1995: 33). Neighborhoods characterized by this new diversity are best described as "diverse by circumstance," given that little conscious neighborhood organizing intervention held their racial mix (Nyden, Maly, and Lukehart 1997; Nyden et al. 1998). Integration was more a product of social and economic factors initially beyond the control of residents. Unlike the conscious and biracial makeup of communities outlined in the previous chapter, the composition of these communities extends to a more complex blending of multiple racial and ethnic groups, class interests, and cultures.

Diverse-by-Circumstance Neighborhoods

In 1995 and 1996, a major study sought to interpret the new forms of neighborhood racial mixing. Eight research teams consisting of university researchers and community leaders collected, analyzed, and reported data in fourteen communities in nine cities. This research project, led by Philip Nyden and John Lukehart, identified two types of integrated communities—diverse by direction and diverse by circumstance (Nyden, Maly, and Lukehart 1997; Nyden et al. 1998). The researchers noted that communities that had sustained integration the longest were those that had become mixed as a result of the pro-integration movement (described in Chapter One). Equally noteworthy was their finding of more recently integrated neighborhoods that did not follow an intentional, directed course. These communities represent the new diversity emerging in U.S. urban areas over the last two decades. They require a distinctive shift in our understanding of the social character of such communities and their path toward racial mixing. Diverse-by-circumstance neighborhoods are different in character than diverse-by-direction ones. Three key features distinguish them from earlier forms of integrated neighborhoods: the extent of the diversity, how the diversity came about, and the focus of organizing efforts once the integration emerged. First, these neighborhoods are diverse on a variety of dimensions. They often are composed of more than two racial and ethnic groups, usually assuming a multiethnic and multiracial composition. The level of diversity helps prevent the numerical (and political and social) dominance of one group. As a city councilman from Jackson Heights told me in a May 1996 interview: "If there was one ethnic group taking over the neighborhood, then there might be problems . . . but because we have South Asians, because we have Central and South Americans, . . . but not so dominating that it overwhelms anyone, I think that helps maintain things." These communities are also economically and culturally mixed, containing both immigrant and native-born residents and a mixed housing stock. Immigrants, usually from multiple nations of origin, are attracted to these communities by their affordable (rental) housing and in turn contribute to a greater racially, economically, and culturally mixed residential base.

Second, diverse-by-circumstance communities illustrate the various paths neighborhoods take in becoming racially integrated. Unlike diverse-by-direction communities where the entry of minorities into the community was followed by an organized biracial response to prevent racial transition and promote integration, the integration that emerged in diverse-by-circumstance neighborhoods resulted from social processes not directly related to resident or community actions, including the influx of immigrant groups, a change in neighborhood composition as an aging white population moves out or dies and new residents take their place, investment or revitalization of a commercial strip within the community or near the community that attracts whites and minorities, gentrification, or a stalled real estate market that keeps people from moving (Nyden et al. 1998: 11–12). In the chapters that follow, I demonstrate that integration in Uptown, Jackson Heights, and San Antonio–Fruitvale emerged as a result of a complex confluence of factors not directly related to an organized response to maintain the racial mix.

Third, unlike many diverse-by-direction neighborhoods where local organizations see maintaining integration as the central organizing principle, integration in diverse-by-circumstance neighborhoods is not the primary goal. While it may be a goal for some organizations, it competes with a variety of other goals and objectives. If a primary organizing principle exists in such neighborhoods, it is the broad issue of maintaining and improving the quality of community life. Most diverse-by-circumstance communities lack a unified umbrella organization that explicitly promotes integration. Instead, the community organization network generally consists of a number of small groups, most of which serve specific ethnic group interests and needs. These groups, however, often form or join coalitions to protect community interests, such as safety, education, and economic development, and even to promote interethnic and interracial harmony. As integration emerges, groups tend to work together to negotiate differences and in the process become aware that racial integration is a community asset. As they do with other community strengths, community organizations work to develop and nurture integration, even attempting to promote or "sell" the community based on its racial mix.

The pro-integrative efforts that produced stable racial integration in dozens of communities across the nation were extremely conscious of their racial mix and the efforts required to maintain it. As Oak Park, Illinois, activist Bobbie Raymond argued: "Until somebody decides that long-term integration is worth keeping, . . . there will never be such a thing as a stable integrated neighborhood. There is no such thing as a stable integrated neighborhood. They're all unstable. . . . If any of these communities stopped for one day, one week, one month, one year, what they're doing, they would resegregate. . . . If we stop doing this tomorrow, it [integration] wouldn't continue" (quoted in Wiese 1995: 120). Raymond's statement is compelling in that it captures the fragile nature and everyday realities for diverse-by-design communities. However, it fails to capture the experience and complexity of emerging multiethnic and multiracial diverse-by-circumstance communities. Initially, there was little conscious work in these communities to promote integration. These communities are the products of social, political, and economic forces outside their boundaries.

It is not that these communities do not care about or value integration. They differ because they contain diverse and numerous groups that often have varied and competing interests and concerns. Despite the dynamics involved, many neighborhoods that integrated along multiethnic and multiracial lines for several decades show no signs of rapid resegregation. However, this does not mean that diverse-by-circumstance communities' local efforts are not necessary to maintain the integration. Raymond is right that conscious efforts to fight institutionalized practices that promote and profit from segregation are required if integration is to be maintained over the long haul. The racial, ethnic, and economic makeup of these communities depends on local efforts to ensure that federal fair-housing laws are enforced, commercial investment is attracted and managed, and opportunities for affordable housing are present. These outcomes require intervention.

What diverse-by-circumstance communities suggest is that there is not one type of integrated community. Integrated communities become racially and ethnically mixed in different ways, are diverse along different lines, and require different types of organizations and interventions. The nature of integration in diverse-by-circumstance neighborhoods represents a step away from the biracial integrated neighborhoods that emerged from the civil rights movement. These communities emerged from the demographic and economic reshaping of urban areas over the last several decades, including immigration and globalization; pro-integration efforts could not have produced them. To understand race relations in urban areas—how race shapes urban space—diverse-by-circumstance communities deserve close attention as unique and varied urban spaces. They are harbingers of the future of race relations in cities and the nation. As the nation becomes increasingly multiethnic and multiracial, models of cooperation, accommodation, and coalition building are necessary. We need insight into ways we can begin to break down the wall of racial exclusion and segregation that has existed in U.S. cities for over a century.

In the chapters that follow, I examine three diverse-by-circumstance communities: Uptown, Jackson Heights, and San Antonio–Fruitvale.

3   Uptown, Chicago

RESIDENT NARRATIVE: ANDREA "ANDY" LOWRY

In 1992, I moved to the Wicker Park–East Village neighborhood, a rapidly gentrifying neighborhood that was once largely Puerto Rican and Latino.[1] I found a small two-bedroom for four hundred dollars a month and lived there alone till August 1997. Around this time, I switched jobs and returned to school full time. As rents increased and my income decreased, I was quickly priced out of the area and had to look elsewhere. I found a roommate and went in search of a two-bedroom apartment that was close to seven hundred dollars per month and not too far north and west. We looked in numerous neighborhoods (Lincoln Park, Lakeview, Ravenswood, etc.), but we did not find an apartment that fit our budget or was close to the CTA el line. In the summer of 1997, we finally found a neighborhood we could afford and still get a decent-sized apartment: Uptown.

We moved into a large two-bedroom apartment on Malden, west of Broadway and two buildings south of Lawrence. At $725 a month, the rent fit our budget. I had little knowledge of Uptown prior to moving in, though I quickly realized that it is a patchwork. This was obvious just looking at the housing on my block. Several decent Victorian houses and graystone six-flats coexisted with several large SRO buildings and ramshackle apartment buildings. Most of the low-end buildings had numerous broken windows, dirt instead of grass, and missing screens and front doors. My block had a lot of low-income residents, although it seemed to be one of the last low-income areas in the area. For example, my boyfriend at the time lived on the same street, three blocks south, but it was quiet and well cared for. His building was the last on the block to be converted into condominiums. Uptown is really patchy. One block will be really nice Victorian houses, the next block will be run-down large apartment buildings and bars and liquor stores that open at 7 A.M.

I didn't mind living in a low-income neighborhood; however, I was shocked to see such a diverse group of low-income residents. There seemed to be little shame in being poor in Uptown and people appeared to accept it as a reality in the community. I liked the fact that there were so many social services available in the community. For instance, Salvation Army had a large presence in the neighborhood, with a facility on Broadway just south of Wilson. There would be dozens of people waiting as I rode by on my bike in the morning and evening. There were also several storefronts offering mental health and drug rehabilitation services and lots of signs for free food. The churches were also real active. I liked the attempt being made to address the needs of the community. I mean, if people are going hungry and homeless then we need services in the neighborhood to address that. I even ended up volunteering at the Inspiration Café [a restaurant that caters to low-income individuals and families].

I could see the racial and ethnic diversity in Uptown just from living on my street. I had never in my life seen so many racial groups living together under one roof or in one neighborhood. One building in particular had Asian, black, Latino, and Native American families living together. My own building was probably an equal mix of Latino families and white twenty-year-olds. I liked that I could walk down the street, be exposed to racial and ethnic groups with whom I had rarely had the chance to interact. It was exciting to be able to access all those bits of culture at one time. Also, there were a lot of racially mixed families and couples and I felt more comfortable on the street. I felt less conspicuous. In other neighborhoods I always felt like I stuck out like a sore thumb. I'm half Puerto Rican but always identified as black—in Wicker Park there simply weren't that many blacks or any other minority groups.

But for all the positive experiences, I eventually moved out of Uptown after eighteen months. I left for several reasons. First, I didn't like the physical location. I did enjoy the proximity to the lake, but it wasn't convenient. I felt that there wasn't much for me to do, but that's just a matter of preference though. The main reason was the commute. I resented having to spend forty-five minutes or an hour each way out of my day commuting, and I wanted that to change.

Second, the crime was a bit out of control. I've lived in some rough areas in my eleven years of living on my own in Chicago. I always felt that I could take care of myself on the street. However, Uptown really did make me feel unsafe most of the time. I was approached on the street quite often by men and had some real disgusting incidents of sexual harassment, just real vulgar stuff that made me want to go home and take a shower. I consider myself to be street smart, but I was jumpy after a couple of months of feeling like I had to watch my back walking home four blocks from the train. I felt continuously on my guard; I had never seen so much action on the street. I mean, people were passed out on my doorstep, women got into fist fights with their boyfriends outside of my window, and people who drank and smoked pot from 8 AM onward in front of my house. The cops were constantly getting called to my block. Someone always seemed to be getting carted away in a cop car. I got tired of feeling unsafe.

Finally, Uptown was gentrifying. I have never seen a community so divided; there was no subtlety to the gentrification. Working with Inspiration Café gave me a chance to interact with longtime neighborhood residents. We talked about their feelings toward the new residents, and the common opinion was that the outsiders are coming in and don't respect their neighbors. It was all about "What about the property value of the house I just bought?" I witnessed this at several Community Area Policing meetings. Most of the newcomers seemed very arrogant and mostly concerned about cleaning up the neighborhood to improve their property values. For example, many wanted to remove the SROs on my block. Many new residents —including a sizable middle-class gay population—were quick to negatively label the residents of the SROs. They would say, "Those people are the ones bringing down my property values and making all the trouble." There was never talk about letting people remain in the less nice apartment buildings or cleaning up the neighborhood so everyone could benefit from a better area. It was always this self-serving attitude that these buildings should be torn down or converted to attract "a different element." There are battle lines drawn by class and race, between the longtime residents and the newly landed residents. I saw little respect for the existing community and a real willingness to label longtime residents as deviant.

Maybe I'm kidding myself, but I like to think that somehow I would be doing less damage by staying in Uptown. I did not want to be part of the new landowners (and renters) forcing out affordable housing. That's what is happening; being low income is seen as criminal. I remember several instances of seeing families or sets of roommates getting kicked out on the street and then having their building go condo. Even if they did owe back rent, it was still an odd coincidence that they would be forced out on the street just before their buildings turned over. Uptown is changing rapidly and part of me did not want to stick around to witness it. It is interesting to note that when I moved from Uptown I looked at rents in the area and they have skyrocketed. The apartment I left now goes for $850, up $125 in eighteen months. Even if I wanted to, I wouldn't be able to afford to live in Uptown anymore.

WELCOME TO UPTOWN

As a new graduate student, I was at first negatively impressed with Chicago's north-side community of Uptown. Classmates and professors painted a picture of a community notorious for crime, homeless shelters, faded retail districts, and uninviting streets. My travels confirmed some, though not all, of these warnings. The physical character of Uptown is much more complex than they described. My frequent trips on the Chicago Transit Authority's elevated Red Line, which snakes through Uptown's core, provided a perch from which to take in its unique character. Looking toward the community's eastern edge, scattered high-rises appear as hulks of steel and concrete peering over a mix of two-flats, larger low-rise apartment buildings, and single-family homes. In the central section, Uptown's numerous two-flats come into view, some in the process of being rehabilitated, others broken down, with backyards that served as parking lots for numerous cars. The stop at Wilson Avenue displays a once prominent commercial area, now filled with a mishmash of marginal stores. Arriving at Lawrence Avenue, to the west is the striking Uptown Bank Building and the impressive Aragon Ballroom and Uptown Theater. Not far away is 4848 North Winthrop, an architecturally unimpressive rectangular building converted to affordable housing after years of neglect when it served as a center for drug dealing. A walk east and south along the lakefront reveals large mansions, attractive housing, beautiful tree-lined streets, and a very diverse population. Any trip reveals what residents have known for years: Uptown is not one thing, it is many, often overlapping and contradictory.

Located midway between the Loop and suburban Evanston, Uptown is bounded by Foster Avenue to the north, Ravenswood Avenue to the west, Irving Park Road to the south, and Lake Michigan to the east. Yet, these official boundaries obfuscate the community's shifting and complex character. For years authors and journalists eloquently captured Uptown's memorable physical arrangement. David Fremon writes: "[Uptown] has seen high society and lowlifes, millionaires and paupers, artists, professionals, entertainers, thieves, and common people from virtually everywhere, often located cheek to jowl. In fact, it is hard to believe that such a compact area contains so much variety: everything from stately, neatly kept mansions to mammoth high-rises to vacated buildings whose boarded-up windows serve mainly to display posters for upcoming rock concerts" (1990).

Uptown's patchwork of housing and land uses reflects its racial and ethnic mix, class cleavages, and political conflicts. As will be clear, Uptown is a community of many "voices," often finding it difficult to agree on the nature of its future. The community's storied history of political and class struggles results in periodic contests for defining what Uptown is or will be, evidenced in the various terms applied to it: Hillbilly Ghetto, the New Skid Row, Uptown the Psychiatric Ghetto, and Contested Territory (Bennett 1991). Other terms seem appropriate, given that the area has been a site for urban renewal plans, project-based subsidized housing construction, historic districting, tent cities for the homeless, condominium conversions, ethnic entrepreneurship, gentrification, and battles to secure affordable housing.

Since the 1960s Uptown has emerged as a truly remarkable community—multiethnic, multiracial, and mixed income. Uptown, however, was never a "traditional" neighborhood that was "attacked" by outside forces. The racial and ethnic integration that emerged in the 1960s and 1970s did not result from the work of individuals who "self-consciously" developed organizations, social networks, and institutional accommodations to promote (or prevent) integration early in the process of racial change. Instead, a complex set of demographic and political processes, along with local community interventions and negotiations, were instrumental in maintaining integration. As a result, Uptown is a relatively stable, viable community that remains as integrated as a neighborhood can get in Chicago.

Becoming Integrated: From Middle-class Mecca to Ethnic Polyglot

The story of Uptown begins in the late 1800s, as Chicago's development pushed north and the city annexed Lake View Township along the northern lakefront. Older wealthy families purchased elegant mansions along Lake Michigan. Professionals and junior executives occupied spacious apartments. Lavish hotels popped up along the lake for vacationing beach seekers. The area's growth accelerated around the turn of the century when Chicago's elevated rail system (the "el") extended its northern terminus to Wilson Avenue. El service connected with electric streetcars, which ran north/south along Broadway and Sheridan Road, and east/west along Wilson and Lawrence Avenues. The abundance of transportation made Uptown accessible and sparked construction of new stores, office buildings, and apartments.

In a short time, Uptown became one of Chicago's most successful business and entertainment centers. In 1915, the infant motion-picture industry planted itself in the area, as stars such as Mary Pickford, Charlie Chaplin, Douglas Fairbanks, and Gloria Swanson made silent films at the Essanay Studios on Argyle Street (DeBat 1993). In the first decades of the twentieth century, Uptown was known as a lively entertainment center, as the Uptown, Riviera, and Lakeside Theaters were places to be seen and to see the first motion pictures (Bennett 1991). Most accounts of this time describe Uptown as a playground for celebrities and young Chicagoans who loved music and dancing. Though movie production ended in the 1920s, the nightlife continued with the opening of the Aragon Ballroom and the lavish Uptown Theater. Uptown was an attractive destination for middle-class Chicagoans. By the early 1920s, Uptown had solidified into a lively commercial district with two large banks, an appealing office building for professional services, theaters, and elegant restaurants. With a mix of modest cottages, elevator apartment buildings, common-corridor and courtyard buildings, and elaborate mansions, Uptown's heterogeneous housing stock also added to the allure of the area.[2] Young singles and couples, as well as affluent households, found housing suitable to their needs and tastes.[3]

UPTOWN'S DECLINE

Like that of most communities, Uptown's prosperity did not last. Uptown began to decline during the quarter century between the Great Depression and the mid-1950s. The Depression curbed consumer demand as unemployment rose. The silent-movie industry moved west. In 1933, the city pushed Lake Michigan's shoreline several hundred yards to the east, allowing Lake Shore Drive to be extended to Foster Avenue, Uptown's northern border. This move took away Uptown's direct access to the lake and led traffic away from the commercial district to its eastern rim. As a result, "the retail business of local merchants was devastated; as independent stores in Uptown and elsewhere folded one by one, they were replaced by absentee-owned chain stores" (Marciniak 1981: 19). The heart of Uptown's commercial and entertainment district was undermined; the decline spread to other parts of the community during World War II and the years immediately following.

Uptown's once glamorous and stable image took a hit during this time. As workers poured into Chicago for jobs in the defense industry, the city found itself in the midst of a significant housing shortage. With its large supply of small and relatively cheap apartments, Uptown quickly became crowded. To meet demand, landlords cut apartment buildings up into smaller units. Many apartments were converted into one- and two-room units and rents were kept low. In the central section along Winthrop and Kenmore Avenues this was particularly evident, marking the beginning of the high-density "Winthrop-Kenmore Corridor" (Chicago Fact Book Consortium 1984). Most of the remodeling was "hasty," "shoddy," and violated existing building codes. Conversions and more intensive use played a significant role in building deterioration throughout

Uptown. After the war, the housing shortage eased as suburban out-migration increased. The allure and affordability of new housing on large lots in the suburbs attracted thousands of middle-class residents. The affordability of "a house in the suburbs" depleted Uptown's population base and housing stock. Uptown's population, which climbed to a peak of nearly 85,000 residents in 1950, dropped precipitously thereafter. Many young singles and married couples—largely white—who inhabited the Heart of Uptown apartment buildings moved out. As whites left Uptown for the suburbs and few moved in to take their place, landlords were left with more vacancies than they could afford. Many deferred routine maintenance and lowered rent standards in response (Marciniak 1981).

UPTOWN TRANSFORMED

Until 1950, Uptown's population was almost entirely white. However, in the following decades, the community underwent a dramatic racial and ethnic transformation. Diverse waves of migrants were attracted to Uptown's varied and affordable housing. In the 1950s and 1960s the mechanization of coal mining brought thousands of Appalachian white migrants to Uptown, which became known as a hillbilly slum (Backes 1968). In the late 1960s thousands of Native Americans began arriving after the Bureau of Indian Affairs changed its policies by stressing integration into cities (Chicago Fact Book Consortium 1995). One community leader commented that more Native Americans lived in Uptown than on any single reservation.[4] While the inmigration of numerous poor Appalachians and Native Americans did not significantly alter the area's census figures, Uptown's social character was affected.

Known for its large supply of small, affordable, and multifamily housing, Uptown in the 1960s and 1970s became an easy target for the city's subsidized housing. Pressured to satisfy federal requirements for providing affordable housing units for low- and moderate-income families, Richard J. Daley and his administration used their legal authority to broker the placement of massive numbers of such units in the community (Marciniak 1981: 99). Although the community received more than its fair share of subsidized housing, unlike several south- and west-side communities, it was never dominated by gigantic and infamous housing projects like the Robert Taylor or Cabrini Green homes. The addition of subsidized housing did, however, further alter the community's social and demographic character.

Large numbers of low-income and disadvantaged individuals moved in, leading many to believe that the community was a slum in the making. The presence of affordable and less-desirable housing in Uptown attracted low-income residents who sought to escape even worse conditions in other Chicago neighborhoods. In addition, various federal and state policy initiatives made Uptown an attractive site for low-income and needy individuals. For instance, in the late 1960s urban renewal was breaking up Skid Row on the city's west side; many of the homeless moved to Uptown (Bennett 1991). The area surrounding Broadway and Wilson Avenue, as well as the parallel Winthrop and Kenmore Streets (the "corridor"), became overrun by taverns, flophouses, dozens of day-labor outfits, and social welfare agencies. Soon Uptown was being referred to as the "New Skid Row" (Oppenheim 1974).

As Uptown's population shifted, it developed a social service infrastructure to serve the needs of its incoming population. In the 1960s and 1970s, social service agencies began to appear in the neighborhood en masse. The 1960s Great Society programs provided cities like Chicago significant federal aid for social welfare programs. The result was quite visible in Uptown, as one human service agency after another opened. As stores and offices closed, social service agencies moved in. This posed a dilemma for many Uptown residents. Indeed, social welfare agencies were necessary to serve the neighborhood's growing needy population, providing everything from basic survival tools to language training, legal assistance, and help acclimating to new surroundings. Those concerned that Uptown was being overrun by social services found it difficult to argue against the proliferation of such agencies as the density of poor households and agencies increased. In certain parts of the community, "Uptown's center of gravity shifted to welfare. That became the main business and the biggest new source of jobs. With the help of the state, the Winthrop-Kenmore corridor was converted into the city's unofficial poorhouse on the north side" (quoted in Marciniak 1981: 23). The debate over the presence of such agencies and their effect on Uptown continues today.

In the late 1960s and early 1970s numerous other groups entered Uptown. Blacks and Latinos came from other parts of the city; as a resident told me in an interview on August 28, 1996, many were "people coming off other worse situations looking for a diverse community . . . and like everybody else they liked the advantages Uptown offered." For many people of color, Uptown was a step up from run-down, homogeneous communities on the south and west sides.

The community's racial and ethnic shift continued with the transformation of Argyle Avenue into an Asian shopping district. In 1974, a restaurateur, Jimmy Wong, unveiled plans to transform Argyle Avenue between Broadway and Sheridan into "Chinatown North." At the time, Argyle Avenue was a deteriorated and nearly vacant commercial strip, where the "El station during the day and rough-and-tumble taverns at night were the only real signs of life" (Dailey 1993). Wong's plans for a Chinatown North never fully materialized, although Asian entrepreneurs began to purchase property on Argyle. The arrival of Indochinese "boat people" spurred development, providing an economic boost for the strip of restaurants and grocery stores. The growth of the Argyle strip—now called "Asian Village"—along with affordable housing made Uptown an attractive place for many Southeast Asians. "If they are coming into the country they're going to look to settle where people who know their language and culture and customs are, . . . so Uptown was kind of [a] logical place for them to settle," noted a leader of an immigrant and refugee agency that serves Uptown.[5] The Argyle strip, in particular, was part of this attraction, serving as a connection to native languages, cultures, and foods. In the late 1970s, refugee Vietnamese, Cambodians, and Laotians moved to Uptown. And while less publicized, immigrants and refugees from Central and South America, Haiti, and Ethiopia also landed there.

Another change was in store for Uptown when the State of Illinois instituted a program that brought thousands of mentally disabled residents to the neighborhood. Seeking to save money, the state instituted a policy that shifted much of the financial and custodial responsibility for mental patients from state-operated asylums to local communities. Numerous old apartment hotels were converted into halfway houses or shelter-care homes for these dependent individuals. The state transformed several Chicago communities, including Uptown, into mental wards. Edward Marciniak notes that some seven thousand "deinstutionalized" mental patients were shipped to Uptown in one year alone (1981: 23). In a short time, Uptown garnered another moniker: the Psychiatric Ghetto.

Uptown thus experienced significant private sector commercial and residential disinvestment, as well as an influx of impoverished and needy families and households, in the decades after the war. This fueled the perception of Uptown as a "poorhouse." Yet things were not that simple. The area continued to attract and hold middle-income and affluent residents as well (and does to this day), particularly along its lakefront sections. For instance, Buena Park along the southeast lakefront and Margate Park along the northern lakefront sustained affluent populations, with median family incomes well above the city and community average in the 1970s and 1980s (Chicago Fact Book Consortium 1984, 1995). A newspaper account in the early 1980s suggested that Margate Park was a "boomtown in Uptown," saved from the conversion and deterioration experienced in other parts of the neighborhood (Bernstein 1987). Upgrading also occurred in other parts of Uptown during this time. So while large sections underwent urban degeneration, other parts experienced rejuvenation. This rejuvenation, along with Uptown's amenities, helped prevent rapid white flight and kept the neighborhood from turning into a slum.

These various waves of in-migration, deterioration, and revitalization have shaped Uptown's current multiethnic, multiracial, and mixed-income nature. Between the 1950s and the 1980s the demographic character of Uptown was significantly altered. Since the 1980s the racial, ethnic, and class mix has remained stable. Decline was slowed by various cycles of new construction, condominium conversion, renovation, and deconversion of previously subdivided buildings. These changes insured that middle- and upper-income residents remained in the community. The continued presence of affordable housing and social services, meanwhile, anchored minorities, low-income, and immigrant residents in Uptown.

INTEGRATION IN UPTOWN: ETHNIC POLYGLOT AND CULTURAL PATCHWORK

The changes that have occurred since the 1950s helped Uptown develop into one of Chicago's most racially and ethnically integrated neighborhoods. Unlike the pro-integration communities discussed in Chapter One, Uptown's racial integration has never been a biracial, black-white affair. Indeed, for over two decades, the area has been home to a multiethnic and multiracial population, setting it apart from Chicago's storied history of racial segregation and isolation. Uptown's racial and ethnic integration, however, just part of the unique character of the community, has maintained a mix that extends along economic, social, and cultural lines. Uptown is "hyperdiverse"—mixed on numerous dimensions. In this sense, Uptown's multifarious character puts it at the "far end of a spectrum of neighborhoods running from the relatively fixed and homogenous to the shifting and complex" (Bennett 1993: 256).

Multiracial and Multiethnic Integration

Compared to other communities in the city, Uptown has never been a stable residential community. The number of affordable rental properties made it a relatively transient community. Uptown's reputation as a community in flux is indeed related to the various cycles of physical, demographic, and economic expansion and decline. After World War II, as the neighborhood experienced another decline, so did its population. Uptown's population dipped from roughly 84,000 residents in 1950 to just over 63,000 in 2000 as families and individuals left in relatively large numbers.[6] The decline might have been worse if numerous and varied newcomers had not replaced them. These groups sparked racial change between 1960 and 1990. Unlike communities undergoing racial transition on the west and south sides of Chicago, Uptown experienced no single racial group moving in and thus little fear that it would "tip." The steady streams of poor Appalachian whites, blacks, Latinos, Asians, refugees and immigrants, and young white professionals into Uptown ensured a multiethnic and multiracial change without rapid white flight or resegregation.

Figure 3.1 offers a snapshot of this racial change. In 1960 whites comprised over 95 percent of the population. This changed as the black, Latino, and Asian populations increased steadily between the 1960s and 1980s. Surprisingly, Uptown did not meet the fate of other once integrated communities in Chicago (e.g., Austin, South Shore); complete racial transition did not occur. While Uptown steadily lost white residents after 1960, the number of white residents slightly increased in 2000 and in that year whites remained the largest population group in Uptown (42 percent). But Uptown had evolved—without intent or direction—into a multiethnic and multiracial community. This shows up strikingly in 1990 and 2000, where large percentages of each of the four main racial groups are represented.

The racial makeup of area schools further illustrates the extent of integration in Uptown. Figure 3.2 displays the racial breakdown of Uptown's public elementary and middle schools from 1987 to 1999.[7] Since the late 1980s Uptown schools have been largely black and Latino, on average, 70 to 75 percent of the student population. Asians constitute just over 15 percent of the school population; whites, roughly 10 percent. The percentage of whites, blacks, and Asians remained relatively stable. Only the Latino population increased, supporting anecdotal accounts that Uptown's Latinos—particularly Mexicans—increased during the 1990s. These data

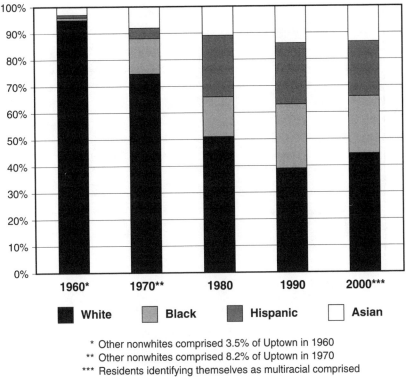

100%
90%
80%
70%
60%
50%
40%
30%
20%
10%
0%

1960*   1970**   1980   1990   2000***

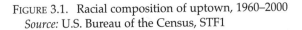

■ White   ▨ Black   ▨ Hispanic   □ Asian

* Other nonwhites comprised 3.5% of Uptown in 1960
** Other nonwhites comprised 8.2% of Uptown in 1970
*** Residents identifying themselves as multiracial comprised
3% of Uptown in 2000

FIGURE 3.1.   Racial composition of uptown, 1960–2000
   Source: U.S. Bureau of the Census, STF1

offer a different picture of integration in Uptown. The percentage of minority children in local schools outpaces each group's overall population in the neighborhood, partly because nonwhite Uptown households have more school-age children. A third of the Latino and black residents of Uptown, and a quarter of the Asians, are less than eighteen years of age, compared to only 16 percent of white residents.

Perceptions of school quality are also an issue. Although students are performing fairly well, Uptown public schools appear to reflect a subset of the community that is low income, racially and ethnically diverse, and transient. In 2001, 93 percent of students in Uptown schools were considered "low-income."[8] This percentage is higher than in the city overall (84.9 percent) and more than double the state average (37.9 percent). Uptown public schools face other "resource pressures." The average

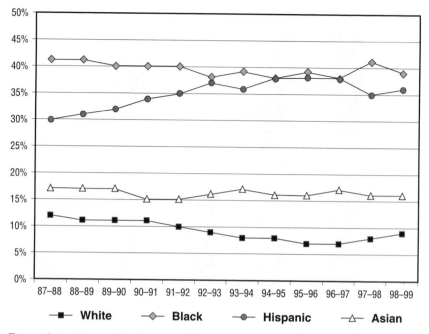

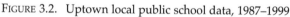

FIGURE 3.2.   Uptown local public school data, 1987–1999
   Source: U.S. Department of Education. 2000. National Center for Education
Statistics. Common Core of Data program. Public Elementary/Secondary School
Universe Survey Data. [http://nces.ed.gov/ccd/]

mobility rate for Uptown schools is much higher than the city average
(37.1 percent to 24.8 percent) and the percentage of Limited English Proficiency students (31.3 percent) is twice the city's and four times the
state's average.[9] However, these pressures, undoubtedly intensified by
recent immigrants, have not significantly affected student achievement.
Chicago Public School data suggest that while the percentage of Uptown
public students meeting or exceeding the Illinois Learning Standards was
considerably lower than the state average, it exceeded the city average.[10]
Nonetheless, these pressures create challenges for Uptown schools to
provide the education quality available in more homogenous communities; although by all indications the schools in Uptown are not below
average, these same data may be perceived differently by Uptown's
white families. And while Uptown's white population consists of a larger number of single and childless couples (related to a substantial gay
population), informants note that most white families with school-age
children opt for private or magnet schools elsewhere in the city.

THE GEOGRAPHY OF INTEGRATION

The racial character of Uptown is played out spatially. In the 1990s, Uptown's racial and ethnic mix was not uniformly distributed throughout its various subareas, although a large section remained either diverse or moderately diverse. For instance, in 1990 the central core of Uptown, including the Heart of Uptown/Sheridan Park and Kenmore-Winthrop Corridor areas, was integrated.[11] Part of Uptown's southeast section has remained moderately diverse, due to the presence of several affordable residential high-rises. The west and northwest sections also were moderately diverse, occupied largely by working- and middle-class Latinos. In both cases, no racial or ethnic group was overrepresented. Finally, two sections in Uptown were relatively homogeneous. One area runs the length of the lakefront and is largely white and affluent to the southeast, and white and gentrifying to the north. The second is southeast, although west of the lakefront, where less-prosperous Latinos live.

By 2000, Uptown's subsections had remained relatively stable. As displayed in Map 3.1, much of the central core of Uptown remained stably integrated. The Heart of Uptown/Sheridan Park and Winthrop-Kenmore Corridor continue to consist of a multiethnic and multiracial mix of residents. Moderately integrated areas in 1990 around this core had become increasingly mixed by 2000. Uptown's lakefront areas remain largely white, although the number of minority residents increased in these areas from 1990 to 2000. Finally, the western sections of Uptown appear to be undergoing some change. Although the areas northwest of Lawrence and Broadway remain moderately integrated, these areas witnessed an increase in white residents. The section north of Montrose and west of Clark became a majority-white section in 2000. These changes are due to a home-purchase and condo-conversion boom in the mid- to late 1990s. In sum, examining the spatial trends between 1990 and 2000 reveals that although the overall integration in Uptown is represented in each of its subsections, there are pockets of racial and ethnic homogeneity.

Ethnic Heterogeneity

Broad racial and ethnic categories, though assumed homogeneous by most white Americans, fail to reveal the ethnically heterogeneous nature of the populations. The numerous and often conflicting cultural and ethnic backgrounds of the various groups further complicate understandings of Uptown's demographic character. For instance, not all residents considered black or African American are native born. In the 1980s and

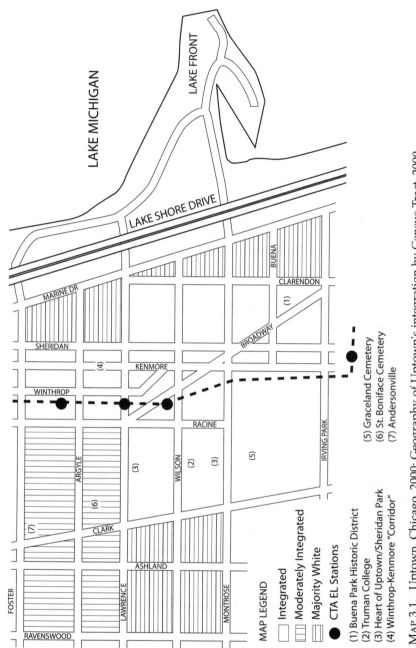

MAP 3.1. Uptown, Chicago, 2000: Geography of Uptown's integration by Census Tract, 2000

MAP LEGEND

☐ Integrated
▨ Moderately Integrated
▧ Majority White
● CTA EL Stations

(1) Buena Park Historic District
(2) Truman College
(3) Heart of Uptown/Sheridan Park
(4) Winthrop-Kenmore "Corridor"

(5) Graceland Cemetery
(6) St. Boniface Cemetery
(7) Andersonville

1990s, a number of recently arrived Caribbean, Nigerian, Eritrean, and Ethiopian families and individuals moved to Uptown. While these immigrants are often labeled "black," their self-identity and perception in the community is different. Leaders note that tension exists not only between the immigrants and black Americans, but also among some of the African immigrants.[12] Ethnic heterogeneity is also visible among Latino populations. Mexicans (54 percent) and Puerto Ricans (18 percent) are the largest Latino groups; however, "in Uptown you have a real mixed Latino community, . . . [including] Mexicans, Puerto Ricans, Salvadorians, . . . Cubans, Guatemalans, and Chileans."[13] The varied concentration of Latinos in Uptown is unique in Chicago, which has two main Latino communities, one largely Mexican and one Puerto Rican. As these areas became overcrowded and people moved to other parts of the city, some moved to the southeast side and others went north to Uptown. Finally, Uptown's Asian population is its most ethnically diverse group. In the 1970s and 1980s, the community drew not only Asian immigrants, but also refugees from Southeast Asia. Census data indicate that the Asian population in the neighborhood includes Chinese (18 percent), Vietnamese (19 percent), Filipino (13 percent), Korean (12 percent), Cambodian (10 percent), and Japanese (8 percent) residents, as well as smaller numbers from India, Laos, and Thailand. Many of these immigrants, particularly those from Cambodia, Vietnam, and Laos, are refugees who relocated to Uptown because of the availability of housing and services, I was told on June 12, 2002, by Edwin Silverman of the Illinois Department of Human Services Refugee Relocation Program. Uptown's Asian subpopulations have different needs. While some came in the mid-1970s with money, education, and political connections, those entering in the late 1970s and 1980s were largely rural, lacking education and English-language skills (Franczyk 1989). National and cultural differences have produced tensions between some of the groups. Solomon Chu, director of the Uptown Chamber of Commerce, commented on this tension in our May 5, 1996, interview: "The Southeast Asians, Chinese, and Vietnamese have existed somewhat uncomfortably, largely because the Chinese have a very imperial attitude towards anyone. . . . I mean, the original meaning for China is 'center,' meaning center of the universe. If that doesn't explain the ethnocentric nature, . . . that is how they look at it."

In part, Uptown has remained an ethnically heterogeneous population as a result of its port-of-entry status for many of Chicago's immigrants since World War II. Most of the neighborhood's immigrants are recent arrivals not only to the city, but also to the United States. Of all foreign-born residents in Uptown, 17 percent reported entering the United States in the 1990s, and 32 percent as late as 1995. The percentage of foreign-born residents has increased from just under 20 percent in 1970 to around 33 percent in 2000 (significantly higher than the city average of 18 percent). Although, as is true for most port-of-entry locations, not all immigrants stay in Uptown, a significant number remain, serving as a magnet for later arrivals, who naturally draw upon existing ties of kinship, culture, language, and friendship (Massey 1998). The presence of mutual aid associations for various groups reveals that Uptown continues to serve as an entry point for immigrants from all over the globe, including Chinese, Vietnamese, Laotian, Cambodian, Ethiopian, Bosnian, and Iraqi. Uptown schools reflect this as well. In 2000, the principal of Goudy Elementary, on the border of Uptown and Edgewater, described his school as a "veritable United Nations," with pupils from thirty-eight countries who speak twenty-six languages (M. Martinez 2000).

Uptown's Economic Mix

Racial and ethnic integration in Uptown intersects with significant socioeconomic differences. At the low end, a large dependent or needy population exists; in 1990, only 42 percent of Uptown's households had incomes of over $20,000 and 29 percent of the residents received some form of public aid (Chicago Fact Book Consortium 1995). No public elementary school in the 1990s had a percentage of low-income students below 90 percent (U.S. Department of Education 2000). The percentage of Uptown families living below the poverty line increased from 16 to 28 percent between 1970 and 2000 (U.S. Bureau of the Census 2000).

Most of Uptown's less prosperous households and residents are non-white. Just under 20 percent of black, Latino, and Asian households had incomes of greater than $35,000, compared to 32 percent of white households. Poverty rates, unsurprisingly, are much higher for nonwhites than whites: roughly 27 percent of whites in Uptown lived below the poverty line, compared to 38 percent of blacks, 36 percent of Latinos, and 43 percent of Asians. A similar trend shows up in poverty rates for children by race.

Uptown's low-income population is quite visible, as a trip down Wilson or Broadway reveals. On a given day or night, one can see individuals—some homeless or marginally homeless, others mentally ill or transient—outside day-labor agencies, shelters, and taverns. This population remains due to the established infrastructure, including nonprofit agencies that provide services to needy families and individuals. The

Uptown Chamber of Commerce's summer 1996 demographic fact sheet reports approximately 153 "professional medical and personal service" establishments in Uptown, outnumbering general merchandise stores. As we will see, the community also possesses a substantial number of affordable housing units.

Yet Uptown has never been a center for the down-and-out. Its location along Lake Michigan, access to public transportation, proximity to the Loop, stately mansions and high-end housing, and relative affordability compared to other neighborhoods attract affluent and upward-mobile Chicagoans. During the 1980s Uptown experienced a 32 percent increase in the number of upper-income households (29 percent higher than the city's), ranking very high among low- to moderate-income communities (Woodstock Institute 1994). Uptown continued to attract middle-to upper-income residents in the 1990s. Housing trends reveal that Uptown's average home-selling price has nearly tripled since 1985, from nearly $127,000 then to close to $400,000 in 2000 ("Living in Greater Chicago" 2000; Obejas 1999). The high sales price ranks Uptown near the top of communities in Chicago.

The more affluent residents in Uptown, however, live in select sections of the community. The neighborhood's "gold coast" lies along the lakefront to the southeast, running from Irving Park to Montrose Avenue. Additional pockets of affluence exist north of Montrose along the lakefront and in the gentrifying areas of Buena Park and Sheridan Park. During the 1980s, residential developers invested million of dollars in housing renovation and new construction, a move tied to the winning of historic district status for Sheridan Park and Buena Park by local residents and real estate interests. The historic district designation allowed developers to seek tax credits, enabling them to secure seed money to buy buildings in the area. The availability of tax credits created a building boom in both areas. As one developer told me on July 26, 1996, tax credits gave him "the money to buy a lot of those vacant buildings. Without the credits those buildings would have probably been abandoned." These efforts are responsible for the noticeable increase in homeownership, from 5 percent in 1970 to nearly 15 percent in 1990 (and estimated around 20 percent in 2000). Uptown continues to attract middle-income residents and is shedding its image of a community locked into "an unbreakable spiral of disinvestment and population loss" (Bennett 1997: 44). The area is holding onto and, in fact, attracting affluent residents.

Unplanned Integration

As Uptown's social and cultural character shifted, there was little conscious resistance to or support for racial and ethnic integration. Initial reactions did not involve either violent protest or rapid racial transition, as happened in other racially changing Chicago neighborhoods. In part, initial reactions were shaped by the community's social and physical structure, which was being depleted; at the least, rehabilitation projects were being deferred. Sue Ellen Long, a longtime resident, developer, and prominent leader in the area, told me in a July 25, 1996, interview that as new racial, ethnic, and class groups came to Uptown, there "wasn't really anybody not to accept them. After the Depression when they cut up the buildings into those small units and Uptown became the affordable area, . . . people weren't organized against them. [In fact] there was some acceptance." At the same time, integration developed without the conscious or goal-oriented actions of a few leaders promoting it or fighting racial transition. Integration was never a primary goal of community organizational efforts. As Solomon Chu, executive director of the Uptown Chamber of Commerce, noted in our May 10, 1996, interview: "The mixture [of racial and income groups] makes us strong in some ways; . . . it is not something we actively pursue, it is almost like laissez faire. We are not stopping it; . . . I mean, it happened because nobody obstructed it, not necessarily because somebody nurtured it."

Uptown's multiethnic, multiracial, and mixed-income character is due in part to a variety of external forces or processes not directly related to resident or community organizational action. Immigrants, minorities, and low-income residents were attracted to the large supply of affordable housing and necessary social service agencies. These agencies soon expanded, providing a solid infrastructure of support for such groups that continues to attract individuals and families, maintaining the influx of immigrants and minorities. Affluent residents (primarily white) were also attracted to Uptown. In the 1960s, and again in the 1980s and 1990s, the corporate sector expanded, fueling a need for high-wage labor and upscale housing. A housing boom resulted along the northern lakefront. By the 1980s, Uptown's two southern neighbors, Lakeview and Lincoln Park, had been secured for the professional and managerial middle class. Uptown, with its lakefront access, convenient transportation, and unique housing stock, became the next beachhead for gentrification. Over the last two decades, a largely white middle class has viewed Uptown as a viable option for home purchase. Market forces helped maintain Uptown's middle-income white population.

Demographic forces offer a partial explanation for stable integration in Uptown. Groups responded to changes, and internal actions affected neighborhood stability. Most community action, however, came after racial change had occurred, and organizational efforts were not centered on maintaining integration. In fact, since the 1960s, efforts to stabilize or improve Uptown have involved contentious battles over the nature and meaning of "improvement." Conflict forced groups to negotiate their various visions, ultimately leading to cooperation on community-development and -building projects. Conflict and negotiation revitalized Uptown without resegregation. The process of maintaining integration in Uptown is quite different than what occurs in diverse-by-direction communities, which makes it a place that requires us to rethink what neighborhood integration means and how it can be maintained.

NEGOTIATING INTEGRATION BY MANAGING CONFLICT

How did stable integration occur in Uptown? Let's begin with the obvious. As in most integrated communities, it is common in Uptown to hear positive statements about living in a diverse, even cosmopolitan, neighborhood. Residents and leaders generally value racial and ethnic integration; as one community leader told me July 25, 1996: "People like being in a community where almost anybody walking down the street doesn't look like us." Another mentioned that "people like [Uptown] because they feel accepted; . . . it is a place where you can get to know people from virtually every corner of the world right here in your own neighborhood and learn to appreciate different cultures and lifestyles."[14] A third suggested in our interview on August 8, 1996, that Uptown's greatest attribute is that it is the "cheapest way to take a trip around the world; . . . for the price of a bus fare you can experience so many different parts of the world." Little evidence exists, however, that individual appreciation translates into community groups adopting, or even, suggesting pro-integrative strategies. Community organizations did not develop plans, rally resources, or intervene to stabilize integration early in the process of racial change.

The seeds of Uptown's stable integration were sown in community conflict. When a diverse population shares residential space, it is rare that groups share common values, norms, and even goals. Racially and ethnically heterogeneous neighborhoods thus produce a certain amount of conflict (Robinson 1989), ranging from overt resistance (e.g., violence) to flight from the community by incumbent residents to clashes over heterogeneous values, norms, or community plans. But conflict is not always negative, as it can serve to sharpen the goals of various groups and force compromise and negotiation. The history of Uptown, a community lacking a unifying culture, shows that tension and conflict can be a stabilizing factor.

Uptown has a long history of conflict over land use and the future of the community, as we will see. Since the 1950s, residents and leaders have clashed over plans for urban renewal, gentrification, and preservation of affordable housing. Painting local political battles with a broad brush, we find that two opposing groups emerged. One side sees Uptown's future as resting on redevelopment plans, gentrification, and commercial upgrading. The other, fearful such plans will displace incumbent low-income residents and families, opposes gentrification efforts. This is an obvious oversimplification; in fact, there are multiple divisions arising from Uptown's diverse population and the sometimes opposing views of groups that appear to be seeking similar goals (Bennett 1997). I use these two groups, however, to simplify the analysis.

Over the last two decades, each side progressed, albeit slowly and with opposition, toward its goals. The presence of each forces the other to negotiate its varying visions of development and of the community's future. These conflicts have produced concrete results that, to the surprise of many, help stabilize the community and integration.

Neighborhood Improvement for Whom?

After 1950, Uptown lost population, saw a decline in its housing and commercial stock, and found new residents from varied racial and economic locations moving in. These changes raised concern over the future of the community. Incumbent residents were rightly troubled with the neighborhood's growing reputation as a rowdy slum. In an effort to alter this image, a variety of residents got behind efforts to encourage homeownership and attract new, more affluent residents. At the same time, the arrival of a large dependent and low-income population spurred the development of a social service infrastructure. Uptown soon had a sizable number of advocates for this population. Fearful that the low-income residents would be displaced, numerous activists and organizations organized not only to fight gentrification efforts but also to secure affordable housing in Uptown.

This political cleavage led to contentious struggles over development and the rights of different groups that reflect conflicting visions of what Uptown "should be" and what it "should become," and truly different understandings of the meaning of "improvement." Soon, "no proposed zoning variance, no plan to renovate an older residential building, no plan to develop even a playground [was] without ambiguous implications for surrounding residents and the future of the neighborhood" (Bennett 1991: 20). Three general and distinct attempts were made to revitalize Uptown's physical, and thus social, character. First, in the 1960s, urban renewal plans were formulated in an attempt to redevelop some of Uptown's most rundown housing. Second, gentrification came to Uptown in waves that ranged from a rash of condo conversions to development in two designated historical sites to new construction on vacant properties. Finally, in the mid-1980s, private developers attempted to "prepay" government-subsidized mortgages and turn moderate- to low-income housing to market rates; local groups and residents successfully blocked their efforts and secured a significant amount of affordable housing. Each of these three moves not only demonstrates the varying visions of Uptown, but the way in which seemingly opposed groups can contribute to maintaining racial integration.

Urban Renewal

The contemporary physical, social, racial, and political character of Uptown is directly tied to early urban renewal plans. The seeds for urban renewal were sown in 1955 with the formation of the Uptown Chicago Commission (UCC). The UCC received support from such local business institutions as Uptown National Bank, Uptown Federal Savings and Loan, Kemper Insurance, and Combined Insurance, as well as Mayor Richard J. Daley's administration. From its beginning, the UCC committed itself to promoting an urban renewal program to prevent Uptown from physically (and socially) deteriorating. The UCC urban renewal proposal grew out of a belief that the area had been afflicted by deterioration, illegal uses, lack of physical maintenance, and an "intense density of population and overuse of community facilities," creating a blighted situation that was spreading rapidly (quoted in Bennett 1997: 77). The UCC's urban renewal proposal covered a wide area, from east of Broadway in the Winthrop-Kenmore area and moving west past the CTA el tracks into the Heart of Uptown/Sheridan Park area. The area selected was deemed the most rundown and in need of improvement. The UCC's urban renewal proposal slowly went through the local and federal approval processes, allowing dissenters to vocalize their opposition. When plans were finally approved, the most significant effort for physical improvement involved plans for a new Chicago City College campus on land west of the el, in a northern corner of the Heart of Uptown/Sheridan Park.

In the debate over the construction of a community-college campus, distinct battle lines formed. On one side, the UCC backed the plan, arguing that the community college would serve the neighborhood's undereducated and economically marginal population, spur economic development around the campus, and replace "substandard" housing, cheap hotels, and bars (Bennett 1997). On the other side, a coalition formed of those who feared the school would displace several thousand residents and hundreds of decent affordable housing units (Gray 1970). This coalition emerged as a result of the demographic changes and the unexpected appearance of the New Left in the community, whose adherents were particularly interested in protecting the rights of the poor and minorities.[15] The coalition argued that minorities and low-income residents, the very groups likely to be displaced by urban renewal, were not represented in urban renewal plans. It proposed an alternative plan—referred to as Hank Williams Village—that sought to preserve much of the existing housing, introduce social service facilities and commercial development, and maintain affordable rents (Graber 1968). After several years of acrimonious debate over urban renewal plans, the alternative plan was rejected, and in March 1976, the Chicago City Colleges opened the Harry S Truman campus in the Heart of Uptown.[16]

The results of the battle over urban renewal were mixed. The UCC did not get what it had envisioned for Uptown. The campus did not cover the entire area planned, and deterioration around the campus actually increased in subsequent years. Rents did not increase as urban renewal advocates had anticipated. In one of the urban renewal areas, developers erected several federally subsidized apartment towers, which coincided with the increase of blacks and Latinos in Uptown. The Heart of Uptown/Sheridan Park area retained the rundown image that city planners and the UCC were trying to reverse. The activists attempting to preserve affordable housing found their alternative proposal rejected, and the construction of the community college led to significant loss of affordable housing in the Heart of Uptown/Sheridan Park area. The physical changes were not the bitter urban renewal battle's most significant result, which rather was the division into "mutually hostile pro- and antidevelopment camps" (Bennett 1997: 88).

Urban renewal established several groups that perpetuate this political cleavage. On the prodevelopment side, the UCC and real estate forces consistently support efforts to increase the area's stock of upscale housing and commercial upgrading. The UCC also regularly weighs in against local proposals advocating additional subsidized housing and the opening of new social service agencies. In our September 19, 1996, interview, a past president of the UCC expressed an underlying belief shared by many supporters of efforts by the UCC and block clubs: "All the poor people don't live in Uptown yet and they don't have to all live in Uptown. I mean, we have been accused in Uptown of trying to get rid of all the poor. And the people that accuse us are the ones who practice the politics of poverty." UCC members and supporters accuse the many social service providers not of helping the poor get out of poverty, but rather of maintaining a dependent and needy population to serve. They claim that Uptown should not become overrun by social service agencies. Instead, promotion of neighborhood upgrading is necessary to prevent it from becoming a slum and to maintain integration.

On the antidevelopment side, organizations emerged with "the end in mind of protecting incumbent and low-income residents" (Bennett 1991: 26). The identity of many of these organizations grew directly out of the early urban renewal battles. As former ONE executive director Josh Hoyt told me on August 28, 1996: "There's a big coalition [that formed] around the building of Truman College. A lot of the identity among the poor was forged in that battle. They were really aware of what was creeping towards them and that was the issue that they were organizing around. There have been different generations at different times in these institutions and organizations that have taken the lead, fighting for maintaining or creating low-income housing. They've operated in different ways; some are more mainstream, some are more radical." This coalition split into two groups, Hoyt said—the "liberal caregivers and the more radical, hard-nosed advocates for the needs and rights of the poor." The latter include prominent activists like Slim Coleman, who took the lead in the late 1960s and early 1970s in providing services to the area's indigent population, from bags of groceries to assistance in dealing with landlords.[17] Coleman and his supporters began to organize Uptown's low-income population. These activists became strong and successful advocates for the area's low-income population, and pushed their agenda of "development without displacement" (Eisendrath 1983). This political movement ultimately helped elect Helen Shiller, representing this coalition, as Forty-sixth Ward alderman.[18] Since her election in 1987, Alderman Shiller has been decidedly antigentrification and has worked to secure affordable housing in Uptown. The faction Hoyt refers to as "liberal caregivers" is represented by numerous community groups, such as the Organization of the Northeast (ONE) and Voice of the People (VOP), both rooted in the urban renewal era. ONE and VOP, more mainstream that Coleman and his supporters, worked for decades advocating for low-income residents and ensuring that affordable housing remained available in Uptown. By the 1990s, ONE and VOP had become less anti-development than they were in the 1970s, although they remained reasonably strong grassroots organizations dedicated to stopping or slowing gentrification in Uptown. The genesis of these groups and their efforts to fight for low-income residents' rights has had a lasting effect on the ability of Uptown to remain diverse.

Gentrification

The end of the urban renewal battle did not signal the end of land-use conflict in Uptown. Debate continues over whether or not a concerted effort should be made to physically (and thus, socially) upgrade the neighborhood. Like most inner-city neighborhoods across the country, Uptown found little assistance for redevelopment from City Hall. As cities became less involved in neighborhood improvement, the private sector became a key proponent of revitalization, particularly through attempts at gentrification. This was evident along Chicago's north lakefront as changes in the region's economy and housing market spurred gentrification efforts. In the 1960s, with the corporate sector booming, Chicago's office economy expanded, bringing a reinvasion of yuppies with the consequent rehabilitation of individual structures, expansive upgrading by real estate entrepreneurs, and spinoff commercial development. The city's first large-scale gentrification began in Lincoln Park and then in Lakeview, Uptown's southern neighbor.[19] By the 1980s, Lakeview and Lincoln Park were secured for the professional and managerial middle class, and Uptown was the next beachhead (Bennett 1993: 253).

Since the 1970s, Uptown has attracted real estate entrepreneurs. "Uptown has always been close to other gentrifying communities," one leader told me in an interview on August 28, 1996. "It has always been the next neighborhood to go upscale, white yuppie. It's close to the lake, it's got good transportation, [and] it's got some very nice housing stock." Uptown's location and proximity to rapidly developing Lakeview made it a logical next choice for gentrification (Juárez Robles 1988). In our June 15, 1996, interview, Alderman Shiller aptly expressed the real estate trends impacting the north side: "I always talk about the cycle of speculation. It is a cycle that moves around the city or has moved around the city. It started on the north side in the Gold Coast, moving north over the last twenty to thirty years. When I first came to Chicago, it was ravaging its way through Lincoln Park. In Lincoln Park, buildings were being built and people were being forced out and displacement was just beginning. The dye had already been set for some time and was already being set for Lakeview and Uptown." Gentrification had certainly arrived by the late 1970s and early 1980s and continued into the mid-1990s. Yet, as we shall see, gentrification's impact in Uptown was never complete, given the presence and action of antigentrification groups.

The most significant real estate activity during this time centered on apartment-to-condominium conversions along the neighborhood's lakefront sections. While real estate investment dipped in the mid-1980s, it surged again late in the decade. During this time, local groups petitioned for historic district status for two subareas of Uptown: Buena Park and Sheridan Park. Neighbors in Buena Park petitioned state and federal authorities for historic district status, receiving the designation from the National Register of Historic Places in 1984. The designation spurred development and upgrading throughout this area. Within months of Buena Park's receiving its historic district status, a resident group (with the help of some developers) in the Heart of Uptown/Sheridan Park area started work on its own petition. A local block group affiliated with the UCC, a local political consultant, and a developer who had been acquiring properties in Uptown since the early 1980s promoted their petition. After several rounds of debate and opposition from an antigentrification coalition, the area was designated a historic district in 1985.[20]

Historic designation in Sheridan Park sparked significant real estate activity. Between 1984 and 1988 the number of private loans in Sheridan Park doubled and investment dollars skyrocketed (Bennett 1997). Building renovations and apartment-to-condominium conversions began to dot the landscape. While condominium prices did not significantly increase, two- to six-unit buildings—the residential structures most likely to be purchased for renovation and conversion into condominiums—significantly increased in market value.[21] Developers began to purchase vacant buildings and lots in an attempt to gentrify the area. Undoubtedly, such real estate activity was driven by fear that vacant land would be used for more low-income housing. As an active developer in Sheridan Park told me on July 29, 1996: "We came into [Uptown] and saw this vacant land around. It was owned by the county and [we] went through the process of buying the land. Then we found out we had competition and it was coming from the City of Chicago. And this area has so much low-income housing and so much social services, it is so heavily

TABLE 3.1.   Residential Lending Patterns by Race, Class, and Type—Uptown, 1992–1998: Mortgage Loans Reported from Home Mortgage Disclosure Act

	Fiscal Year							
	1992	1993	1994	1995	1996	1997	1998	1992–98
Total Loans*	427	616	644	530	743	785	946	4,688
Race								
White	75%	77%	73%	73%	74%	76%	80%	76%
Black	6%	4%	9%	8%	8%	8%	3%	6%
Hispanic	6%	5%	4%	7%	5%	4%	3%	5%
Asian	6%	5%	7%	5%	4%	4%	3%	5%
Income as % of MSA Median Income								
<51%	8%	5%	8%	7%	3%	3%	1%	5%
51–80%	20%	19%	26%	25%	15%	14%	12%	19%
81–95%	15%	11%	11%	12%	10%	10%	12%	12%
96–120%	15%	16%	15%	16%	17%	14%	18%	16%
>120%	28%	32%	27%	27%	47%	51%	64%	39%
Total Loans by Uptown Subarea								
Buena Park	67	108	86	83	134	96	159	733
Heart of Uptown/Sheridan Park	30	68	75	82	94	111	146	606
Lakefront	203	241	240	216	257	260	302	1,719
Ravenswood/Glenwood	90	143	170	97	153	196	216	1,065
Winthrop-Kenmore Corridor	37	56	73	52	105	119	123	565

*Excludes home improvement or refinancing lending activity.

Source: Right to Know Network (RTK) [http://www.rtk.net]; Federal Financial Institutions Examination Council, Federal Reserve, Washington, D.C.

weighed toward the low-income stratosphere. We thought more low income would really hurt the neighborhood, hurt our investments up here." Given Uptown's proximity to other gentrifying neighborhoods, it is not surprising that real estate developers were concerned about vacant properties. This concern, along with tax credits available for developers in historic districts, kept Uptown's condo market strong into the early 1990s.

The positive real estate trends of the 1980s intensified in the 1990s. Table 3.1 displays the distribution of home-mortgage loans in Uptown from 1992 to 1998 by race, income, and subarea.[22] The data reflect significant real estate expansion in Uptown during the last decade. Several trends are worthy of note. First, the volume of loans granted more than doubled from 1992 to 1998, with 90 percent of all loans going toward home purchase. Second, over three-quarters of the loans went to white applicants, with only a small percentage going to minorities. Third, home-mortgage investment went to higher-income families. Over half of all loans in Uptown between 1992 and 1998 went to families or individuals with incomes near or greater than the median for the metropolitan area ($42,761).[23] The economic disparity between income groups who received loans is pronounced between 1996 and 1998. In 1996 and 1997, approximately 65 percent of all loans went to higher-income families; this jumped to 82 percent by 1998. Finally, mortgage loans are not evenly distributed across Uptown's landscape: the largest number of loans went to Uptown's lakefront sections. As in the 1980s, year in and year out more mortgage money flowed into the lakefront section than to any other area. Yet this is only part of the story. Each subsection saw increases in the number of loans received, particularly western and northwestern sections. Particularly striking is the fourfold increase in the number of loans going to applicants purchasing homes in the Sheridan Park historic district. While this trend began in the late 1980s, there was even greater investment in that area in the 1990s.

Mortgage-lending data in Uptown suggest that homeownership is dramatically increasing, particularly for white middle- and upper-income residents. Affluent home and condo purchasers inflated land values in Uptown during the 1990s ("January Home Sales" 1996). Thus, while individuals or families with incomes between 50 and 81 percent of the metropolitan median income received loans, as property values soar it is difficult for residents with lower incomes to obtain loans and afford housing in Uptown. Recent lending patterns show that residents buying property in Uptown resemble home buyers in gentrified Lakeview and Lincoln Park. Like these areas, the community attracted a large number of white middle- to upper-income residents. This, in turn, helps explain the racial character of homeowners. It seems that the gentrification of Lakeview and Lincoln Park crept north, and many potential buyers dissuaded by soaring prices in those neighborhoods found housing in Uptown a more reasonable buy.

The flurry of real estate activity in Uptown is not an anomaly in Chicago. Many city neighborhoods experienced dramatic real estate investment during the 1990s, thanks to a strong economy and a citywide building boom. But local reaction to real estate trends sets Uptown apart and reveals the underlying tension among leaders and residents over what the community should be. When gentrification began to occur, the argument among leaders was transformed from whether gentrification was going to happen to how good it is for the community. "Development is not an either/or situation," an ONE representative told me on July 25, 1996. "It brings money into the community, but it can also be detrimental." Gentrification is a contentious issue, although groups do not fit neatly into pro- and antigentrification camps. Development is needed in every community to stave off deterioration and maintain a healthy neighborhood. However, the issue becomes touchy in a racially and economically mixed community, especially when most low-income residents are people of color. The reactions to gentrification reveal the difficulties of development in an integrated environment.

Many laud new development in Uptown because it brings middle-income residents into the community. Progentrification advocates hold a long-standing belief that if the neighborhood is to remain integrated, part of the mix must include people with money. "One of the big weaknesses of Uptown is that it hasn't had a recognizable middle class," a leader active in economic development told me on August 8, 1996. "It has been skewed toward the lower end and I don't find that dynamic very good for anyone." As is evident from Table 3.1, new development, particularly in the sale of condominium conversions, has brought more middle-class residents to Uptown. A recognizable middle class keeps the community from being skewed to the low end of the economic scale and positively affects the community in various ways. For example, a middle-income presence generates economic development, as business ventures seek to profit from the disposable income of middle-income residents. According to progentrification leaders, such economic development benefits everyone in the community by bringing businesses back to Uptown.

Efforts by developers to gentrify Uptown are lauded for helping stabilize the neighborhood by rehabilitating vacant and deteriorating buildings in some of the most rundown sections of the area. A tour of Uptown in the early 1990s would have revealed buildings in various stages of disrepair, as well as vacant lots and buildings. Not only were some of these buildings unsafe and potential sites for criminal activity, they conveyed an image of disorder and decline. Redevelopment in Uptown is viewed as necessary to reverse this negative image. Randall Langer, a prominent for-profit developer, feels justified in his efforts to rehabilitate properties that would otherwise still be vacant.[24] "We don't get grant money, we don't get federal money," Langer told me contentedly in our July 29, 1996, interview. "More than half of the buildings that we've done up here were vacant and they'd be empty vacant lots right now." Langer is not alone. Other for-profit developers, such as Peter Holsten, reconstructed abandoned and mismanaged buildings in Uptown.

A noteworthy attempt to change Uptown's image involved historic plans in Sheridan Park. Beyond local pride, historic district status offers fiscal benefits to developers and homeowners. For example, individual rehabilitators and developers are eligible for tax credits to use for renovation of income-generating property. Financial incentives encourage developers to upgrade and build in the area. Also, developers who use federal money to rehabilitate buildings in Sheridan Park (or any historic district) are subject to a design review of any proposed changes to building facades. Because such design reviews require extensive time and money, they act as a disincentive for low-income housing producers. As a result, Sheridan Park became a prime area to generate middle- to upper-income housing in the late 1980s and 1990s. The historic district status also functioned to distance the area from common perceptions of Uptown, such as "Psychiatric Ghetto" or the "center for the down-and-out." Developers and real estate–marketing firms advertised new condominium conversions as located in "historic Sheridan Park," rather than in Uptown. That descriptor became an effective marketing tool and worked to quell the fears of potential middle-class residents that Uptown was a risky investment (Kleine 1998a).[25]

A significant and vocal group in Uptown opposes gentrification. Although not in these terms, most antigentrification leaders have questioned who Uptown was being redeveloped for and have been concerned with the possibility (and reality) that rising rents would price long-term residents out of Uptown and displace low-income residents. Developers of rehabilitated properties claim that new units are affordable, but affordability is clearly a matter of opinion. Before Sheridan Park's application for historic district status, this coalition publicly questioned the affordability of various rehabilitated buildings in the area. The group rallied to challenge developers believed to be deliberately attempting to "turn" or gentrify the community by displacing low-income and minority residents.

All communities struggle with market forces that encourage speculation. How speculation is handled is the difference. Not everyone applauds real estate activity aimed at attracting middle-income residents; some clearly view it as threatening to the existing community. The movement to designate Sheridan Park as a historic district is a good example. Not surprisingly, there was concerted local opposition to Sheridan Park's historic district application by leaders and residents who saw it as an effort to symbolically set the area apart from other parts of Uptown—as an area that is "safe," attractive, a solid investment, and (subtly) less diverse. Critics also have argued that seeking historic status for an area with questionable historical significance is a veiled attempt to fuel gentrification. Alderman Shiller captured this complaint in our interview:

"Uptown has connotations of diversity which the development community doesn't necessarily want it to have. So, there's a tension between building a community, fighting and having it where you live, raising your family, . . . from the point of view of the people who live there and want to make it their home. Then with the perspective of the development community that really just looks at it as a commodity that they can turn over for a profit. [And] there have been real efforts, primarily by real estate forces to redefine this area from a marketing standpoint and their own speculative business interests." The coalition, less concerned with "selling" the community, is fearful that real estate activity in Sheridan Park will threaten Uptown's racial and economic integration by displacing long-term minority and low-income residents.

Claims of displacement of long-term residents are not without foundation. Gentrification in Uptown has hurt those with the fewest resources. For example, Langer emptied out several buildings in Sheridan Park in the mid-1980s; his most controversial move involved thirty-three Southeast Asian families.[26] Fully aware of gentrification's ill effects, members of Voice of the People, the Heart of Uptown Coalition, and the Organization for the Northeast formed the Uptown Task Force on Displacement and Housing Development. "Most of the time people talk about the market being a positive thing that is forward and always improves things," a representative of the coalition told me on July 15, 1996. "But the market is raging; . . . people are being displaced and have to go somewhere." This coalition, "a second-generation, [even] third-generation embodiment of the will of the poor and their representatives in Uptown," as one interviewee told me on August 28, 1996, carried on a campaign against developers like Langer, picketing offices and drawing public attention to displacement and homelessness in Uptown (Juárez Robles 1988).

"Secondary displacement" is also a concern of leaders. The flurry of real estate activity that involves affluent home buyers and property owners increases land and housing values, consequently reducing the number of affordable housing units. A leader describes this trend: "When mass rehabbing was done here, we estimated that 1,000 low-income or affordable units were lost; rates in general were raised, and the residual effect of that made fewer places available."[27] Apartment-to-condominium conversions reduced the number of rental units, while redevelopment brought an increase in housing values and rents. As a result, low- to moderate-income individuals and families got priced out of the market. While people were not directly "put out," the effect remains significant. Numerous anecdotal and journalistic accounts highlight the effect of rising rents and costs on households at the low end of the income scale. For example, a newspaper article recounted the story of a retired couple who had lived in the same one-bedroom apartment in Uptown for thirty-four years. In 1998, after paying around $450 a month in rent for years, the couple received notification that their building was to be gutted and rehabilitated. After spending half their lives in Uptown, they could not find an apartment of comparable rent and had to leave the neighborhood. A year later and after complete renovation, units in their old building rented for $925 a month. The building's owner stated that he had no problem renting the new, high-priced units because "there's nothing else out there" (quoted in Kleine 1998b).

These conflicting views on gentrification are not easily reconciled. Private development brings some benefits to Uptown. Deteriorating and vacant buildings are upgraded and "thrown back into the community's usable pool of housing stock."[28] New development attracts middle-income residents with disposable income. Such activity attracts economic development, makes the community more attractive, and increases the number of its resources. Development has benefits for the whole community, a fact gentrification foes are not quick to recognize. Indeed, private investment has stabilized Uptown by upgrading its physical character and preventing deterioration. At the same time, gentrification opponents have stabilized the community by curbing widespread gentrification and displacement.

Affordable Housing

The pace and nature of real estate activity in Uptown in the 1990s suggests that a "developer's holiday" is working its way through the neighborhood, pushing renters out to more affordable areas of the city (Kleine 1999: 20). Gentrification and market forces, however, are always tempered by local responses. In Uptown, efforts by real estate forces to gentrify the neighborhood coincide with grassroots efforts to secure and maintain affordable housing units to prevent displacement of the neighborhood's poor, immigrants, and minorities. Such grassroots efforts date back to the urban renewal era and the conflict over the future of the neighborhood. While contentious debate over the presence and number of affordable housing units in Uptown goes on, the work of affordable housing activists is a stabilizing factor for integration in Uptown. Like middle-class development, preserving affordable housing is a leveling force, keeping gentrification from sweeping through the neighborhood. It would be misleading, however, to claim that these efforts have come easily.

Uptown's affordable housing stock ranges from project-based high-rises to scattered site developments to for-profit mixed-income initiatives. In the 1960s and 1970s the U.S. Department of Housing and Urban Development (HUD) granted subsidies to private developers to build ten below-market rental buildings, to be reserved for low-income residents for at least twenty-five years (Nyden and Adams 1996). The ten high-rise properties, which contained more than 2,600 units of housing, provided a "base of 10,000 people who live in affordable housing, who are overwhelmingly minority and immigrant," one community leader told me on August 28, 1996. (Other leaders estimated the number at 11,000.) In addition to the high-rise buildings, federally subsidized scattered-site units, SRO buildings, and other affordable units dot Uptown's landscape and offered low-income residents the chance to stay in the neighborhood.

Several organizations have been particularly active in providing and managing affordable housing. The Habitat Company, which manages the Chicago Housing Authority's scattered-site program, built and manages several hundred scattered-site units in Uptown (Chung 1995). In the last decade and a half, Lakefront SRO, a community-development corporation whose mission was to "rehabilitate and manage singe room occupancy (SRO) buildings in the Uptown, Edgewater, and Lakeview neighborhoods," has been active in preserving hundreds of affordable units (Levavi 1996: 17). By the end of 1996, Lakefront had rehabilitated approximately seven hundred units in seven SRO buildings in Uptown, many of which had been slated for demolition (Dobmeyer 1996). Lakefront also provides social support programs and has built a solid track record and garnered support with both Uptown and the city. Another group, Voice of the People, collaborated with a steering committee made up of various mutual aid associations in the construction of twenty-eight duplexes and townhouses on vacant property at the northern end of the Winthrop-Kenmore corridor (Podgorski 1993).[29] The project, dubbed International Homes, sought to produce affordable houses for working families with incomes of between $20,000 and $50,000 per year. The project received the land and an estimated $20,000 subsidy as part of the city's New Homes for Chicago project. The International Homes project attracted buyers from ten ethnic groups; the last of the twenty-eight homes sold in December 1995 (Hein 1995).

Similar to progentrification condo conversions and rehabilitation projects, Lakefront SRO's rehabilitation of seven buildings and the twenty-eight International Homes produce visible results that will impact who lives in the community. Sue Ellen Long, a developer and owner of several buildings, told me in an animated tone in our 1996 interview: "I cannot imagine how [Uptown] would ever be gentrified with the numbers of affordable housing initiatives that we have. It can't happen. It won't happen." Affordable housing restrains gentrification efforts by offering lower-income families and individuals (including incumbent residents) the opportunity to live in the neighborhood. Since most of the low-income residents relying on affordable housing are minorities and immigrants, efforts to guarantee affordable housing bodes well for maintaining integration. Many leaders and residents, including a number of for-profit and prodevelopment leaders and groups, applaud the presence of some affordable housing initiatives for fulfilling the needs of Uptown's different groups. However, such positive feelings fade, especially among prodevelopment groups, when the discussion turns to the extent of such affordable housing.

Some leaders believe Uptown has too many subsidized buildings. This sentiment dates back to the 1960s, when many Uptown leaders argued that the area had more than its fair share of affordable housing (Marciniak 1981). Michael Pavilon, resident, landlord, and former UCC president, expresses this frustration: "We think that Uptown in general has enough [low-income] housing [and] that it should be placed elsewhere. If you walk to the northwest side, you won't see anything like it" (quoted in Kleine 1999: 21). However, housing alone is not the whole story; whom the housing attracts is a key issue. Leaders argue that housing produced by nonprofit developers increases the number of "dependent populations and agencies providing for these groups," as one leader told me on September 19, 1996. Compared to other moderate- to low-income communities, Uptown possesses a greater share of affordable housing units and social service agencies serving poor, immigrant, and needy residents. Some leaders assert that continued subsidized housing initiatives make the community a dumping ground for poor residents from other communities.

Opposition to affordable housing rises out of the same ideology that guides efforts to attract middle-income residents to the community. This opposition speaks to the differing views of the presence and rights of low-income residents in Uptown. Those involved in protecting and providing affordable housing options place a premium on the rights of the poor to stay in Uptown. This view recognizes the importance of affordable housing for maintaining racial integration. The opposing view places a higher premium on stabilizing the community by balancing out the large number of subsidized housing units, poor residents, and social service agencies with middle-income development. An example of just how divergent these views can be is clear in a remarkably candid statement by a former UCC president and current board member, who told me on September 19, 1996: "All the poor people don't live in Uptown and they don't have to live in Uptown. You have to explain to me, if you will, why a person who is permanently locked into poverty has to have a lake view! I don't understand it, . . . and I have a real problem with why there has to be a lot of properties on the lakefront for poor people. Certainly not the highest and best use!" Many efforts to gentrify or attract middle-income development are guided by this sentiment that the "highest and best use" of Uptown's attractive housing locations—including the most scenic vistas—should be reserved for more affluent residents. Poor residents living in desirable locations are not perceived by some as capable of improving the community. From this perspective, the needs of middle-income residents should be given priority (including the best views of Lake Michigan) for Uptown to stabilize. In the late 1980s the struggle over affordable housing was played out in dramatic fashion. The commotion surrounded the ten high-rise HUD "prepayment" buildings and their 2,600 units of affordable housing. During the neighborhood's urban renewal era, private developers were awarded HUD subsidies to back the construction of ten below-market rental buildings. These buildings—many of which are close to the lake—locked in affordable housing and a racial mix, as a racially and ethnically diverse group of residents occupied their units.[30] In the late 1980s and early 1990s, the affordability of these buildings was threatened. The subsidy agreement between HUD and the various developers specified that after twenty years, owners could "prepay" the remainder of their mortgages and convert their buildings to market-rate properties (Nyden and Adams 1996).[31] In several cases, owners gave clear indication of their intention to exercise the prepayment option (Joravsky 1989; Stuenkel 1993). The prepayment threat was considerable, given that very few of the current residents of these buildings would be able to afford prevailing market rents. The effort to preserve the affordability of these buildings is an incredible tale in which community organizing, resident involvement, and local organizations substantially affected local and national policy issues and neighborhood outcomes. The individual stories of the "prepayment buildings" will not be retold here (see Nyden and Adams 1996), but the organizing campaign requires attention. ONE was a key player, organizing tenants and institutions in the fight to preserve affordable housing. ONE viewed preserving affordable housing in Uptown as critical to its mission, as one mailer put it, of "building a successful multi-ethnic, mixed-economic community." The organization worked with residents of several buildings as part of a larger political campaign to publicize and ease residential displacement from upscale redevelopment. ONE staff members stepped up their organizing around the prepayment issue as they realized just how many families would be affected if building owners opted to prepay their mortgages. In 1986, Susan Gahm, an ONE staff member, began working with one building to raise consciousness over the issues. She expanded to other buildings and in some cases formed indigenous tenant groups (Bennett 1997). Given that each of the buildings became eligible over a five-year span, organizing tenant groups became a key strategy in saving some of the housing. ONE coordinated tenant association actions in all the buildings, created lines of communication between buildings, and cooperated with other community organizations and institutions (Nyden and Adams 1996). ONE decided to organize all the tenant groups together to fight on the larger policy issue of affordable housing, while also fighting on the condition and status of the individual buildings. The strategy enabled individuals to see their connection to a larger battle. A tenant leader comments on working with ONE:

> ONE forged us together as a group and started teaching us that if we joined in each other's struggles—even though each struggle was different—[and] if we came together and formed a common agenda, we were going to be stronger together than if each one of us went separately. It took a little time but as we saw that other people came along with us, and when we started talking about the issues and got publicity, then we began to see our identity. When someone would go to Washington, the people who went spoke for the entire neighborhood. (quoted in ibid.: 45)

Residents' and ONE's effort to preserve affordable housing proved largely effective. To simplify a complex process: two of the buildings were converted to market-rate housing; one building became the nation's first tenant buyout under the 1990 Federal Housing Act; three were preserved when community economic development organizations purchased the buildings; community pressure convinced one landlord to work with tenants in preserving below-market rents; and the fate of two other buildings remained uncertain. While some buildings were lost, affordable housing was preserved in Uptown. And as Josh Hoyt noted in our interview, the key variable in preserving it was the "intentionality with which the advocates of affordable housing have fought for, building by building and block by block, their right to keep living in the community." The presence of individuals and groups who not only advocate for the maintenance of affordable housing, but also fight for the right of low-income, minority, and immigrant families to remain is a familiar scenario in Uptown. This story reflects a distinct viewpoint on how to stabilize and improve the neighborhood, and sheds a different light on claims that gentrification is going to steamroll through Uptown.

SINCE THE 1960s, spirited battles have occurred over efforts to improve and stabilize Uptown. Their contentiousness arises from very different definitions of what "improvement" means and for whom the community is being improved. The presence of conflicting views, however, is not without merit. Land-use conflicts have produced concrete results. Prodevelopment groups have made inroads in upgrading Uptown's housing stock and attracting an until-then relatively absent middle class, keeping the neighborhood from deteriorating into a slum and threatening its racial integration. Antidevelopment groups have staved off gentrification enough to keep the neighborhood open to low-income households—most of whom are minority and immigrants—by preserving and maintaining a significant number of affordable housing units in the community. Past conflicts have forced groups to negotiate their visions of what the community should or will become. While there has been no meeting of the minds on what Uptown should be like, groups have negotiated. Negotiation has not led to closure; not everyone has signed on. Nevertheless, while the meaning of "improvement" varies from person to person, the ability of groups to balance competing views of Uptown's future cannot be underestimated as key to maintaining racial integration.

CONFLICT, COOPERATION, AND REDEFINING UPTOWN

The negotiations taking place signify a shift in the way things get done in Uptown. A sense of balance is forming among groups. "Uptown's way has seemed to be twenty to twenty-five years of knockdown, drag-out battles between different forces until at this point there is a sense of equilibrium, that we can live together," Josh Hoyt noted in our interview. "And not everybody is happy, but there is some equilibrium." In the late 1980s, this equilibrium led to cooperation among groups. Ironically, such cooperation appears to start in the same place as the conflict. No clear winners emerged from the battles over urban renewal, gentrification, and affordable housing. Low-income minorities and immigrants were not pushed out, and gentrification and affluent residents came to Uptown.

Moreover, no clear vision of what Uptown "should be" was developed. Indeed, Uptown's racial and economic diversity, its mix of affordable and high-end housing stock, remained relatively stable for several decades. As a result of the lack of agreement that emerged from Uptown's battles, a new attitude toward cooperation developed. "I really believe that all of us who are involved in community organizations want to support cooperation and involvement among different neighbors in the neighborhood," says a former president of the UCC. "I don't think any of us feel we can be successful in such a diverse community by trying to serve the interests of one group at the expense of the other."[32]

Does this mean that the conflicting groups are suddenly working together and agreeing? After years of acrimonious conflict, a sudden shift toward collaboration would be shocking. Overall, this is not the case. Conflict and tension remain among organizations; groups are not working hand-in-hand or even meeting to discuss how to work together. By and large, groups stick to their primary focus of serving the needs of specific interest groups (e.g., ethnic associations, middle-income block groups). However, conflict is proving functional in the sense of stabilizing the neighborhood by helping groups define the important issues, and leading to group cohesion and the formation of alliances.[33] My fieldwork suggests that groups recognize—after years of conflict—that Uptown is going to be mixed racially and economically, and this recognition brings groups together to work on improving the community in ways beneficial to all. A long-term resident and board member of ONE notes:

> Things have changed in Uptown. There'll be disagreement over things, but at least there's more talking. In the 1970s and mid-1980s there were really divisive battles on lots of issues, particularly housing. Groups fell into more traditional camps: one camp of low-income advocates and one camp of property-owning or gentrifying advocates. They would battle, and each time there'd be a new issue it would fall into the traditional camps and they'd fight it out. I think people were tired of fighting. I think [there's a realization] that it's gonna be mixed-income, it's gonna be mixed ethnically, in the future why don't we see what we can do together. We still will disagree on some things, but let's see what we can do together.[34]

This does not mean that they necessarily work together on all projects. The difference now is that groups are working toward some of the same goals or, at the very least, recognizing the needs of other groups and supporting initiatives beneficial to all. Vocal and organized community-based groups are discovering connections to other groups and movements focused on common concerns that bring groups across traditional lines. Cooperation occurs in a variety of ways. A primary unifying factor among community groups, leaders, and residents is a desire to redefine Uptown by altering negative perceptions and portraying the community as stable and attractive. Image-maintenance efforts, as they might be called, involve collaborations to challenge Uptown's shortcomings and build on its strengths. There appear to be two general types of community-based effort being used to redefine the community as stable. The most popular, community development, involves working on Uptown's physical, social, and economic character. This is exemplified by attempts to spur economic development along Uptown's main commercial corridors and professionalize affordable housing initiatives. These efforts stem from the awareness that disparate groups are good allies when it comes to achieving basic community concerns, such as safe streets, decent shopping alternatives, quality community resources, and decent housing. The other type, community-building efforts, involves specific actions to emphasize the value of integration and improve communication among groups. Such actions challenge the negative perception of integrated neighborhoods as unstable. Both community-development and community-building efforts are integral in stabilizing the community and its racial and ethnic integration. Since the 1960s, prodevelopment groups have worked to redefine Uptown as attractive to the middle class, while antigentrification groups have sought to keep it open to various racial, ethnic, and income groups. These seemingly opposed efforts share a common understanding that communities are not only physical and social, but also symbolic, entities. In this light, definitions of a community are of great importance in determining an area's stability. To understand the importance of perceptions, it is useful to note the "incivilities thesis," developed primarily by criminologists to explain what causes residents to stop investing socially and economically in, or ultimately to leave, a community. The thesis contends that residents look to the surrounding social and physical environment for reinforcement of desirable public norms (Hunter 1978; Lewis and Maxfield 1980; Skogan and Maxfield 1981).[35] If the norms displayed are not viewed as positive, residents' commitment to the neighborhood may drop. Individuals and community groups may be less willing to volunteer time to improve or beautify public spaces, spend money on improving public or private property, and frequent local shopping areas or public areas. The withdrawal of economic and social investment becomes an impediment to community viability.

All communities must address images of incivility or perceived instability, since negative perceptions can erode the viability of a neighborhood. For years, leaders have been trying to shed Uptown's "gritty image," which it earned in the 1950s and 1960s when it was depicted as going from "a promising, vibrant neighborhood to a troubled community inhabited mostly by poor immigrants, known for its burned-out buildings and abandoned cars" (Hartstein 1996). This image is slightly overblown, as the community is not a slum beset by complete disinvestment or racial tension. Yet the neighborhood still has problems and symbols that convey a less-than-stable image. Luckily, several generations of leaders of a variety of stripes are addressing the problems and in the process altering Uptown's image. As Mary Ann Smith, alderman of the Forty-eighth Ward, said in our interview: "Our community has been able to recognize and confront its problems. Not every community can recognize what is going on with it, not every community wishes to or is capable of publicly confronting those problems. We have drug dealing. We have prostitution. We periodically have arson. We have these problems, but the water mains are being fixed. Wherever we have total control, we have a plan afoot [and] it is a unifying thing." Issues of community vitality draw consensus among often conflicting groups. Uptown leaders are recognizing the problems, remedying them where possible, and addressing negative perceptions.

Community Development Initiatives

Most efforts to reshape the image and identity of Uptown are centered on improving quality-of-life issues. Leaders are working on enhancing the area's social, physical, and economic vitality by reducing dilapidated buildings, visible poverty, homelessness, and crime, while shoring up economic development, infrastructure, and housing (efforts common in any neighborhood). Economic development and improved affordable housing delivery are two community-improvement issues drawing groups together across racial and class lines. Work in these areas is leveraging changes that prevent Uptown from deteriorating and challenge perceptions that the neighborhood is an unstable "community in transition" or a "gamble."

Since the community's decline in the 1940s and 1950s, Uptown's main commercial arteries are anything but vibrant. Uptown's commercial heart, running along Broadway and Lawrence Avenue, is symbolic of the area's economic decline. Only the stunning Uptown Bank building, the famous Green Mill jazz club, the Aragon Ballroom, and the Riviera nightclub remain as evidence of the once prominent entertainment and business district. The historic Uptown Theater and former neighborhood commercial mainstays (e.g., Goldblatt's department store, Heilig-Meyers furniture) are boarded up and covered with concert posters. In their place came numerous Mom-and-Pop stores, many of which did not survive for more than five years. The slow decline of retail business in Uptown has had negative consequences. Not only are shopping options and a potential source of local jobs compromised, but also the area is viewed as declining and unattractive to potential retailers.

Until recently, Uptown commercial establishments underserved all groups, regardless of race, nativity, or income. Many leaders suggested that the area had been desperate for more commercial stores for some time. A recent study of business patronage in Uptown confirms that a majority of households, particularly middle-income ones, routinely leave Uptown for clothing purchases, restaurants, entertainment, medical services, and banking (Nyden, Bennett, and Adams 1993). In each category, lower-income households were more likely to use local businesses and facilities, although a significant percentage also reported leaving the area to obtain certain services. Leaders in Uptown recognized this as a problem for all residents and implemented programs to boost commercial resources. Recent organized efforts are focused on reviving Uptown's central commercial districts to provide retail services and recast Uptown's image as vibrant and stable.

In the 1990s the most concerted and cooperative effort to strengthen economic development centered on the Broadway-Lawrence corridor. For years, Lawrence Avenue was a site of gang activity, drug dealing, and general neglect. Recasting the Broadway-Lawrence corridor required reclaiming the street through business improvement, beautification, and reduced criminal activity. To accomplish these the Uptown Chamber of Commerce formed the Lawrence Avenue Task Force to improve "security, sanitation, youth development, and business attraction" along Lawrence Avenue ("Task Force" 1996). The task force, made up of sixty-three individuals representing merchants, residents, city services, property owners, and social and community service organizations, set as its goal to "improve Lawrence Avenue and then improve everybody," I was told by Solomon Chu, executive director of the Chamber: "We try to beautify the street, change the image." While the success of this effort remains open to debate, it is a symbolic expression of unity over community concerns.

These cooperative efforts are tied to planning efforts to revitalize retail along Lawrence and Broadway. "We hope that people will be attracted to

Broadway and we will begin to create a good retail mix," Sue Ellen Long told me in our interview. The hope is that people will once again shop in Uptown, because according to leaders "they don't shop here [now]." The recently completed U-shaped shopping center at Broadway and Lawrence (across from the Uptown Theater), Sun Plaza, is a good example. It was built on the site of the Sun Chevrolet automobile dealership, vacant for years and the target of vandals, squatters, and numerous fires. Randall Langer, a key leader of the Sun Plaza's development group, said in our interview that "Sun Plaza happened to be a vacant piece of property, . . . just a bullshit piece of property, for years. We felt that that was a great intersection, so we put a developing proposal together and a marketing proposal. After two years of trying to broker it to an owner, we said let's do it ourselves." The nearly fully occupied shopping center includes a "Westernized" Asian market, pizzeria, Thai restaurant, laundromat, pediatric physician center (the only one in the community), and franchise video store.[36] Sun Plaza is not another "neon plastic strip mall." Langer and his group were responsive to community and alderman input, even agreeing to invest additional money in streetscaping. While Langer freely admits that his foray into commercial development is tied to securing his residential holdings, his effort to bring retail shopping opportunities to the community has evoked positive responses from leaders and residents.

The Sun Plaza development is part of a greater economic development plan that is beginning to produce results. Solomon Chu told me that Uptown is one of three or four neighborhoods in Chicago to show a retail increase in the last twenty years. This increase is snowballing as developers and retailers are being attracted to the Broadway-Lawrence strip. Developers announced plans to renovate the former Goldblatt's property and turn it into a retail center (Petersen 2000) anchored by "big name" tenants (e.g., Borders bookstore). In addition, a Starbucks opened on Wilson several blocks west of Broadway (Obejas 1999). These efforts will be supported by two tax-increment financing (TIF) districts that are planned in Uptown, one along Broadway-Lawrence and the other south of Wilson along Broadway. While neither TIF has been approved by the city, the city's planning department and both aldermen support them. Alderman Smith notes that TIF money would allow the neighborhood to use some economic tools not only to preserve integration in Uptown, but also to highlight it (Petersen 2001). Alderman Shiller sees the TIF districts as encouraging both new and improved commercial, residential, and entertainment developments in the area. The TIF debate, beyond the scope of

FIGURE 3.3. Gold-
blatts Building in
Lawrence/Broadway
TIF, currently being
converted into con-
dos and retail

my analysis, is the culmination of efforts to revitalize and redefine
Uptown's commercial districts.

Community-development projects aimed at reviving Uptown's commercial districts elicit some degree of cooperation. Arguably, all groups
stand to benefit from the shopping opportunities offered through the
retail development along Broadway and Lawrence. In fact, leaders realize that low-income residents will feel the potential effect of retail development most significantly. "Less affluent people need more shopping
opportunities, because they are less mobile," noted Alderman Mary Ann
Smith. "They should be able to put less money into transportation and
more money into the essentials of life." Another leader suggested to me
on August 8, 1996, that "just because you have a lower income you
should [not] have to get on a bus or a cab and go to another neighborhood
to get your goods and services." So far, the commercial redevelopment
being attracted serves Uptown's diverse economic mix. Most of the businesses are not out of reach for those with the fewest resources, and
middle-income residents are finding stores and services they frequent.
Commercial development thus can serve all groups. Commercial growth
also affects perceptions of community safety. A community informant

told me on August 8, 1996: "Once you have a viable commercial district where you have people coming and going, you have security implicit in that. If you don't feel safe on streets in your neighborhood, and you feel more comfortable in another neighborhood, you will go there. But as this new retail comes in, . . . that if people perceive that 'Oh, this is all cleaned up' and begin to shop . . . [now] it may not be true, but perception becomes reality!" Retail developments along the Broadway-Lawrence corridor complement evening entertainment venues and bring more "eyes on the street" throughout the day. The issue of improved safety is a bridge that joins groups together.

Finally, leaders recognize the need to improve the balance between the abundance of social services and development attractive to middle-income groups. For many years, nonprofits and banks have been the main economic sources in Uptown. This imbalance puts a damper on neighborhood revitalization. As Sue Ellen Long told me: "The bank cannot continue to be the heart of a community without people with some disposable income living here—that is part of the mix too. The approach we've taken through our development corporation is to build up supportive services that are needed for someone to come in here and develop. Because when they come in, they look at it, they say, 'Sorry, we don't want to do anything here because there is nothing else that is going to draw people out here.'" Long is correct that a healthy neighborhood needs disposable income to thrive, and this depends on an active commercial center. Leaders serving the low-income residents recognize this as well. One leader notes that "you have more . . . opportunities to shop [and] . . . a better range of services . . . if more middle-income people are moving into the neighborhood."[37] Greater safety and increased retail attracts other businesses, which increases opportunities for everyone. Leaders believe that these efforts help redefine Uptown as viable and stable.

Professionally Managed Affordable Housing

Another aspect of redefining Uptown's image involves efforts to improve affordable-housing initiatives. Low-income housing in Uptown has meant many things, from poorly maintained rental properties to project-based subsidized projects to SRO buildings. In the 1970s and 1980s, many affordable units were rentals in poor condition. A developer, Randall Langer, told me that "low-income housing in the 1980s was not professionally managed. It was slum buildings. Landlords charged cheaper rents because they couldn't get better tenants." Even some subsidized housing was of poor quality. Remnants of low-income housing of this type are still present, for example, the Wilson Club Hotel at the corner of Wilson and Clifton Street, which Josh Hoyt described to me as "one of the only remaining cage hotels in the city. It's the cheapest kind of SRO housing which is allowed. It is plywood walls and chicken wire, front and top . . . whole floors of these little cubicles. You pay by the night, I think it is seven dollars a night. The reason they are in cages is that the sprinkling system, in case there is a fire, can turn on and sprinkle the whole thing." While such spaces provide affordable housing for Uptown's poorest residents, they also convey an image of deterioration and instability.

Advocates for more affordable housing *and* developers of market-rate housing agree that low-income housing—a hot-button issue—must be well managed and residents need to be organized to get their needs met. Alderman Smith told me that residents said that "everything we do, whether it is upscale or SRO or senior [housing], should be of the highest caliber." Even conservative groups applaud organizing efforts that provide quality and well-managed affordable housing.

Lakefront SRO is one nonprofit that is not only revitalizing properties in Uptown, but also implementing a well-managed structure to effectively serve low-income residents. In the last decade, Lakefront converted numerous deteriorated buildings. Some leaders are critical of Lakefront's efforts, claiming that Uptown is oversaturated with subsidized housing, but even prodevelopment leaders praise the results. Solomon Chu commented to me on the reaction to Lakefront's rehabilitation work: "A lot of the builders argued that the more low-income housing we provide the less homeownership you have, . . . and then the less stable. My point is, what do you want? 'Do you want this boarded-up, rat-infested house sitting there?' I challenge them. 'None of you want to touch it in over seven years, because it is not commercially viable.' The only way you can change it and make it viable is to have it done through a not-for-profit."

Lakefront, however, plays a larger role than simple housing provision. A leader from Lakefront stresses: "After the housing is built we want to involve the people as much as possible and give them the skills to become involved. We have tenant councils in each building and tenants can be on any of our board committees. And according to our bylaws, residents are the majority of our board of directors."[38] Creating affordable housing by revitalizing existing buildings is just one part of Lakefront's success; the other part, key for stabilizing residents, involves resident management and a professionally run building with full-time social services on site.

Lakefront's outreach to the community earns it points as well. Lakefront made connections with groups not considered traditional allies. Its goal is to "go out and say, 'Here, look, this is what we're trying to do, here's why we're trying to do it. What do you think about that?' And [then] be responsive to some of their issues."[39] The approach is paying off as more conservative groups and for-profit developers are supporting Lakefront's efforts, thus recognizing its provision of well-managed affordable housing and altering the perception of affordable housing in Uptown. Randy Langer told me: "When we came in, [groups like Lakefront SRO] were just forming to professionalize low-income housing. I think that is what has changed in Uptown—we are building right next to Lakefront SRO. You typically don't see condos wanting to go next to low-income buildings, but we are seeing the tolerance from the people we sell to." This tolerance appears driven in part by the way affordable housing is being handled.

Lakefront SRO is not alone. There is evidence of less "us versus them" when it comes to affordable housing. Groups are beginning to see their common interests. For-profit developers are even getting into the act. For

FIGURE 3.4.   Affordable housing projects in Uptown. *Left*, 300-unit apartment building at Carmen Avenue and the lakefront (first group of renters in nation to buy a HUD prepayment building); *right*, Lakefront SRO building in Sheridan Park

example, J. R. Graves is known as an owner committed to maintaining economic diversity in Uptown. Graves, with thirteen apartment buildings in the community, is working at creating affordable homeownership. He sold several dozen condos to tenants with incomes far below the city's median. "I think the community should have a mixture of people—not just poor people and not just rich people," he says. "I thought if we could increase ownership residents would be more likely to be involved in the community" (quoted in Terry Wilson 1995: 2). Graves does profit from these sales and is also protecting his other buildings by increasing ownership. Yet his attitude is evidence that leaders are recognizing that providing quality affordable housing and ownership stabilizes Uptown. Such development challenges the myth that affordable housing means slums and crime. Alderman Smith commented to me that because of certain affordable housing initiatives, "not only are those buildings themselves more beautiful, [but you get] better neighbors . . . [and] the whole area is safer. And the real estate values have gone up for everybody."

The approach Uptown leaders take to planning retail development and dealing with professionally managed affordable housing is not typical of most communities. Political cleavages force groups to align on various issues and in the process to realize that development does not have to be a zero-sum game. Equitable planning and development efforts are creating equilibrium in the community. A leader summed this up when he told me, on July 27, 1996: "I think there is less us versus them. Some people are trying real hard to maintain the us versus them, . . . but I think less and less, in reality, people are permitting themselves to be pitted against the other." Through cooperative efforts to prevent disinvestment, disorder, and decline, leaders are redefining Uptown as viable and stable. In the process community-development initiatives are increasing the likelihood that Uptown's racial and class mix will be preserved.

Community-building Efforts to Promote Integration

All communities hoping to remain stable and vibrant need community-development projects that address the physical and economic infrastructure to create a positive image. Maintaining racial, ethnic, and class integration is even more complex. For a community to be stably integrated, local interventions are required beyond economic and physical improvement projects to channel conflict and create positive images of integration. Organizations are needed to redefine community values and norms by going beyond brick-and-mortar projects to promote integration as a community good. In many diverse-by-direction communities like

Oak Park, Illinois, leaders quickly forged a positive take on the changes taking place. Leaders shifted the emphasis from "white flight" and "black invasion" to an image of "multiethnic and multicultural" convergence (Goodwin 1979: 127). This did not immediately occur in Uptown. In fact, as racial change began, neither was community intervention intentionally aimed at maintaining integration nor was integration put "front and center" in local discussions. This does not mean that community groups were not involved in stabilizing integration. Urban community theory suggests that when a community experiences change, organizations can stabilize or redefine the community as stable by strengthening social networks. This strategy, referred to as an "interactionist" approach, does not accept the inevitability of decline in racially integrated neighborhoods, instead positing that neighborhood stability is possible through the creation of a strong sense of community (Saltman 1990; Suttles 1968, 1972; Fischer 1984). In Uptown several generations of leaders have worked to stabilize integration through community-building efforts to strengthen social ties and networks among varied groups, and through efforts to recast the ethnic mix as a community strength.

The most visible community group attempting to stabilize Uptown by reinforcing social support networks among groups is ONE. For over two decades, ONE has brought organizations and leaders together to deal with community concerns, including maintenance of the area's racial and economic mix. And while ONE's legitimacy in the community has fluctuated, since the mid-1980s it has positioned itself as a key community organization working to stabilize integration in Uptown. This is explicit in its stated mission, mentioned earlier, of "building a successful multiethnic, mixed-economic community." Josh Hoyt told me that ONE is committed to the idea "that there has to be a place where we can work together, . . . a place where we work together on diversity, as it's valued." The prodevelopment and antigentrification poles in Uptown create a space where people could come together with the potential for working together. ONE consists of members from around sixty community organizations, including churches, banks, businesses, ethnic associations, tenant and housing associations, and local universities and colleges. Driven by members who reflect the diversity in the community, ONE created in the last decade a level of organization that ensured that integration is talked about, and that the rights and needs of various groups are addressed. By fostering dialogue, ONE provides space for the needs of those with low and middle incomes to be considered, and in the process creates a sense of equilibrium.

As an alliance of smaller groups, ONE finds its main strength in the relationships based on mutual interests it cultivates among groups that normally would not collaborate. A former member of ONE's board notes: "I think there are people who are working together . . . at ONE [and through] communitywide efforts people are getting together. Then I think relationships form. I don't think they normally form easily."[40] By facilitating relationships, ONE is building community and creating new values of cooperation. This was evident in ONE's organizing efforts around the prepayment issue. The multicultural organizing effort, by nature local and interpersonal, strengthened community networks by creating links among various groups. ONE's organizers assisted in drawing groups together across racial and ethnic lines, as well as in building multicultural task forces to work together and see their common fate. The effort created a positive image for residents of Uptown. The struggles and successes, at both local and national levels, cultivated the perception that Uptown residents are not doormats, but organized and willing to fight for societal and governmental goods. These community-building efforts help stabilize integration in Uptown.

Another community-building effort surrounds, ironically, the proposed TIF districts and other neighborhood issues. Many antigentrification representatives are concerned that the TIF proposals that further commercial development will have negative effects, such as displacing smaller businesses and residually affecting low-income residents by raising property values (and thus rents) (Joravsky 1999). Others see the TIF proposals as necessary for revitalizing Uptown. This might appear to be business as usual in Uptown, as prodevelopment and antigentrification groups battle over low-income housing and defining improvement (Allee 2000; Hepp 2001), but something else is occurring—what I term "structured cooperation."[41] For example, Alderman Shiller, viewed by her opponents as the "champion of the poor" or as "practicing the politics of poverty," has organized forums where all sides present their views. Although tension exists over the type of residential and retail development (estimated at around $135 million) generated by TIF money, groups are cooperating through structured meetings. Shiller views these forums as a basket where "everyone's idea was put in" and respect is given to "the full diversity of the community" (quoted in Tardy 2000: 1). Shiller's willingness to engage those at odds with her political agenda represents a shift in community dynamics that is reflected in the nature of Uptown's

TIF proposals. Different from any others in the city, they seek "balanced development" by attempting to jump-start development and boost property values, while also using development as a "tool for financing low-income housing and supporting low-rent businesses" (Petersen 2001). Shiller supports the TIF, as she sees it protecting "the continued diverse, multi-cultural, mixed income nature of the community."[42]

Such cooperation is also visible in other recent actions by Alderman Shiller. She recently turned an expected clash between herself and a community group, the Buena Park Neighbors (BPN), into a positive encounter by requesting that the BPN form a committee to advise her on the feasibility of permit parking in the area and the placement of benches at bus stops throughout the ward. "It's a fairness question," said Shiller, noting that she herself is not sure what should be done (quoted in Butler 1999). Members of the BPN were pleased and somewhat surprised by Shiller's willingness to open lines of communication and cooperation. A representative of the BPN notes: "In the past, the alderman hasn't had a history of seeking the input of community organizations, or at least not ours" (cited in ibid.). Whether cooperation will remain is open to debate; however, Alderman Shiller's reaching out to these groups is a positive sign. In contrast to the 1970s and 1980s, there appears to be a greater chance for dialogue and thus cooperation in the twenty-first century.

Finally, there is evidence that Uptown leaders are working to redefine the community through creating a "distinguishable" image for it. As the community became integrated, its multicultural and economically diverse mix became a defining symbol. In the process, an awareness of, pride in, and promotion of integration emerged. Leaders quickly applaud the area's diverse populations and are even working to "sell" certain identifiers of the community's integration as an asset. Organizations from both the private and public sectors are beginning to publicly recast integration as positive and worthy of promotion.

For example, Uptown boasts two "unplanned" economic developments along Argyle Avenue and the area known as Andersonville (running north on Clark at Foster Avenue). Both areas were commercially revitalized through entrepreneurial activity. Argyle has approximately twenty food markets and bakeries, more than twenty restaurants, and numerous businesses bordering on wholesale, making it an Asian food center for the Midwest and attracting customers from as many as four states. Andersonville, located in the northwest edge of Uptown, was the former center for Chicago's Swedish community. In the late 1970s and 1980s, an exodus of older residents spurred the closing of numerous

Swedish businesses. Since the late 1980s, however, Andersonville has attracted new merchants who represent several ethnic communities (e.g., Greek, Italian, Japanese, Middle Eastern, and Iranian), as well as a number of female and gay businesspersons (Nyden, Bennett, and Adams 1993). These commercial strips, reflective of the changing globalized economy, are identifiable symbols of multiethnic and multiracial integration in Uptown.

While Argyle Avenue and Andersonville were not planned efforts at economic revitalization, they are experiencing tremendous economic success, which is good for promoting racial and ethnic integration in Uptown. Numerous leaders recognize the value of these areas to the community. Both aldermen, ONE, the Uptown Chamber of Commerce, and the Andersonville Chamber of Commerce are supporting and touting these areas as what is right with Uptown. Alderman Smith, who supports improving the area by strengthening the commercial district's infrastructure, told me: "We have brought the full power and authority and resources of the mayor's office to Argyle . . . to bring more major improvement to that area. And we are piece by piece providing more resources and some adjustments to the infrastructure." The Andersonville Chamber of Commerce rigorously promotes the area, particularly through a heavily attended summer festival. The success of these areas,

FIGURE 3.5.   "Asian Village" or Argyle Street looking west

the subject of numerous newspaper articles, generates a positive community image (Denney 1989; Lauerman 1999; Hein and Domke 1999). Uptown leaders use these successes to challenge the perception that racially mixed areas are not viable. By latching onto the success of these global zones, leaders are redefining Uptown as integrated, accepting, and successful.

THE CASE of Uptown reveals the complexity of maintaining a racial, ethnic, cultural, and economic mix of residents over time. Uptown's diverse mix of residents was not planned or directed, at least not in the sense that there was conscious, goal-oriented action by groups working together to promote the benefits of integration. The community's multiethnic, multiracial, and mixed-income character ensured that no single group dominated. Demographics alone, however, do not account for Uptown's stable integration. Its social, demographic, and residential evolution since the end of World War II involved numerous negotiations over redevelopment, housing, and land use. Disparate community organizations negotiated issues and initiated community-development projects to keep Uptown a stable and vital area. Groups, albeit late in the process of racial change, went beyond bricks-and-mortar projects to reaffirm the value of integration. Generations of leaders struggled to manage Uptown's symbolic identifiers, successfully creating a distinguishable image of Uptown as an organized, empowered, and stably integrated community.

4   Jackson Heights, New York

Resident Narrative: John Nicholson

Prior to moving to Jackson Heights I lived in various NY neighborhoods.[1] I lived in Brooklyn's Park Slope from 1980 to '82, then the Upper West Side (103rd Street and West End Avenue) from 1982 to '84, and finally Riverside Drive from 1984 to '86. During most of this time, I worked during the day and went to graduate school at night. I and most people I knew were forced to live in "emerging" or gentrifying neighborhoods. These neighborhoods were in beautiful old sections that had fallen out of favor and into disarray/disrepair in the 1960s and 1970s. These neighborhoods were "cool" and with more upwardly mobile folks came a better image, and better stores, restaurants, et cetera. Despite the pretensions of trendiness, it was an economic reality to choose these neighborhoods, as prices for both rentals and for cooperatives/condominiums were increasing at an alarming rate.

In the mid-1980s, when I finished my MBA and found a decent job with potential, I wanted a place of my own. Prices in the cool neighborhoods were out of reach, except for small studios. So given the choice between a studio in a trendy neighborhood, and more space in a less trendy neighborhood, I opted for space and started to search. I had friends throughout the metropolitan region and began visiting a variety of neighborhoods. In 1986 I purchased a co-op apartment in Jackson Heights. I opted for Jackson Heights because of location. It is close to midtown, twenty minutes via a number of subway lines. It also had great prewar apartments, which meant more space, better detailing in each apartment, and reasonable prices. I bought my large one bedroom for $75,000 in early 1986. I was offered $85,000 at the beginning of 1987, and a real estate broker suggested I list the apartment for $95,000 (with the intention of settling at $90,000). I had no intention of selling but wanted to see what was out there. However in the fall of 1987, the real estate picture changed dramatically. Within a few years the same apartment was valued at $35,000. Neighborhoods like Jackson Heights or Sunnyside suffered the largest decrease in values. Even today, ten years later, the apartment is only worth $40,000 to $45,000. The slack in the real estate market was disappointing, but compared to other neighborhoods, the cost of living in Jackson Heights was low.

In the spring of 1990 I met my partner, Carlos, and settled into domestic bliss. As a Colombian immigrant, he chose Jackson Heights because he had a cousin, married to an American, living there. When he first came to the United States he stayed with them for a few months, and then rented his own apartment a few blocks away. Family and the rather large South American community, especially the Colombian community, including restaurants, ethnic food, and music stores, were appealing and comforting. Most of the Colombian stores and restaurants are in the Seventy-ninth Street to Ninetieth Street area, between Roosevelt Avenue and Northern Boulevard.

Although not influential in my decision to move to the community, I came to appreciate some of Jackson Heights' unique amenities. For example, the spirit of community was strong in Jackson Heights, especially among new arrivals. I found it easy to meet new neighbors. In developing neighborhoods like Jackson Heights, people are not as reluctant to talk with strangers. The sense of community became increasingly important as I lived there. I became involved in the co-op board and feel we were able to improve the building's gardens via landscaping. We also opened the backyard to tenants, further offering a bond between neighbors.

I also liked the freedom of being in a very diverse atmosphere. And although I had heard there was a gay community, I didn't realize it was as large or as active as it was until after moving in. The gay community was a less important factor in my life, being settled down and all, although it was nice not to be the only gay couple in the building. There are a number of gay bars in the community. They tend to cater to a bit older, blue-collar, and immigrant crowd. For many cultures where homosexuality is more repressed than in the United States, moving here is a way of escaping repression and exploring one's sexuality. The trendy bars in Manhattan, however, are overwhelmingly white and upper middle class, and a bit intimidating to recent immigrants.

The ethnic diversity in Jackson Heights was also intriguing. It was most notable in the wide selection of all kinds of ethnic cuisine, and at very affordable prices. I learned a lot about different cultures via neighbors and restaurants. I also saw the ethnic diversity in my building. When I first arrived, the building was evenly split between owners and renters. Renters were predominately older retired folks—generally German Jewish and Irish Catholic—who were protected by rent control, and the owners tended to be young, ethnically diverse upwardly mobile couples. As time when on, it was a sad reality that the older couples died or moved out. And as prices fell, the new owners became more diversified, and generally more recent immigrants. The diversity impacted me subtly and over time. For example, just in talking with your neighbors, you find that they're from a region of the world you don't know much about—or with very different customs. Slowly you begin to expand your cultural and geographic frame of reference.

I did not, however, find everything about living in Jackson Heights positive. First, travel back and forth to Manhattan became tiresome. Although it is not far in distance or in time, there is a psychological distance that is an impediment. Second, Jackson Heights also lacked upscale products and services. For a good bookstore, art-house movies, or Starbucks, you had to leave the neighborhood. Local businesses were primarily food stores, either grocery stores or fruit markets, or dry cleaners and utensils. To purchase clothes, books, or gourmet foods, it was Manhattan.

Also, the diverse ethnic and cultural mix was occasionally bothersome. Different cultures have such drastically different concepts of order, personal space, and reactions. Dealing with all those differences can at times be difficult. I am sure these differences led to the friction between older residents and new arrivals that was there when I moved in 1986. There were a lot of brief fearful comments made by older residents about the recent immigrants. It always sort of puzzled me because most were immigrants themselves—albeit from Europe. Happily, the fear seems to go away with time and experience. Also, the Jackson Heights Preservation Committee and other community groups fostered greater sharing and interaction between groups.

In the ten years that I lived in Jackson Heights, there were changes. When I moved in, there were still remnants of an older German population (visible through delicatessens, restaurants), but this has all but disappeared. The Seventy-third–Seventy-fourth Street shopping hub became Indian/Pakistani. Parking and traffic became more problematic—especially on the weekend. The increased traffic without new infrastructure was annoying. There was a little ditty: "Hindus honking at parking Pakistanis." It was overwhelming at times, but I was aware that this activity was bringing life into the neighborhood.

I eventually left Jackson Heights for Colombia, South America. Carlos's petition to receive a U.S. work visa was denied, since as an accountant he could not meet the standard of "offering a service/skill that no U.S. citizen could be found for." He had a choice of either remaining in the United States as an illegal or to return to Colombia. We discussed the options and decided that we could have a better quality of life living in Colombia. We proceeded to obtain all the legal permissions necessary for me to live and work in Colombia. After all was obtained, Carlos went down to get a job and set up a home, while I continued to work in the United States, saving as much money as possible to give us more options later. I eventually took the plunge in 1996 and moved. I have sublet my apartment since 1996. All interested parties have been Indian. The sublet process was not too difficult. The co-op board based their approval of each *sublet on the individual and not on ethnic background. Each new sublet is interviewed and their credit profile studied. It has been difficult, however, to find a buyer. Several buyers were found but rejected by the Cooperative Board of Directors, who aren't under obligation of explaining why applicants are rejected. The rejection of the buyers and the denial of permission for further sublets resulted in my defaulting on the apartment, hence losing a ten-year-plus investment. It was a sad turn of events, but my life in Colombia has been an extremely positive experience, expanding my vision to a much larger frame of reference.*

Exiting the Number 7 Train at Seventy-fourth Street

On an overcast lazy autumn day, I board the Number 7 train traveling east to Jackson Heights, Queens. Leaving behind the rail yards, taxicab headquarters, warehouses, and small industry, the train nears Jackson Heights, where brick single-family homes and six- to seven-story high-rise apartments scatter over the landscape. I exit the train at Seventy-fourth Street and Roosevelt Avenue at 10:30 AM, the crossroads of Little India and Little Colombia, as well as two of the nation's most ethnically diverse neighborhoods, Jackson Heights and Elmhurst. I walk along Jackson Heights' commercial streets, where the number and variety of stores are remarkable. Along Roosevelt Avenue, they range from an Asian hair-and-nail salon, a Korean/Japanese restaurant, and a grocery store advertising Halal meat, to a Latin dance club and numerous second-floor offices providing travel and legal services. Street merchants share the sidewalks with men handing out flyers. Along a three-block strip of Seventy-fourth Street, informally known as Little India, dozens of shops sell goods ranging from Indian clothing to gold jewelry to groceries unique to the Asian subcontinent. The old Eagle Theater, a shade of a different era, carries colorful advertisements for Bollywood films.

The mix of street and pedestrian traffic, smells, and large, bright, colorful signs along these commercial strips attack my senses. People of color dominate the sidewalks and stores. After forty-five minutes, I find myself looking for someone like me or a store I like or something "American." Everyone speaks differently, not just than I, but than each other. The foods are foreign to me. The amount of signage and the visual medley are disconcerting. Suddenly quite aware of what it means to be a Midwestern middle-class white male, I realize that this too is part of the

United States and likely what it will increasingly look like in the coming decades.

The ethnic-based commercial districts serving the masses of Latinos and Asians that in-migrated to Jackson Heights and neighboring Elmhurst contrast with the streets north of Thirty-seventh Avenue lined with large co-ops and stately one- and two-family homes. The sidewalks widen on these streets and landscaping and a canopy of well-maintained trees create a counterpoint to the commercial districts just blocks away. Here there is less traffic, noise, and clutter. The historic co-ops and single-family homes provide a distinctive and stately ambiance for all who pass by. I marvel at the intricate architectural features and plush interior gardens of the renowned Towers and Chateau co-op structures, stretching over a full city block. Jackson Heights' geography mirrors the complexity of a community that over the past quarter century has become one of the nation's most ethnically mixed.

Jackson Heights arose from a unique vision of a planned, restrictive, and suburbanlike residential community. From its inception in the early 1900s until after World War II, the neighborhood maintained a distinctive architectural and racially homogeneous identity. As demographic and cultural shifts made their way through Jackson Heights (and much of the rest of northern Queens), the area was transformed into an amazing multi-

FIGURE 4.1. Jackson Heights historic co-ops. *Left*, the Towers; *right*, the Chateau

ethnic and multiracial community. This integration was far from planned; few long-term or newly arrived residents consciously chose to live in a diverse community. Yet Jackson Heights did not experience the pattern of resegregation that so often accompanies racial and ethnic transition. White, Latino, and Asian residents from different economic backgrounds today live alongside each other, not always in harmony, but striving to make their neighborhood succeed. Jackson Heights as a viable and stably integrated neighborhood is the result of a confluence of demographic processes and community negotiations and interventions, as we will see.

From Restrictive Community to Multiracial Mix

Jackson Heights is located close to Shea Stadium and just south of La Guardia airport. Until the late nineteenth century, like most of Queens County, the area that would become Jackson Heights (then referred to as Trains Meadow) was predominately rural. Between 1900 and 1910, Queens remained a network of autonomous townships surrounded by farms and fields. Since residents could reach Manhattan only by trolley and ferry, Queens was not a viable bedroom community until 1908, when the Queensboro Bridge and plans for the construction of a subway mass-transit line made commuting to Manhattan practical. The promise of accessibility sparked a real estate boom, as speculators began to buy up open land in western Queens.

The most significant investor, Edward MacDougall's Queensboro Corporation, purchased a 325-acre parcel of undeveloped land and labeled it Jackson Heights. Lacking a master plan for the property, the Queensboro Corporation developed portions of the property, dividing it into lots for quick sale to other builders. Soon, however, a unified vision of Jackson Heights evolved. Inspired by the low-density, garden-city model of British planner Ebenezer Howard, MacDougall envisioned a unified "Garden Apartment" community that emphasized light, space, and greenery (Karatzas 1992). He built large Tudor-style residential buildings that covered only 30–50 percent of a city block (buildings in Manhattan covered 70 percent), featuring interior gardens and rooms that allowed for more light and ventilation. Many of these buildings stretched from sidewalk to sidewalk, built around common courtyards. Streets were shaded by trees, and it was not uncommon to see single- and two-family homes blending in between modern apartment buildings. MacDougall intended Jackson Heights to be a city within a city, with churches, shopping, and recreational activities that would make it a cohesive community. He donated land for churches, planned a main commercial district along Thirty-seventh Avenue and Eighty-second Street, and built tennis courts and even a golf course (ibid.). In 1917, as the elevated Number 7 train reduced the trip to Manhattan to twenty minutes, Jackson Heights became a convenient alternative for individuals and families who wanted to escape overcrowded Manhattan. MacDougall endeavored to give Jackson Heights a suburban feel to attract young, educated, sophisticated, and affluent professionals.

Jackson Heights was thus not designed for everyone. Early advertisements made it clear that Jackson Heights was envisioned as an exclusive suburb for a native white middle class fleeing the increasingly crowded and culturally diverse city.[2] The social inclusiveness of the utopian garden-city proposals of Ebenezer Howard was not for Jackson Heights, which was advertised as a "restricted residential community" and barred Jews, African Americans, and Catholics by both custom and restrictive covenants. Daniel Karatzas notes: "Whether or not it was explicitly stated in promotional material, it was widely known at the time that only white Anglo-Saxon Protestants were welcome in Jackson Heights, Forest Hills Gardens, or Garden City. In addition the prices MacDougall charged for his apartments and homes removed the vast majority of New Yorkers from the pool of potential residents. Apartments costing as much as $25,000 and homes which commanded $38,500 were well beyond the reach of most of the people that restrictive communities did not welcome" (1992: 79). As a result of these policies, integration in Jackson Heights before the 1950s was confined to the housing stock, as the population remained racially and ethnically homogeneous. While Jews began to move into the neighborhood after restrictive covenants were ruled illegal, blacks were openly discriminated against until the Fair Housing Act of 1968.

Driving the growth of Jackson Heights was the Queensboro Corporation's cooperative ownership plan. Families who had previously rented were offered the chance to buy their apartments at a flat fee, paying a monthly maintenance fee for the management of the building. Tenants not only owned their apartments, but also became shareholders in the cooperative (or co-op). This setup had several advantages for home buyers. First, co-op residents enjoyed the benefits of home ownership while living in professionally managed apartments. Second, and of more importance to the tenant owners, was the ability to protect themselves from owners who might sell their stock interest in the building at a low price to an "undesirable person" (Karatzas 1992: 46).[3] This feature, which contributed to the community's racial homogeneity and exclusiveness by keeping "undesirable" people out of buildings, continues today, making enforcement of antidiscrimination housing ordinances difficult (Rozhon and Kleinfield 1995). To this day, co-ops make up a substantial portion of Jackson Heights' housing stock.

Jackson Heights grew steadily through the boom years of the 1920s, as new residential properties covered the remaining open areas. Fifteen apartment complexes and hundreds of private English garden homes filled in the gaps of the thirty-three square blocks. By 1930, Jackson Heights had become a racially homogeneous, architecturally unified, middle-class community of more than 44,500 residents. Development continued, albeit without strict adherence to MacDougall's suburban vision; for instance, the golf course and tennis courts were leveled in 1950 to make way for more residential development. By 1954, local development in the MacDougall model came to a halt, although the legacy of MacDougall's vision and development remains today. The neighborhood continues to possess a strong, although often architecturally defined, sense of community. The area corresponds to no political jurisdiction for electoral office at the city, state, or federal level. Even Jackson Heights' local community board is shared with two smaller neighboring areas, Corona and East Elmhurst.[4] Jackson Heights continues to maintain an identifiable sense of self, which is in no small part due to the community's undeniable visual distinctiveness. The large co-op buildings with their interior gardens, the unique architecture of the Towers and the Chateau, and the mix of single-family, co-op, and rental buildings are crucial to maintaining its identity as a distinct and unique entity.

In the early to mid-1960s, Jackson Heights began to lose its appeal for young middle-class families, as the postwar building boom on Long Island and Robert Moses's highway development drew families out of the city. By the late 1960s, residents of Jackson Heights saw white residents "fleeing" to the suburbs, fewer whites moving in, and the neighborhood physically declining. Once-manicured courtyard gardens were covered over with asphalt, sandboxes, and playground equipment. Many of the single-family homes and even garages were illegally converted to apartments. "In the 1960s Jackson Heights was really sliding down," noted a resident of twenty-five years in our November 21, 1995, interview. "The apartments and the co-ops went down in price. The Towers was a symbol of that—they were renting, the gardens were not maintained. They were really in shambles." Many residents sensed that this "neighborhood was not what it had been" and feared further decline. As a result, there was "a certain amount of white flight in the sense that couples with kids moved out." While decline occurred, two very different yet simultaneous trends prevented residents' fears from being realized: post-1965 mass immigration to New York City (in particular, to Queens), and the attraction of and movement toward historic preservation by middle-class whites during the 1980s and 1990s.

The Hart-Cellar Immigration Act of 1965 brought a massive influx of immigrants from Latin America, Asia, and the Caribbean to the United States. The New York metropolitan area was a principal destination for newcomers. The arrival of immigrants was instrumental in revitalizing numerous neighborhoods throughout the city, particularly in Brooklyn, the Bronx, and Queens (Winnick 1990). In northern Queens, communities like Woodside, Jackson Heights, Elmhurst, Corona, and Flushing quickly became ports of entry for a diverse group of immigrants. The influx of immigrants to the borough of Queens in recent decades brought Jackson Heights new neighbors and a different racial, ethnic, and cultural character. For example, according to New York City Department of City Planning data, between 1983 and 1987 close to 430,000 immigrants legally entered New York, with approximately 130,000 (30 percent) arriving in Queens (ibid.) While many settled in Manhattan's traditional immigrant and minority enclaves of Chinatown, El Barrio, and the Lower East Side (see Lin 1998; Abu-Lughod 1994), a large number moved to neighborhoods in Queens. Immigrants entering Queens after 1970 offered a stark contrast to the second- and third-generation European ethnic groups that had called the borough home for decades. Between 1983 and 1987, of all immigrants arriving in New York, 42 percent from Asia and 47 percent from Central and South America settled in Queens. These trends continued: more than 180,000 immigrants entered Queens in the first six years of the 1990s, with immigration escalating in 1995 and 1996 (Howell 1999a). By 1996, nearly half the 700,000 households in Queens were headed by a foreign-born resident. In the 1990s, immigrants arrived from 180 countries, particularly from Asia and to a lesser extent from South America, Europe, and the Caribbean. The varied immigrant streams altered Queens demographically and socially.[5] Their magnitude and variety led residents to label the borough the most ethnically diverse county in the United States.

These demographic realities became increasingly visible on the streets and in the shopping centers and housing of Jackson Heights. In the 1970s, a significant concentration of South American immigrants began to emerge, especially along the commercial artery of Roosevelt Avenue. A traditional boundary between the older white population of Jackson Heights and the Asian and Latino populations of Elmhurst, Roosevelt Avenue soon housed the city's growing Colombian, Peruvian, and Ecuadorian communities. At the same time, a smaller percentage of Asians migrated into Jackson Heights, although most Asian immigrants settled in Elmhurst or Flushing (now the city's second Chinatown). While no Asian residential enclave formed, a three-block stretch of Seventy-fourth Street (and spilling onto other streets) became the center of Asian business activity, soon identified by newspaper accounts as "Little India" (Khandelwal 1994).

Why did immigrants settle in Jackson Heights, a planned community that historically restricted access by minorities? Timing is a reasonable explanation. The influx of immigrants into New York, and particularly Queens, came when neighborhoods were losing residents. The transportation and housing amenities attractive to early Jackson Heights residents also drew recently arrived immigrants. A sagging housing market and a decline in neighborhood upkeep made it easier for immigrants to find landlords willing to rent or sell. However, there needs to be something worth buying or renting, and despite periods of decline, Jackson Heights maintained an attractive and varied housing stock, consisting of MacDougall-era single-family houses, affordable boxy frame houses, rental apartments, newer co-op conversions, and the stately and original co-op buildings. Helen Sears, a resident of thirty years and former Democratic Party district leader, told me in an interview on August 21, 1996: "We cannot ignore the housing to recognize why it has been diverse. The housing mix is very unique . . . [and] it brought together a mixture of people that were very diverse but would be able to find the kind of housing that suited their needs. When you have the housing and accessibility to public transportation, you are going to be a magnet for newly arrived immigrants [and] people who come from the city who can no longer afford Manhattan prices." Immigrants, especially those with the fewest skills and resources, came to Jackson Heights because of the tight housing market, often residing in overcrowded and illegally converted but affordable houses.

In addition, Jackson Heights' location and access to transportation cannot be discounted. In our November 21, 1995, interview, I asked Rudy Greco, former Jackson Heights Beautification Group president and long-time Towers resident, why immigrants came to Jackson Heights rather than to other neighborhoods; he offered a one-word explanation—"location"—then elaborated:

> This is the geographic center of New York City. Proximity to public transport is a big reason. We are very, very well served by public transportation. We have service transit and the subway line. We are extraordinarily well served by those things. So, that stop here at Seventy-fourth and Roosevelt Avenue is about the third busiest in the city, after Times Square and Grand Central Station. The volume over there is spectacular. And so that has been a big plus [and so has our] proximity to the airports. I mean, immigrants are generally not adventurous once they make the jump, depending where they land, is where they stay for a while, at least for a generation or so.

The area is well served by Metropolitan Transit Authority trains and buses. The elevated Number 7 train, or International Express, made famous by baseball player John Rocker, provides cheap transportation to factory jobs in Long Island City, babysitting jobs in Manhattan, various kitchen jobs, and numerous other low-paying but necessary jobs along the subway route.[6] The E and F subway trains provide express service from Seventy-fourth and Roosevelt to the Citicorp building at Fifty-third Street in Manhattan. These subway lines offer fifteen-minute access to midtown Manhattan. Ease of transportation is key to the livelihood of immigrants, especially the many who work late shifts. Late-night use of the subway by immigrants is one of the reasons ridership has increased significantly along the Number 7 (Pierre-Pierre 1997). This fact is not lost on local leaders. "You can go to the 90th Street subway station in Jackson Heights at one in the morning," says Councilman John Sabini, "and it looks like rush hour" (quoted in Barry and Ojito 1997).

These advantages did not just appeal only to immigrants. Location, transportation, housing costs, and the historical character of the Mac-Dougall-plan housing continued to attract and keep middle-class whites in the community. The visual distinctiveness and quality of MacDougall's garden apartments are striking. For example, the Chateau includes twelve co-op buildings that connect, each sharing a common garden and each an individual corporation governed by a cooperative board. These buildings, along with the calm tree-lined streets, are attractive to many middle-class families and individuals. In the 1970s and 1980s, these co-ops were quite affordable compared to housing in other parts of the city, particularly Manhattan, attracting middle-class whites. "Where are you going to move and get a place located like this for those prices?" queried a resident in our November 22, 1995, interview. "There aren't too many places like it in New York City." This distinctiveness also stemmed white flight. A core of white middle-class residents has remained, many committed to and active in maintaining Jackson Heights. Helen Sears commented in our 1996 interview on the "choice" some whites have made: "There is a core that has chosen to live in Jackson Heights. They aren't here because they have no options or economic chains. They are here by choice. The groups in the co-ops, the groups that have been in the straight rentals, . . . when they went through conversions, they bought. There are also those who decided to stay in those [co-op] conversions and are above that economic level . . . and choose to stay. The purchasing power of that population is very strong. They have been a stabilizing force." The community involvement of this group centers on neighborhood improvement and community building. Certainly, individuals have different motives for remaining in a community; however, the presence of dedicated individuals is essential for staving off neighborhood disinvestment and decline, and for maintaining racial and ethnic integration.

Jackson Heights has experienced an incredible shift from an elite, racially and culturally homogeneous, and restrictive community to a multiethnic, multiracial, and multicultural mix that borders on the overwhelming. Integration in Jackson Heights was never planned; in fact, for most of its history it was actively discouraged. As we will see, the diversity in this neighborhood runs along many dimensions—race, ethnicity, nativity, sexual orientation, and class. Like Chicago's Uptown, Jackson Heights can be best described as "hyperdiverse." And while the Jackson Heights of today is very different from the Jackson Heights of twenty or thirty years ago, the neighborhood maintains a distinctive character. For years, the defining feature of Jackson Heights was MacDougall's unique architectural scheme imprinted on the local landscape. In recent years, the racial and ethnic mix has become another defining feature.

JACKSON HEIGHTS' UNPLANNED AND IMPROBABLE INTEGRATION

Various social and demographic shifts in the 1960s and 1970s helped Jackson Heights develop into one of New York City's most racially and ethnically integrated neighborhoods. As in Uptown, a population of different racial, economic, and social groups defines Jackson Heights. While the neighborhood is racially and ethnically integrated, it does not fit conventional views of residential integration. Few blacks have ever lived within its boundaries. Residents of Jackson Heights do not share the same cultural traditions, norms, identities, and concerns. International connections and language differences act as barriers between groups. The neighborhood's integrated mix sets it apart from fixed, homogeneous communities and from the invasion-succession model of neighborhood change. Integration here is not a black-white affair; it extends along multiple social lines. Jackson Heights is now comprised of a polyglot of races and cultures that shares a densely populated urban space.[7] Yet, as we will see, even with the significant changes in the neighborhood, integration has remained relatively stable.

Jackson Heights as a Microcosm of the World

In 1960, Jackson Heights had just over 81,000 residents. Unlike many areas undergoing racial change, however, the neighborhood gained population. In 1990, Jackson Heights had approximately 85,000 residents; by 2000, the population had swelled to over 109,000. The numbers are somewhat misleading, as the U.S. Bureau of the Census admittedly did a better job of counting in 2000.[8] But since the 1980s, immigration helped Queens become one of the fastest-growing boroughs in the city.

Figure 4.2 offers a snapshot of racial change in Jackson Heights. In 1960 the neighborhood was almost exclusively white (98.5 percent)—European immigrants and their descendents, primarily Italian, Irish, German, and Jewish families (Jones-Correa 1998). The percentage of whites declined in every subsequent decade, a trend the neighborhood shares with the borough.[9] In 1990, whites constituted two-fifths of the Jackson Heights population; by 2000, one-fifth. Hispanics meanwhile increased from 6 percent in 1970 to 41 percent in 1990 and 54 percent in 2000. Jackson Heights' Asian population also increased in every decade, albeit at a slower pace, comprising approximately 20 percent of the residents in 2000. Yet white flight does not seem to be correlated with the influx of immigrants. Roger Sanjek, a noted authority on Queens, states that "the white population didn't leave because the immigrants came. The population was already leaving in the '50s and housing was available [for immigrants]" (quoted in Cheng 2001).

Since 1980, only about 2 percent of the area's residents have been African Americans, remarkable given that Jackson Heights borders two smaller neighborhoods (Corona and East Elmhurst) with longstanding black populations (Gregory 1998). Explanations vary as to why so few blacks live in or are moving into Jackson Heights. Rudy Greco shared in our 1996 interview a belief common among community leaders: "Adjacent to us is North Corona. It is a vast area . . . that is segregated and all black. That is where blacks settled and they were all middle class to

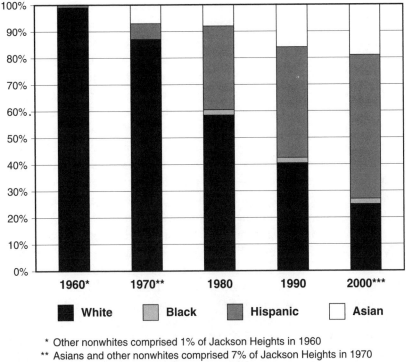

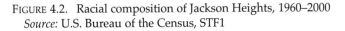

* Other nonwhites comprised 1% of Jackson Heights in 1960
** Asians and other nonwhites comprised 7% of Jackson Heights in 1970
*** Residents identifying themselves as multiracial comprised
    3% of Jackson Heights in 2000

FIGURE 4.2. Racial composition of Jackson Heights, 1960–2000
   Source: U.S. Bureau of the Census, STF1

upper middle class. Louie Armstrong lived there. Malcolm X lived there. And if you go there now, you would see that this is a wealthy and well-ensconced middle-class black community. So blacks have had a place established of their own a long time ago. Now the walls are breaking down to the extent that in these formerly restricted co-ops in Jackson Heights there are the beginnings of black presence, maybe just tokenism but it is happening." Many leaders intimated that blacks in adjacent communities did not attempt to move to Jackson Heights because of the presence of a homogeneous black community nearby. Such a statement assumes that blacks have preferred to live in racially homogenous communities. There is, however, more to the story.

Jackson Heights' history involves racial antagonism and discrimination against blacks. The commonly accepted eastern border of Jackson

Heights has been defined as the street that divides that community from blacks in East Elmhurst and Corona. This street, Junction Boulevard, was called the "Mason-Dixon Line" in 1964, after an attempt by the board of education to integrate schools in Jackson Heights and Corona (Powledge 1964). The board's integration plan was met with significant resistance from Jackson Heights whites. Though there is today little indication of that level of racial friction, indicators of the color line between Corona and Jackson Heights remain. That many community leaders continue to refer to Junction Boulevard as the Mason-Dixon Line indicates some resistance to black residents. Several leaders candidly suggested that while Jackson Heights may be ready for integration with Asian and Latino residents, this willingness does not extend to African Americans. "I think that on the whole this neighborhood is not ready for racial integration, . . . not racial integration with blacks," a thirty-year resident and activist told me in a November 21, 1995, interview. "I think if African Americans moved in here rapidly, the neighborhood would simply—. . . a lot of apartments would be sold very fast. Because many of the tenant owners are elderly, they have enough problems dealing with Hispanics or gays." Integration with Asians and Latinos appears more acceptable to many residents. Another leader notes that "Latinos or Hispanics are here and are coming in large numbers; . . . they're tenant owners. You had this thing where the Hispanics and the Asians were kind of the buffers between the blacks and the whites, and that is certainly true here." Such assertions are difficult to confirm, as there is little direct evidence of housing discrimination against blacks. A balanced explanation for the small number of blacks appears to lie somewhere in between.

Finally, Jackson Heights' multiethnic and multiracial character is most visible in the racial and ethnic composition of local public schools (see Figure 4.3).[10] Since the late 1980s, Jackson Heights students have been increasingly Hispanic. Asians constitute slightly less than 20 percent of the student population. Whites, once one-fifth of the student body, have slipped to a mere 14 percent. The percentage of black students in Jackson Heights schools is almost as negligible as the number of black residents in the community. For the most part, the percentage of minority students in local schools mirrors each group's overall population in the community. Indeed, because Jackson Heights' white population consists of a substantial number of retirees and childless couples, there is a lower percentage of white children in local schools than the percentage of whites in the population.

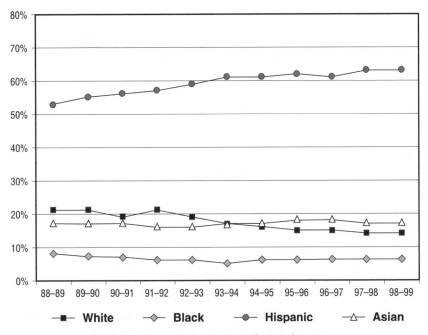

FIGURE 4.3.   Racial composition of Jackson Heights's Schools, 1986–1999
Source: U.S. Department of Education. 2000. National Center for Education
Statistics. 1986–1999. Common Core of Data program. Public Elementary/Secondary School Universe Survey Data. [http://nces.ed.gov/ccd/]

The growing immigrant population also significantly impacts the Jackson Heights schools, which are tremendously overcrowded. For example, in the 1999–2000 school year, 1,528 students filled Jackson Heights Elementary School (PS 69) to 126 percent of its capacity; 22.3 percent of these had immigrated to the United States within the past three years.[11] PS 69 has students from seventy countries who speak forty languages (Breslin 2001). Indeed, in the 2001–2002 school year, 24 percent of Jackson Heights students were "English Language Learners," nearly twice the average for the city.[12] While many public school (and some private school) officials boast of the diversity, the fact remains that it creates additional pressures on teachers and administrators. The good news is that students in Jackson Heights schools are performing above average on city and state tests. In 2001, 45.2 percent of students met or exceeded the learning standards for reading and 43.3 percent met the standards for mathematics, compared to 39.5 percent and 35.1 percent for the city.[13] Jackson Heights schools also have far fewer students failing to meet the city and state learning standards. Thus, while overcrowded and facing resource pressures, Jackson Heights' diverse schools appear to be good educational options for Jackson Heights families. With this said, white families continue to stay away, possibly because of the options of various charter and magnet schools in the area (e.g., Renaissance School).

The Geography of Integration

Integration in Jackson Heights is also articulated spatially. I identify four recognizable subareas: the historic district, north of Northern Boulevard, the low Seventies, and the upper Nineties.[14] Like Uptown's, Jackson Heights' racial and ethnic groups are not uniformly distributed throughout these subareas. While most of Jackson Heights can be defined as moderately integrated by the Neighborhood Diversity Index, different subsections had one racial or ethnic group that made up a majority of the residents. For example, in 1990 a significant portion of the historic district was moderately integrated, although over half its residents were white. The area north of Northern Boulevard, the part of Jackson Heights without MacDougall developments, was racially and ethnically mixed, with no one group constituting a majority. Only the eastern end of the historic district to Junction Boulevard (between Northern and Roosevelt) was segregated, consisting of Latino residents. By 2000, the racial and ethnic changes in the community were quite visible geographically. As the overall population became more Latino—so did the geography.

Many of Jackson Heights' census tracts were majority Hispanic by 2000 (see Map 4.1). The upper Nineties, the eastern section near Junction Boulevard, remained segregated, populated by a large Hispanic population. Other sections of the neighborhood, namely north of Northern Boulevard (i.e., the eastern section), witnessed an increase in the number of Hispanic residents. These findings might give the impression that Jackson Heights is transitioning to Latino. Yet such a conclusion is premature, as the historic district (considered by many to be the heart of Jackson Heights), the low Seventies, and north of Northern Boulevard to the west continue to consist of a multiethnic and multiracial mix. In these census tracts, there was no clear majority racial or ethnic group. In fact, these areas consisted of a fairly even mix of white, Hispanic, and Asian residents. In sum, the spatial trends between 1990 and 2000 reveal that while integration remains in certain subsections of the community, there are pockets of racial and ethnic homogeneity.

MAP 4.1. Jackson Heights, Queens, 2000. Geography of Jackson Heights's integration by Census Tract

Ethnic Heterogeneity

Over the past three decades, Jackson Heights has become a polyglot of ethnic groups and cultural traditions. Yet broad racial and ethnic categories alone, such as Asian and Hispanic, cannot capture the ethnically heterogeneous nature of Jackson Heights residents and the community's astonishing integration. The Hispanic or Latino population is the most ethnically diverse group. For example, of the more than 35,000 Hispanic residents that reported living in Jackson Heights in 1990, 52 percent are of South American and 41 percent of Central American descent.[15] Dominicans (15 percent), Puerto Ricans (10 percent), and Cubans (7 percent) are the largest Central American groups, and Colombians (28 percent), Ecuadorians (12 percent), and Peruvians (6 percent) the largest South American. Data reveal that the ethnic diversification of the Latino population continues. In the 1990s, Jackson Heights was one of the top six destinations for immigrants arriving in Queens. Of the 11,079 immigrants who legally arrived in the borough, 15 percent were from the Dominican Republic and 14 percent were from Colombia. Jackson Heights is also attracting a growing Mexican population.

The presence of residents of Latin descent is not new. Immigration from Central and South America began in the late 1950s, slowly gathered pace, and in the process dramatically transformed the community. While the Colombian and Puerto Rican presences remain, the ethnic mix has become even more diverse and has spread out geographically. The surrounding neighborhoods of Elmhurst, Corona, and Woodside received more legal Latino immigrants in the 1980s and 1990s than did Jackson Heights (Jones-Correa 1998; Howell 1999a). The Elmhurst-Corona area quickly became a Latino and Asian community, as whites left more rapidly (Sanjek 1998). These neighborhoods all share commercial strips with Jackson Heights.

Ethnic heterogeneity also exists among the Asian population in Jackson Heights, which increased from approximately 7,000 residents in 1980 to around 14,000 in 1990 and to over 20,000 in 2000. The umbrella Asian category masks an internal diversity of Chinese (42 percent), Asian Indian (20 percent), Korean (14 percent), and Filipino (9 percent) residents. Smaller numbers of Japanese, Vietnamese, Thai, and Cambodian residents round out the Asian population. Although no Asian enclaves exist within Jackson Heights, leaders note that a significant number of Asian residents are buying co-ops in the historic district, as well as single-family homes north of Northern Boulevard. Leaders attribute the influx of Asians to housing pressures in Flushing, northeast of Jackson Heights, which began to attract Asian entrepreneurs and residents in the 1970s and is now recognized as the city's second Chinatown (Deutsch 1994). Flushing's boom has pushed Asian residents to adjoining neighborhoods, such as Bayside and Jackson Heights.

As an immigrant port of entry, Jackson Heights quickly achieved an ethnically diverse population. Immigrants have been attracted to northern Queens communities like Jackson Heights, Elmhurst, and Corona dating back to the 1950s and 1960s. Jackson Heights' large share of immigrants is reflected in the nativity status of its residents. In 1990, 54 percent were born outside the United States; by 2000, it was 65 percent. Foreign-born residents are not confined to one part of the community. In 1990, only five of the seventeen census tracts that make up Jackson Heights had populations less than 50 percent foreign born. In 2000, every tract was over 50 percent foreign born. An extreme example of this is one tract in the upper Nineties near Junction Boulevard, where 74 percent of the population is foreign born. A significant number of immigrants to Jackson Heights are recent arrivals not only to the community, but also to the United States. Of all foreign-born residents in Jackson Heights, 25 percent reported entering the country between 1995 and March of 2000, and 46 percent reported entering in the 1990s. Of the approximately 71,000 foreign-born residents, 62 percent are not citizens. Leaders suggest that the number of immigrants is even greater than reported, due to census undercounts and a high number of undocumented residents. Ethnic heterogeneity in Jackson Heights adds another layer of complexity to understanding its integration. And as in Uptown, the multiracial and multiethnic character of the community is compounded by economic and social differences.

Economic Diversity

Racial and ethnic integration in Jackson Heights intersects with socioeconomic and social differences. Although the socioeconomic mix is neither as overt nor as central to community organizing as it is in Uptown, Jackson Heights' economic mix is more complex than it may seem. From its inception, Jackson Heights has been a middle- to upper-middle-income community. The area's stunning architecture, historic district, and solid middle class has done little to change that. Jackson Heights' median family income in 1999 was $43,197, slightly below the median for Queens County ($48,608). Traditional indicators suggest that Jackson Heights is indeed largely middle class. For example, 63 percent of Jackson Heights' households had incomes over $30,000 and only 4 percent of the residents received public assistance income. Also, a third of housing units in the area are owner occupied, a figure that is higher than the city average, but lower than the borough.

The housing market reaffirms Jackson Heights' middle-income status. The housing market in Jackson Heights crashed in the 1970s, then rebounded in the 1980s when a significant number of young professionals priced out of Manhattan gravitated to the community. After hitting a peak in the late 1980s, housing values leveled off, then picked up again in the 1990s. Table 4.1 displays the distribution of home-mortgage loans in Jackson Heights from 1992 to 1998 by race, income, and subarea. The data reveal real estate expansion in the community over the decade. The volume of loans increased steadily over the seven years, with nearly 95 percent of the loans going toward home purchase. Also, over two-thirds of all loans in Jackson Heights during this period went to families or individuals with incomes near or greater than the median for the metropolitan area ($37,515). Data suggest that property values in Jackson Heights are rising. The average cost of a one- or two-family house increased from $183,000 in 1995 to $240,000 in 1999 (Reed 2000). The increase both in the number of loans and in property values is evidence that Jackson Heights remains (at least on the surface) a middle-income community located within a solidly middle-income borough.

However, over the last three decades an economic change has occurred, and some suggest that many residents and leaders do not want to recognize it. As Father Bernard Poppe, pastor of St. Mark's Episcopal Church, noted in our September 23, 1996, interview: "[Jackson Heights] tends to be—with some exceptions—a lower-white-collar, blue-collar area, and that I believe is also a transition, which I think occurred years ago, but occurred nevertheless. And some of the older people still view it as a middle- to upper-middle-class, essentially closed community. And that has changed and there are some people who don't want to recognize that has ever changed. Well, guess what? You can't go back." Father Poppe appears correct. Various indicators suggest that economic disparities are emerging in Jackson Heights that do not mesh with its longstanding middle-income image.

While real estate trends reveal a relatively strong market, a closer look sheds light on the class divide. For example, 42 percent of all loans between 1992 and 1998 were granted to Hispanic applicants (see Table 4.1). However, homeownership is decidedly skewed in favor of Jackson Heights' non-Hispanic residents. The ratio of white renters to white homeowners is 1.2:1; for blacks, 1.5:1; for Asians, 1.2:1, and for Hispanics, 3.7:1.[16] Despite the increase in mortgage lending to Hispanics in Jackson Heights, they are far less likely to own homes. This may be explained by the overcrowding of recently arrived immigrants in various sections of

TABLE 4.1. Residential Lending Patterns by Race, Class, and Type—
Jackson Heights, 1992–1998: Mortgage Loans Reported from Home Mortgage
Disclosure Act

	Fiscal Year							
	1992	1993	1994	1995	1996	1997	1998	1992–98
Total Loans*	256	352	478	471	503	1,122	551	3,733
Race								
White	25%	16%	17%	17%	16%	14%	19%	17%
Black	3%	4%	4%	5%	6%	4%	3%	4%
Hispanic	25%	31%	40%	44%	41%	51%	41%	42%
Asian	27%	33%	26%	21%	21%	19%	22%	23%
Income as % of MSA Median Income								
<51%	1%	1%	4%	1%	1%	0%	1%	1%
51–80%	8%	9%	11%	10%	8%	3%	5%	7%
81–95%	8%	8%	5%	10%	6%	2%	3%	5%
96–120%	13%	13%	14%	16%	9%	9%	8%	11%
>120%	44%	46%	50%	53%	63%	72%	69%	61%
Total Loans by Uptown Subarea								
Historic District	30%	28%	25%	27%	30%	28%	27%	28%
Upper Eighties	13%	14%	16%	16%	17%	14%	18%	16%
North of Northern Blvd.	42%	47%	50%	50%	44%	49%	44%	47%
Low Seventies	14%	11%	9%	7%	8%	8%	10%	9%

*Excludes home improvement or refinancing lending activity.
Source: Right to Know Network (RTK) [http://www.rtk.net]; Federal Financial Institutions
Examination Council, Federal Reserve, Washington, D.C.

the community. Anecdotal and news accounts suggest that many Hispanic renters are working low-wage jobs and paying inflated rents in illegally converted single-family homes (Barry and Ojito 1997; Bruni and Sontag 1996; Howell 1999b).

Census figures and field research indicate that income levels and homeownership rates also vary geographically. For instance, median family incomes range from roughly $32,000 to $54,000 among census tracts. Homeownership ranges from 19 percent in some parts of Jackson Heights to 65 percent in others. Also, leaders note that co-ops and rentals in the historic district contain high-income individuals and families, while residents outside that area have fewer resources. This seems related to how concentrated the MacDougall-era co-ops are within the community. An Asian Indian merchant and resident told me in an interview on May 16, 1996: "The density [of the co-ops] drives property values up and pushes people away because they can't afford it. The people in the co-ops are doing fine but others aren't; . . . the rentals mainly house immigrants." While there are immigrants that earn middle-class incomes, data suggest that a substantial number of immigrants, particularly recently arrived and undocumented, earn very little and live in Jackson Heights' worst and most cramped housing.

A Dominican organizer suggested in our August 18, 1996, interview that middle-income residents in Jackson Heights "want to believe that we are all middle income and above and they don't want to deal with it. And they put blinders on, . . . and what is happening in the community is that those that need the services, like for housing or social services, they don't get the services . . . because they don't exist in the community." The evidence is mounting, however, that the population needing such services does exist. This reality is apparent in the public schools, where during the 1997-1998 school year three-quarters of all students were eligible for "free lunch" by federal standards (U.S. Department of Education 2000). Census data reveal that a third of all rental housing is overcrowded.[17] In some sections, particularly between Eighty-ninth Street and Junction Boulevard between Northern and Roosevelt, over 50 percent of the housing is overcrowded. This area has received a good deal of media attention for its violations of city housing codes. The most infamous case involved the discovery of sixty-two deaf immigrants, smuggled into the country and held in servitude, living in two houses. The victims-men, women, and children-slept side by side on bunk beds, mattresses, and sleeping bags (Sontag 1997; Barry and Ojito 1997).

Jackson Heights' socioeconomic mix is thus more complex than it appears at first glance or than many residents wish to acknowledge. While the community contains a solid middle-class base that cuts across race and ethnic lines, another segment of the population is less affluent and appears to be largely Hispanic (recently arrived) immigrant, located on the edges of the community, and invisible even to official population counts. These class fissures add to the complexity of Jackson Heights' multiethnic and multiracial integration, making it difficult to separate race and class in community discussions.

Jackson Heights as a Gay Enclave

A large gay and lesbian enclave also bolsters Jackson Heights' multicultural status. Early in its development as a bedroom community, Jackson Heights attracted a colony of vaudevillians, many of whom were gay. These performers worked in the theater district around Times Square in Manhattan, which coincidentally is the final stop on the west end of the Number 7 subway line. Jackson Heights was a convenient and pleasant alternative to smaller apartments and rooming houses in midtown Manhattan. Slowly and with little public notice, "Jackson Heights developed as a gay haven, a remarkable contrast to the area's intolerance towards ethnic and racial minorities" (Kasinitz, Bazzi, and Doane 1998: 163). Since the 1960s, Jackson Heights' gay population has grown, and the community is now home to the city's "second-largest" gay and lesbian community outside of Manhattan (Serant 1996). While the precise number is difficult to assess, informants note that the gay population has not only grown but also become more diverse. For example, in 1994 approximately 40 percent of the Jackson Heights Lesbian and Gay Pride Day committee was Hispanic. The committee's annual summer parade down Thirty-seventh Avenue now attracts between thirty and forty thousand participants (Varghese 2001). The parade attracts dozens of very different organizations and is more ethnically diverse than the more commercial Pride parade along Fifth Avenue in Manhattan. In Jackson Heights, the parade features groups of gay Colombians, Venezuelans, West Indians, Filipinos, blacks, Asians, and Pacific Islanders. The gay community is also aging. Ed Sedarbaum, founder of the Queens Gays and Lesbians United, recently received grant money to develop a gay senior citizens center in the neighborhood.

Traditionally, the gay community in Jackson Heights has been relatively invisible. Father Poppe noted in our 1996 interview that "because of the socioeconomic status and the cultural backgrounds, many of the gay men . . . are more closeted than you would find in the city, if you were to go into Chelsea, for example. I mean it is all out there; nobody cares. But here, because of the mores among the families and the extended families, it is not talked about; . . . you don't find Jackson Heights to be a self-identified gay area. You don't find the kind of activism, although the Gay Pride parades get bigger each year." Similarly, while the community has always had a gay nightlife, it was "kept secret for self-protection" (Serant 1996). However, the visibility and activism of the gay and lesbian community changed in the early to mid-1990s, following the 1990 gay-bashing killing of a local resident and bartender, Julio Rivera. The twenty-nine-year-old Rivera was lured to a Jackson Heights schoolyard, where he was beaten and stabbed to death (Serant 1996). Rivera's murder galvanized gay residents into a budding political force. As Sedarbaum recalls: "We felt fear, the kind of fear any community feels when one of its members is attacked. We also felt abandoned by the police department, who not only refused to classify the case as a bias attack, but lied and classified it as drug related" (quoted in Kasinitz, Bazzi, and Doane 1998: 168). The gay community's activism also led to the Gay and Lesbian Anti-

Violence Project, a social services agency that monitors criminal acts against and within the community citywide, to open a satellite office on Thirty-seventh Avenue.

This increased visibility and activism has been necessary, as there are still barriers facing gay and lesbian individuals and couples. Several leaders noted the lack of tolerance by some co-op boards. A resident of the Chateau co-op building recalled a conversation with a neighboring gay couple in our November 21, 1995, interview: "They are aware that they would be accepted in this particular Chateau building, but not in others. They mentioned the others, and I said that they were right. I couldn't lie about it. They wouldn't have been accepted, they wouldn't have been welcome." Over time, the activism of numerous gay and lesbian individuals and couples appears to be overcoming intolerance and resistance in the community. Informants note that the gay community is a pioneering force that adds to the overall stability of the area. Many leaders credit the gay "community" for maintaining safety, tolerance, and property values, and thus stabilizing the neighborhood. This dimension, more openly discussed than in Uptown, adds another layer of complexity to Jackson Heights' diversity.

Stable and Unplanned Integration

Is Jackson Heights a model of stable integration? It depends on whom one talks to. Some residents believe the neighborhood is transitioning. A pastor at a local church told me in our interview on September 23, 1996: "It is my feeling that Jackson Heights is in a period of transition. It may take a generation or so, but I believe it is in that period of transition. And as it becomes more Hispanic, more Asian, the church has to prepare for that." Demographics do not lie; the number of white residents has significantly decreased since 1960 and Latinos and Asians are now the largest majority. Yet some residents do not see a transition, pointing out that racial change did not involve racial transition and resegregation. Also, there is no evidence of panic selling and rapid white flight. White flight may have occurred in the 1960s and 1970s, but Jackson Heights continued to attract new white residents in the 1980s and 1990s. "I think those who have flown, have flown," noted Father Poppe in 1996. "I think those that have taken flight because of the racial diversity have already gone twenty years ago. But I don't think anyone is leaving now because the area is too 'whatever.'" And leaders point out that although whites have left the neighborhood, a sizable number of whites remain who are committed to Jackson Heights and active in the community. Leaders also acknowledge that the decrease in white residents is less about "flight" and more about the failure to attract enough younger white residents to replace older residents. As one leader put it in an interview on May 15, 1996: "The children of the old guard are the ones most likely to move."

Jackson Heights is *one* model of stable integration. The pattern of racial transition and resegregation predicted by models of neighborhood change did not occur here. Racial change has occurred, but not a rapid pace. It appears, ironically, that the multiracial and multiethnic mix is partly responsible for preventing resegregation. "I think there is a certain attraction to diversity in the neighborhood," noted Councilman John Sabini in our interview on March 13, 1996. "If there was one ethnic group taking over the neighborhood, that might be a problem, but because we have South Asians, because we have East Asians, because we have Central and South Americans, but not so dominating that it overwhelms anyone, I think that that helps maintain things." The multiracial and multiethnic character creates a dynamic where the most common link among people is their differences. "This community is unique in the sense that it doesn't belong to one person," Rev. Austin Armitstead, retired pastor of the Community United Methodist Church, told me in our March 13, 1996, interview. "One person doesn't own all the turf. All of us own the turf. If we reduce that down to one or two ethnic groups then the battle ensues." Lacking a dominant group, fears of the community being "invaded" are reduced and potential tensions are more easily diffused before they can escalate.

Jackson Heights is also unique among racially integrated residential areas in that there is little evidence that its mix was planned or directed. "Diversity has been thrust upon the neighborhood," Rudy Greco told me. "Nobody asked for it, it is here. It is more of a question of dealing with that which has been thrust here. It is not that we are out recruiting for diversity. It is a fact of life here." Most leaders share this sentiment—integration is less something people seek or encourage than it is an outcome. As Father Poppe candidly stated: "I don't think people have a commitment to make [integration] happen. I think it is more of a by-product when it happens. I never hear people talk about a philosophical commitment to living together. It is more of a reactive kind of thing than a proactive kind of thing, but even the reactive tends to be a little bit more favorable." Integration developed in Jackson Heights without conscious or goal-oriented actions of leaders to promote it. As one leader told me on May 15, 1996, their response to integration involves figuring out "how to operate programs or facilitate things that bridge the gaps between the ethnic diversity of different populations," whether this involves economic development or running housing or cultural programs. In many ways, it does not matter how integration emerged. Fortunately for Jackson Heights reactions to integration have by and large been favorable. More importantly, various groups in different ways and at different times have taken the lead to negotiate competing cultures, needs, and interests. While far from a perfect process, these negotiations create greater understanding among groups and help maintain the neighborhood's multiracial and multiethnic mix.

NEW NEIGHBORS IN AN OLD NEIGHBORHOOD

The racial, ethnic, and social changes in Jackson Heights did not happen overnight. Various waves of immigrants entering Jackson Heights altered the social and demographic landscape, gradually transforming the neighborhood. "Forty years ago it was white, Anglo-Saxon, Christian," noted Gloria Diani, a former schoolteacher and active board member of a MacDougall co-op, in our May 15, 1996, interview. "I mean it really was. I always laughed and said we were the token Italians. We are second-generation Italians. I think what happened was the first big wave came in the 1960s, when we had a tremendous influx of Hispanics, and they were primarily Colombians and Puerto Ricans." As a result, Jackson Heights is not the same as it was three or even two decades ago. Older white residents, the "old guard," living in the historic co-op buildings witnessed the culture of the neighborhood change from one based on a "British kind of good manners," where you "didn't hear any other language other than English," to a mix of racial, ethnic, and cultural groups.[18] As a result, older white residents now coexist with new, diverse, and nonwhite populations. Neither population has a history of relations with the other.

The demographic and cultural change is visible in local institutions, as well as public spaces. The Community United Methodist Church offers masses in four languages—English, Korean, Chinese, and Spanish. The principal of St. Joan of Arc Catholic School boasts that the student body reflects nearly a hundred countries. On the street, the smell of exotic spices permeates the air. The Seventy-fourth Street shopping strip, between Thirty-seventh and Roosevelt, resembles an open-air market. The stores sell everything from groceries and Bollywood movies to gold jewelry and saris. A newspaper vendor stationed on Seventy-fourth Street sells a variety of newspapers from the Asian subcontinent; he sells no U.S. papers. Along Thirty-seventh Street, older stores compete with street vendors. Spanish is now a dominant language in the neighborhood. Cars and trucks blaring Mexican salsa drive through neighborhood streets. The Jackson Heights public library, one of the busiest in Queens, has separate book and periodical sections in various non-English languages. An interracial mix of patrons quietly catches up on news from all over the world. This is Jackson Heights' new character, born out of immigrants and newcomers blending into an older, established, planned community.

Anytime social, demographic, and cultural change occurs in a community, there are a complex set of effects and local responses. Urban history is replete with examples of negative responses displayed by incumbent residents as different racial and ethnic groups enter the neighborhood. In Jackson Heights, the changes created by newcomers elicited both positive and negative responses, though all subtle in nature. On the one hand, the racial and ethnic transformation of the neighborhood brought new life to an aging neighborhood. Property values are stable and commercial rents are rising. Newcomers revitalized commercial districts and some cultural institutions, especially churches. At nearly all times of the day, the streets and subways serving the neighborhood are abuzz with activity. Disinvestment and decline did not accompany racial and ethnic change in Jackson Heights. In fact, the opposite occurred.

On the other hand, incumbent residents have not always been comfortable or appreciative of newcomers and changes in the community. For relative newcomers, particularly immigrants, navigating a new country, culture, and often a language, there is a sense of being misunderstood. The changes brought by such a multiethnic and multicultural blend of residents are a source of conflict. However, unlike the reaction in Uptown, where overt land-use conflict persisted over three decades, the conflict in Jackson Heights is more complex. No pervasive or incendiary tension exists over defining the neighborhood's future, though such issues have arisen. Absent are clearly identifiable or unified groups standing in opposition to each other. While changes created challenges for leaders and residents, they emerged in different ways and in reaction to different community issues.

The nature of conflict in Jackson Heights can be characterized in two ways. First, the sheer number of newcomers from such varied backgrounds altered the physical and cultural landscape of the community. While newcomers brought new life to the area's housing market and commercial districts, the size of the population and explosive success of unplanned economic development created concerns for many in Jackson

Heights. For over a decade, "quality-of-life" concerns have been a recurring theme in community discussions among leaders.[19] In many cases, complaints take the form of intolerance. "A lot of quality-of-life crimes that get reported are really about immigrants," noted Councilman John Sabini. "People are entitled to their complaints, but if you boil it down, most of it is directed at newcomers. The complaints are 'Those lousy people next door, they don't put out their garbage right.' Those 'filthy spics' . . . or these 'damn Chinks.' Usually there is an ethnic slur at the end." While such bigoted sentiment exists in Jackson Heights, it does not appear pervasive. In fact, most quality-of-life concerns and complaints are grounded in real and everyday challenges resulting from population density and the absence of a supportive infrastructure. These concerns involve practical issues such as congestion, garbage, noise, illegal housing conversions, and criminal activity. These issues have a real bearing on neighborhood stability and vitality.

Ethnic conflict is also articulated in Jackson Heights in debates over aesthetics and community norms. Many incumbent white residents feared and resented newcomers for changing the look and identity of the neighborhood. "It got to a certain point where people started getting nervous," noted Jeffrey Saunders in our March 13, 1996, interview. "Not nervous because there were different people in the neighborhood, but nervous because what they were accustomed to was changing and changing radically. The fact is these differences in personality and approach from the old country manifest themselves in ways which made the current people who are living there uncomfortable, and it is those manifestations, those effects, in my opinion, that they are actually objecting to, not so much the people." The manifestations Saunders speaks of are clearly visible in the changing store facades and commercial signage. Immigrant entrepreneurs have transformed many of the commercial districts, bringing their own vision of what is aesthetically proper and what constitutes acceptable public behavior. Incumbent white residents resent newcomers and changes occurring in what they deem "their" neighborhood. Some residents, particularly those holding onto a vision of Jackson Heights as homogenous, even accuse newcomers of violating the norms and values of the neighborhood.

With newly arrived residents from all over the globe blending with established residents, the prospect for negotiating tension and building community is difficult, though not insurmountable. Fortunately, Jackson Heights has a variety of civic organizations assertively addressing the pressing problems with community-building efforts, negotiating responses to change and allowing the transformation to occur smoothly. Community groups like the Jackson Heights Beautification Group and the Jackson Heights Community Development Corporation mobilized newer and older residents against the negative aspects of recent changes, ranging from the effects of unplanned economic development and overcrowding to prostitution and drugs. Preservation groups have worked to maintain the area's unique architecture and historic identity. There have even been organizational efforts to define Jackson Heights' racial and ethnic character as a positive neighborhood amenity and proud achievement. These efforts range from symbolic acknowledgments of the mix of cultures to efforts to bridge gaps between various ethnic groups and to foster, even at a rudimentary level, interracial and interethnic dialogue. Such diverse efforts are attempts by groups to find ways to ensure a vital, safe, and ordered community.

Local civic groups play an important role in mediating the challenges of such racial and ethnic change, maintaining the community, and stabilizing its diverse mix. Integration in Jackson Heights brought a host of challenges to the community. With each challenge, community leaders organized to stabilize the community and improve the quality of life of all residents. Yet each effort also demonstrates the difficulty in bridging gaps between groups with very different conceptions of what constitutes positive neighborhood life. On the one hand, groups are working not only to define diversity as a positive neighborhood amenity and proud achievement, but also to challenge negative perceptions created by quality-of-life concerns arising from neighborhood changes and immigration. On the other hand, building community is no easy task in such a diverse neighborhood. At times, an undercurrent of intolerance surfaces, where not everyone is included or considered in community-building efforts and differences in culture are ignored.

Commercial Revitalization

Like Uptown's Argyle Street and Andersonville, Jackson Heights' fading commercial strips were revitalized by an influx of ethnic business. In fact, as the large concentration of South American residents emerged in the 1970s, Roosevelt Avenue unofficially became the main commercial strip for Colombian, Ecuadorian, and Peruvian communities in Jackson Heights and neighboring Elmhurst. The strip between Seventieth and Junction Boulevard earned a variety of informal names, most notably "Little Colombia." Also, in the mid-1970s a two- to three-block strip on

Seventy-fourth Street soon became the "nation's largest shopping center for immigrants from India" (S. Myers 1993a). Both commercial strips, described by leaders as "ghost towns" before the ethnic revitalization, are marvels of neighborhood economic development and investment. Ethnic and immigrant entrepreneurs lifted sagging commercial strips to the point where the "whole neighborhood is jumping," as one resident told me on May 16, 1996, and there are no abandoned buildings and few vacancies. Yet understanding these areas is far from a simple process. Commercial success evokes negative reactions from local groups—particularly incumbent white residents living in the historic co-ops adjacent to Roosevelt Avenue and Seventy-fourth Street. Objections center not on the commercial development itself, but on what comes along with it. Leaders note that issues related to the "quality of life," such as increased traffic, litter, noise, overcrowding, and criminal activity, generate the biggest complaints. Some residents even organized meetings, claiming they are "mad as hell," summoning people that are "tired of arrogant, selfish people breaking our laws" (quoted in S. Myers 1993a). The tension centers on open resentment to the changes resulting from immigration. Fortunately for Jackson Heights, local leaders stepped up to negotiate differences and foster compromise.

Roosevelt Avenue

Roosevelt Avenue's Little Colombia, bordering Elmhurst and Jackson Heights, is now the commercial hub of New York's South American community, selling everything from "periodicals from Bogotá, to markets offering Colombian white cheese and tortillas, to restaurants serving papas chirreadas (a dish made with a dark-fleshed potato)" (S. Myers 1993a). This strip along Roosevelt Avenue teems with stores and street vendors and hosts a steady parade of buses, large trucks, cars, and bikes. Add the el roaring overhead and Roosevelt Avenue is not the most attractive center of commerce. Ethnic entrepreneurs, however, have turned it into a prosperous and growing commercial area. "The small businesses have taken some of the least desirable property because the train makes so much noise and turned it into something really good," one leader noted in an interview on November 19, 1995. "It has usually been the home of the more cheaper and more ethnically oriented businesses. They are upgrading. Roosevelt Avenue is bootstrapping itself, and little by little the stores are getting finer and nicer, because they are making a lot of money."

As a result, on any given day pedestrians fill the streets and stores as early as 10 A.M. It is not uncommon to find an Asian hair-and-nail salon next to a Mexican cocina, or an Argentine restaurant near the Magic Lamp Chinese Restaurant. On weekends, this variety brings out numerous families from varied backgrounds who shop for clothing bargains or Latin American foods. Little Colombia is a center where "established, middle class South Americans and poor, recent immigrants alike" frequent restaurants and shops to "refuel on the familiar" (Kasinitz, Bazzi, and Doane 1998: 166).

Residents of Jackson Heights, particularly older white residents, have not always embraced this commercial strip, an attitude tied to the street's negative reputation as a center for drugs, prostitution, and other illegal activities over the last three decades. By the mid-1970s, Jackson Heights and Elmhurst had become the center of cocaine importation and distribution for the northeastern United States, with Roosevelt Avenue considered the center of drug-related activities. By the 1990s, hundreds of millions, maybe billions, of dollars in cash and cocaine were flowing in and around Jackson Heights (I. Fisher 1993). With its large concentration of South American immigrants, northern Queens became the base for several South American organized crime groups affiliated with the Colombian drug trade. To the chagrin of its residents, tree-lined Jackson Heights drew national media attention, much of it sensationalist, as the "Cocaine Capital of the World," a phrase used by many I interviewed. Mark Schorr's 1978 *New York* magazine story, "Gunfights in the Cocaine Corral," shaped many negative perceptions: "Over the past three years, in this nice, quiet neighborhood, 27 people have been killed and dozens have been injured. . . . The violence spreads to surrounding neighborhoods as cops and prosecutors fight a losing battle. Double and triple homicides go unsolved. The biggest unsolved mass murder in New York in recent years—the LaGuardia Airport bombing that killed 11 and injured 75—seems to have a Jackson Heights connection" (48–54).

The drug-related problems plaguing Jackson Heights were on full display in the early 1990s following the execution-style murder of crusading journalist Manuel de Dios Unanue. De Dios, who accused the Cali and Medellín Colombian drug cartels of supplying most of New York City's cocaine during the 1980s through front businesses in Jackson Heights, Corona, and Elmhurst, was gunned down in 1992 in a restaurant on Roosevelt Avenue (I. Fisher 1993; Kalita 2000a). Many leaders and residents sought to distance Jackson Heights from this activity. While Roosevelt Avenue is a few blocks from several of Jackson Heights' most distinctive

MacDougall co-op buildings, residents protested that the *New York Times* misidentified Jackson Heights as the site of the murder. Residents angrily complained that the restaurant where de Dios was killed was on the south side of Roosevelt Avenue, which is in Elmhurst. Many residents, largely white, were willing to cede this area to Elmhurst, even insisting that Jackson Heights ended on the north side of Roosevelt Avenue. In a letter published in the *New York Times* on December 25, 1994, one resident, Tom Lowenhaupt, clearly identifies Roosevelt Avenue and its problems as not part of Jackson Heights: "The drug, noise, and prostitution problems plagued Roosevelt Avenue, the southern border of our community, and were never prevalent throughout Jackson Heights."

The boundary dispute is a symbolic move to distance Jackson Heights from very real neighborhood social problems. Leaders note that while drug activity surely continues along Roosevelt Avenue, the criminal activity has little daily impact on the lives of most residents. "Jackson Heights has been labeled as a high crime area, but that is confusing," noted a representative of Community Board 3 in our November 18, 1995, interview. "All that is going on either behind closed doors or late at night." Yet the shadow of a criminal presence remains; some residents and the media point to the 100 to 150 international money-transfer stores and businesses selling beepers and fax machines as evidence of the continuing drug trade in Jackson heights. Some local businesses, particularly travel agencies, cash-wiring outlets, and check-cashing services, profit directly or indirectly from the drug trade by providing convenient money-transfer channels from Jackson Heights and Latin or South America (Gordy 1996). While these businesses provide vital services for thousands of working immigrants making a new life in the United States, they continue to carry a stigma of illegal behavior and are viewed as having long-term negative effects for the community. "Those stores take away from the commercial stock of the neighborhood," a Jackson Heights Beautification Group member remarked to me on November 21, 1995. "The fact that they are run by drug guys, as odious as that may be, it is not so harmful on a day-to-day basis. What does hurt is that they are taking up these eighty-five to ninety storefronts that could be [used] for other things that would really help the quality of life in the neighborhood."

Residents also view other goings-on along Roosevelt Avenue as evidence of disreputable activities. The presence of Latin American–owned bars and clubs along the avenue, some with tinted windows or iron gates, continues the perception of illicit activities. News stories occasionally confirm that some storefronts are indeed headquarters for illegal behavior, although others attract nothing more than young men wishing to watch soccer matches on satellite television (Kim 1997; LeDuff, 1998). The large number of single immigrant men sparked another service industry along Roosevelt Avenue. Numerous brothels operate in the basements and on the second floors of Roosevelt Avenue storefronts. Jackson Heights assemblyman Ivan Lafayette notes that "Roosevelt Avenue for as long as I can remember—and we are talking about 30 or 40 years—has been a place for people to go to get a little excitement. We've had consistent complaints about prostitution in the area" (quoted in Gardiner 1998). The number of brothels and prostitution peddlers increased in the mid-1990s when a mayoral task force cleaned out prostitution from Midtown Manhattan. Roosevelt Avenue's location right next to the subway made it attractive to the prostitution trade.

While these negative perceptions continue, a loose coalition of community groups is changing Roosevelt Avenue's image. For a brief period in the early 1990s, the United Organizations of North Corona, East Elmhurst, and Jackson Heights formed "as almost a congress of all of the civic groups."[20] Meeting initially to discuss common concerns, the United Organizations parlayed enough political weight to force local officials to hold town meetings and area tours. As a result, local officials worked to obtain increased police presence, responsiveness, and vigilance along Roosevelt. Organizers were specifically concerned with the drug trade and prostitution occurring on Roosevelt Avenue. The organizing paid off. "They have blitzed Roosevelt Avenue," one leader told me on May 15, 1996. "We have put a lot of pressure and they have blitzed it, blitzed the hell out of it. They've got portable police stations there because we screamed for it. The commissioner has paid attention and it is better, much better." The street-drug trade has all but disappeared and the big importers from South America do not appear to be operating out of Jackson Heights anymore, moving to other parts of Queens or the suburbs of New York or New Jersey (Kalita 2000a). The police also targeted brothels along Roosevelt Avenue, at first with large-scale raids and sting operations targeting customers. Law enforcement efforts eventually involved employing the city's nuisance-abatement laws by seeking civil injunctions to have numerous apartments and properties vacated and padlocked, in an effort to punish landlords (Bazzi 1996; Gardiner 1998). As a result, the public presence of prostitution decreased dramatically.

While illicit activity continues along Roosevelt Avenue, it no longer defines the strip. Leaders note that Roosevelt Avenue has stabilized. Yet perception lags behind. Older and European whites hold negative views of the strip, as they no longer see Roosevelt Avenue "for them" and few use it for their shopping. "Roosevelt Avenue is a big buzz word," Councilman John Sabini told me in 1996. "It is a Spanish area. A lot of people will say that we need to take Roosevelt Avenue back." Sabini alludes to the displacement old-timers feel the strip represents, as newcomers enter Jackson Heights. A self-described veteran resident poignantly expresses feelings of displacement in a letter to the *New York Times* published on January 2, 1994: "As for Little Colombia, once again the ethnic balance has been destroyed and traditional businesses been displaced. Anyone who thinks Roosevelt Avenue is a treasure of ethnic diversity should take a weekend walk and hear the Latin music blaring from oversized car speakers, or see the unlicensed street merchants peddling counterfeit videocassettes, the discount junk shops, the cocaine trade." For some, the loss of "traditional" businesses equals decline. The majority of leaders and residents, however, do not appear to share this sentiment. In fact, leaders are active in their efforts to alter perceptions of Roosevelt and be inclusive. Rudy Greco, in his usual blunt style, represented these views when he told me in 1995: "What is lagging behind is public perceptions. The people who have been here for forty years or more still perceive Roosevelt Avenue at its worst. But they haven't walked there in ten to fifteen years. One woman told me, 'This is the belly of the beast.' I said, 'Hon, that is not the belly of the beast. You go to east New York, walk across the housing projects on Newport Avenue, it is fifty-fifty you will make it across the projects without a bulletproof vest. The belly of the beast? What the hell are you talking about? It is not elegant like it used to be, but neither are you and me.'"

Stores that serve only white residents no longer populate Roosevelt Avenue, and yet the strip is an economic success. As a result of neighborhood organizing, Roosevelt Avenue is also a stabilizing force for the neighborhood.

Seventy-fourth Street: Little India

The Seventy-fourth Street shopping district, extending from the subway north to Thirty-seventh Avenue, elicited a similar level of antagonism, albeit for different reasons. In the early 1970s, Seventy-fourth Street began its transformation into the nation's largest shopping center for immigrants from India when Subhash Kapadia and Raj Gandhi opened an electronics and appliance store called Sam and Raj, catering to the demand for appliances that operate on 220 volts (the U.S. standard is 110 volts) to take or send back to India. Kapadia and Gandhi chose to locate on Seventy-fourth Street, given the quality of the space, low rent, and proximity to the Number 7 train, which would draw Indian immigrants from throughout Queens (Murphy 1992). Their success attracted other Indian businesses, such as India Sari Palace, Sinha Appliance, and the Delhi Palace. By the 1980s, Indian merchants had replaced many older merchants as their leases expired or rents increased. Over a hundred Indian establishments now operate on Seventy-fourth Street and several side streets. The area resembles an Indian bazaar, "where the smell of masalas wafts from restaurants and groceries, and thousands of people course through store after store buying saris, spices, and jewelry" (S. Myers 1993a). The Seventy-fourth Street strip is now a commercial center for the metropolitan area, attracting customers from the suburbs and from states as distant as Connecticut, Maryland, Massachusetts, and North Carolina.

Originally, the majority of the shops along Seventy-fourth Street catered to immigrants from India. However, the food, clothing, and electronics were also relevant for the cultures of people from Pakistan and Bangladesh (Shukla 1999). Now merchants and customers from all over the Asian subcontinent find their way in and around Seventy-fourth Street. Noticing this trend, numerous businesses began marketing themselves to "Indo-Pak-Bangla" constituencies, setting aside religious, linguistic, and political differences. Few businesses declare exclusive appeal to their nationals and it is not uncommon to see special sales in Pakistani stores during the essentially Indian festivals of Diwali and Holi (Kalita 2000b). Customers from the Middle East shop for Indian rice and spices, and almost everything in the grocery stores is meant to attract South Asian customers. The strip is now a global marketplace, transcending national and regional boundaries.

The Seventy-fourth Street commercial corridor, now spilling onto Thirty-seventh Avenue and other side streets, reinvigorated an aging and declining shopping center. And not unlike Roosevelt Avenue, the strip elicits bad feelings from community residents, particularly older co-op residents. Ironically, the tension stems from business success and the attendant problems associated with a quick and unplanned economic expansion. For many longtime residents, the flourishing Seventy-fourth Street commercial strip—whatever its economic benefits—has meant the decline of long-established familiar stores and restaurants, those they considered their own. Tension centers on issues such as parking, traffic congestion, trash, rising commercial rents, and the offensive practices of some customers. John Moran, a Community Board 3 member, told me in our November 19, 1995, interview: "The *New York Times* writes about the area as exotic, but the people living there don't see it that way—they deal with the garbage, traffic, and noise." Moran's claims are supported by the dozen or so articles chronicling the problem. An article in *Newsday* captures the reality of the traffic problem on Seventy-fourth Street: "First there is the gridlock: the hundreds of cars that converge here every weekend, creeping slowly up and down the narrow two-lane streets, hunting for parking spaces that hardly exist. Then there are the pedestrians, crowding the crosswalks, making right turns near impossible, leading to clogged roadways and frayed nerves. And that, of course, leads to horn honking. On weekend mornings it can start as early as 9 a.m., residents say, building to a crescendo in the early afternoon and persisting until past nightfall" (Cuza 2000).

The success of Seventy-fourth Street is a complex trade-off between economic development and its effects on an area without the infrastructure to handle it. John Sabini told me: "We'd rather have it than [be like] burned out Camden, New Jersey. But it is a unique situation. It is a mall without walls. What these people did was, store by store, take over a neighborhood shopping strip. They are paying taxes and it is nice that the place is busy. But there's lots of ancillary problems. You've got cars coming in from New Jersey, Pennsylvania, Connecticut, and other parts of the city. You've got people eating fast food on the street and throwing stuff around." It is estimated that ten to fifteen thousand people visit this Indian commercial center each weekend, leaving the area strewn with litter and overflowing garbage bins, even though some merchants sweep three times a day and the Sanitation Department services the area seven days a week. In the process, shoppers and merchants have been cast as "invaders." "These merchants have taken over our neighborhood," a resident complained. "They have invaded us. And they are just standing there not understanding why we're complaining" (quoted in S. Myers 1993a). Many residents see the changes as negative, blaming unresponsive merchants and the "disregard for local quality-of-life issues by shoppers from affluent out-of-town communities."[21] For example, a member of the Jackson Heights Beautification Group (JHBG) told me on November 1, 1995: "The people who live right on the periphery of that are furious, because . . . they do have superficial differences, but those can be overcome—different sights, different smells, and different cultures—but it is not that which is bothering these people. What's bothering these people is these people come in a Mercedes Benz and dump some kid's soiled diapers on the sidewalk, if the kid himself is not defecating or urinating on the sidewalk. They just leave it there; now they wouldn't do that where they come from." Residents report that customers visiting Seventy-fourth Street frequently drop their garbage on the street or in already overflowing garbage bins. More vigilant residents have developed the habit of verbally confronting those who litter, even, as one resident told me on November 20, 1995, picking "it up and throwing it right back into their car, they are so furious, saying, 'This is yours. You take it.'"

As most Indian shoppers and merchants are not Jackson Heights residents, they are easily seen as outsiders.[22] Many residents perceive little benefit from the thriving businesses or the tax revenue. One leader asked rhetorically in an interview on May 16, 1996: "Do they hire from the community? Do the weekend shoppers frequent non-Indian stores?" The answers appear to be no, but merchants see such negative local responses as misdirected. Property values have increased in the last fifteen years. This is due in part to local building codes that limit the size of buildings, which inflates rents as demand exceeds space. Vasantrai Gandhi, a businessman and president of the Northern Queens Chamber of Commerce, suggested in our interview on August 15, 1996, that "some [complaints about Seventy-fourth Street] are legitimate, some exaggerated, and some are just crazy . . . [because much of it] is the natural consequence of development." Gandhi, a merchant and resident, criticized many in Jackson Heights for "shallow thinking" when it comes to the problems of Seventy-fourth Street. He argues that local business owners pay more in property taxes than do residential owners, while neither receiving city garbage pickup nor possessing the corporate muscle to elicit such amenities from the city. Thus, while the city benefits from immigrant businesses as net contributors to the city economy, few think about where tax revenues go or about the city's role in the consequences of rapid economic development. Gandhi and other merchants argue that the city is also responsible for the problems in and around the Seventy-fourth Street shopping district. Former Community Board 3 manager Mary Sarro echoed these views in our May 16, 1996, interview: "It seems like the problem with the Indian shopping strip and visitors is misdirected. Politicians don't put pressure on agencies to enforce laws or get some response, and agencies are shorthanded; in fact, many are overwhelmed."

Civic leaders and Indian business owners have made attempts to bridge the gap between the anger and frustration of local residents and merchant's interests. For example, the JHBG decided against aggressively confronting Seventy-fourth Street merchants. Instead, JHBG leaders attempted to work with merchants, even approaching several to join its board. In the early 1990s, an Indian restaurant owner joined, serving as treasurer for several years. This opened communication lines. For their part, Seventy-fourth Street merchants formed the Jackson Heights Merchants Association (JHMA) to deal with many of these concerns. JHMA, consisting mainly of Indian business leaders, confers with Councilman Sabini, Assemblyman Lafayette, and community groups. JHMA worked with city officials to deal with the traffic concerns; a parking lot recently opened (ironically, next to Sabini's office). Leaders are also working with the New York City Department of Transportation on proposals on how to deal with the traffic congestion (Machleder 1998). As a result, the city created loading-only zones, added eighty new parking spaces, put up No Horn Honking signs, and dramatically stepped up traffic enforcement (Cuza 2000). Positive steps like these open lines of communication between and provide opportunities for interaction among resident leaders and merchants. However, since most users of Little India are not residents, local political and civic institutions cannot provide opportunities for interaction to produce mutual understanding.

The tension in Jackson Heights does not involve interethnic hatred or violent action to prevent groups from entering. As a former JHBG president candidly told me in an interview on September 23, 1995: "It is not, 'You are a fucking Indian, therefore, I hate you, you dot head!' It is not that at all. It is, 'You got to do something about your customers, they just come in here and they are just taking over.'" Some in the community may feel general disdain for Asian and Latino newcomers, but the tension has deeper roots. "The good news is that nobody has killed anybody," a leader told me on November 20, 1995. "We are making headway, but we got some issues." The issues involve a crush of customers, cars, garbage, noise, and residents in a neighborhood once three-quarters the size and almost suburban in feel. Much of the resentment, however, also hinges on feelings of cultural displacement resulting from intensive immigration and the slow acceptance by some of cultural differences (e.g., conceptions of public space, of social graces, and of commerce). The concentration and success of Latino and Asian Indian businesses signify neighborhood changes that arouse feelings of displacement. Some residents no longer see stores catering to their ethnic group, and see instead the disturbing actions of newcomers and the offensive actions of nonresident customers. In our May 16, 1995, interview, one leader explained the tension between long-term residents and newcomers as resulting from Latino and Southeast Asian merchants and customers in Jackson Heights having a "total disrespect for our community." The use of phrases like "our community" or "our laws" suggests a clear sense of neighborhood ownership, one that seems to be eroding.

Overcrowding

Immigration in Northern Queens created a variety of overcrowding challenges, particularly for housing and schools. Jackson Heights' varied housing structure includes the historic cooperative buildings, apartments, and one- and two-family homes east toward Junction Boulevard, and a solid group of single-family houses north of Northern Boulevard. The housing structure shifted with the influx of immigrants. While the co-ops remain relatively stable, the areas east toward Junction and north of Northern Boulevard changed. "The biggest difference that has happened as a result of the diversity is the concentration of people," long-term resident Gloria Diani told me in our 1996 interview. "I moved in 1954 and it was always crowded. But the buildings haven't changed all that much; . . . the number of units has, the difference is the incredible concentrations." Leaders note that the areas deteriorating two decades ago were the ones with apartment buildings, while the single-family homes north of Northern Boulevard were in good condition. John Sabini, a life-long resident of Jackson Heights, noted in 1996:

> That has totally changed now. The area north of Northern, the one- to two-family homes are non-owner-occupied family homes. So now sixteen people are living where one or two used to, and cars are up on blocks, and the owner might be Century 21 or "Mrs. Crapalucci" in Tampa who hasn't seen her property in fifteen years and couldn't give a rat's ass who is in it. So what used to be Ozzie and Harriet mowing the lawn, you now have Miguel and Chang with their car up on the lawns. That is not an ethnic slur, it is just different. You go there looking to find the people that were there twenty years, they are not there. They are brown, they are yellow, and they are not owners anymore, by and large.

Immigration's impact on housing is considerable, punctuated by the sensational, such as the discovery, mentioned earlier, of more than sixty deaf Mexican immigrants living in overcrowded houses. While the extraordinary circumstances of this discovery sparked international outrage, few in Jackson Heights were surprised. For years, leaders complained about owners illegally renting out basements, landlords carving up apartments and renting cubicles, and other unscrupulous practices. One leader noted in our interview on May 16, 1996: "In these single- and two-family homes you have sixteen people living where two or four used to. Many times when there are fires, the fire department doesn't know when to go in, because twenty people will come out and they don't know how many people are in the buildings." Many landlords take advantage of the tight rental market by exploiting immigrants. "There are a lot of landlords who won't give leases," a Dominican activist told me on August 18, 1996. "They are warehousing people, because they will let people sleep on the floor with sleeping bags." When she attempted to organize tenants in her building, her rent doubled and the landlord threatened legal action.

The issue of illegal conversions needs to be put in the context of New York City's urban development. In the late 1800s and early 1900s, it was common within each immigrant neighborhood for residents to take in boarders illegally to make ends meet (Binder and Reimers 1995). What is different today are the faces, legal status, and commitment to stay in the United States. Immigrants in Jackson Heights are not from the same countries as older residents, many are undocumented, and a significant number plan on returning to their home country. Besides the historical context, there are other realities. First, most immigrants come from areas where two to three families living in one unit is not unusual. Second, the most abusive landlords often exploit members of their own ethnic group. "Some of the most abusive people are those of the same ethnicity and they are renting to their own kind because they know that they don't know how to petition government," Bart Goft, a former fair-housing counselor, told me in our August 15, 1996, interview. "Many are coming from countries where the military was the police and money is power."

Finally, overcrowded housing reflects established and rarely discussed arrangements among varying interests. Poor people, including legal and undocumented immigrants, need cheap housing. In fact, given the city's housing shortage at the low end of the market, many tenants are happy with their crowded and illegally subdivided apartments, viewing them as a step up from where they were before (Howell 1999a). The housing need creates a market for landlords who ignore zoning laws or owners who remodel or subdivide their basements (and even garages) to help meet the mortgage payment. And until recently, the city has largely looked the other way. After the *New York Times* ran a series of articles that chronicled the Queens housing problem, the Buildings Department implemented a long overdue plan. They created a "quality-of-life" task force of eight inspectors to work weekends and nights. In four months in 1996, the task force issued 1,770 violations to owners and landlords, for either working without a permit or violating occupancy regulations (Barry and Ojito 1997). Many in the community, including Thomas Raffaele, chair of Community Board 3, are adamant that enforcement regarding illegal conversions is necessary, even to setting up hot lines to make it easier for residents to make complaints.

Enforcement, however, is not the sole answer. Queens borough president Claire Shulman notes that city officials are "betwixt and between." If they hired enough inspectors and mounted enough court battles, they might be able to begin to solve one housing problem, but "it would probably only increase the homeless population" (quoted in Bruni and Sontag 1996). Local agencies operating fair-housing programs find their effectiveness limited. Agencies like the Jackson Heights Community Development Corporation (JHCDC) lack the resources to deal with enforcement or with the dramatic increase in residents. City cutbacks on housing programs, particularly tenant-assistance groups, force groups like the JHCDC to focus on protecting tenants from eviction and educating tenants about their rights. "What do you do with a block like right up here, between Roosevelt and Thirty-seventh Avenue, which is a block of single-family houses with sewers and electric built for single-family houses, but you probably actually have thirty or forty families living on a block that is built for twelve?" asked Eric Jacobs, JHCDC executive director, in our May 15, 1996, interview. "If you do enforcement and you evict them you run the risk of dramatically increasing the homeless population in the city. The city doesn't have the resources to deal with that dramatic increase. If you don't enforce it, then from a neighborhood standpoint the area becomes more and more at risk because of the lack of city services." Few simple answers or policies are available. Enforcement in Jackson Heights would likely push the problem to another community, creating another submarket. If nothing is done, the neighborhood's ability to provide adequate services is strained and the quality of life is threatened.

Illegally converted and overcrowded housing also impacts other local institutions, particularly schools. "Overcrowding is a major issue," former Community Board 3 district manager Mary Sarro told me in 1996. "Unless we address the illegal occupancy issue, we'll be building schools until 2025." Immigrant families are generally large, and Jackson Heights is an older neighborhood. As a result, like the commercial district, local schools were unprepared to handle the influx. Community School Board 30 (which has jurisdiction over Jackson Heights and surrounding areas) is the fourth most-crowded district in the city (Bazzi 1997). By the mid-1990s, every local school was operating between 120 and 150 percent of capacity. Numbers alone, however, do not capture the problems local schools face. During my fieldwork, I toured Joseph Pulitzer Intermediate

School (IS 145) with then principal Perry Sandler. At midmorning, several math and reading classes were being held in the cafeteria and on the gym floor. Grades ate lunch in shifts. A broom closet had been turned into an office. Special education classes were confined to just one or two rooms. Unfortunately, IS 145 is not alone. At PS 69, an elementary school located near the busiest part of Jackson Heights, schoolyard trailers housing classrooms are now permanent, complete with brick walls and air conditioning (Onishi 1996).

Overcrowded housing and overcrowded institutions frustrate leaders and have galvanized them to challenge what they view as an unresponsive governmental bureaucracy. The issue also elicited a strong sense of neighborhood solidarity among leaders and residents. In 1996, Community School Board 30 attempted to alleviate overcrowding at IS 145, offering a rezoning plan that would send students to other district schools. This plan was not received well, as a sizable number of parents and community leaders packed school-board meetings to express their opposition. Many argued that local schools are a key part of the community and rezoning would make the area less attractive to local residents. The president of the parent-teacher association at IS 145 asked: "Why would someone want to purchase a home or co-op in Jackson Heights if their children could not attend neighborhood schools?"[23] The rezoning plans were eventually scrapped, even though the board faces health and safety issues stemming from the overcrowding.

Ironically, the loudest oppositional voices to rezoning were those of white parents, who resisted a plan that would bus their children from predominantly Latino schools to two schools in more heavily white neighborhoods. A major concern raised by rezoning is the long-term neighborhood effects of busing. Zoning lines tend to stay for a long time. Leaders were concerned that zoning would decrease area children's (and ultimately, parents') commitment to and identification with the community. Jeffrey Saunders told me in our 1996 interview: "We resent in Jackson Heights and we fight vigorously the idea of shipping our students out. It teaches students that no particular community matters and there is no distinction and there is not a lot of identity. I went to a good school in Jackson Heights. I walk up and down the streets with lots of trees on them in Jackson Heights. They don't identify. As soon as you start shipping them out, they stop identifying with the community. Graffiti? Well, they don't live there, it doesn't matter. For students, their sense of place is defined by their home and their school, and what they see as they walk in between these two." Another parent, Tom Lowenhaupt, echoed Saunders's sentiment in a letter published in the *New York Times* on January 14, 1996, complaining his children attending a school for the academically gifted in neighboring Astoria no longer felt a commitment to Jackson Heights: "There they learn nothing about our historic district, about our magnificent diversity, or about the great things residents are doing to improve the neighborhood. Their friends and allegiances are Astorian. They now hate Jackson Heights, their mantra is: 'Dad, when are going to move to Astoria?'" Although school overcrowding, like that in the housing market, is fueled by the immigrant influx, most white parents active in school improvement efforts have not openly blamed immigrants. Instead, parents and leaders focused on finding solutions. The PTA, JHBG, Association for Neighborhood Democrats, and active parents formed Advocates for Community Education, a coalition of individuals interested in educational betterment or reform, whether public or private. Advocates for Community Education initially rallied for the construction of additions to existing schools to ease the overcrowding. A representative from this coalition told me in a November 20, 1995, interview: "We fought for those additions very hard. We even had to fight our local politicians, because they tried to . . . sell us out, in a misguided effort. They wanted a fourth school. That is nice, but that is fifteen to twenty years, the way things go around here. By the time they do an environmental impact study and buy land, . . . it is just not effective. We are not interested in a fifteen-year solution, we are interested in the next year or two when we can help these kids."

The additions were a first step. This victory led to an innovative plan to construct a "new vision" magnet school called the Renaissance School. The districtwide school involved converting space in an office building on Thirty-seventh Avenue, adjacent to Jackson Heights' public library. Construction began in 1996 and the school opened in 1997. The Renaissance School, kindergarten through twelfth grade, uses cluster teaching and blends a variety of models of teaching. The school has open registration, although lotteries have been necessary. Leaders note that the school attracts dedicated teachers and parents who are more informed and active in their children's education. The presence of the school is a symbol of the vigilance of community leaders and awareness among leaders of the importance of schools to maintain Jackson Heights' racial and ethnic mix. "We understand that education is a cornerstone for the community," a school activist told me on November 21, 1995. "If you have a good school, you can keep and attract young families to come in and take the place of the old people who are dying off." Another leader said in our

March 13, 1996, interview: "I know people that are moving here particularly for the Renaissance School. They want that school for their children." Underlying these statements is the reality that the Renaissance School is attracting and anchoring white families to Jackson Heights (though its students are not homogeneous). While this creates discomfort for some, it is an effort to prevent resegregation from occurring in the community. Whites are also part of Jackson Heights' integration, and the community needs to find ways to keep and attract white families to preserve it.

Historic Preservation: The Politics of Aesthetics

The decline of the neighborhood in the 1960s and 1970s created a challenge for residents and leaders concerned about the image of the neighborhood. A core group of leaders took up the issue of reworking negative perceptions of Jackson Heights as a drug- and crime-ridden neighborhood. A neighborhood's image is important for influencing everything from entry and exit decisions of individuals and families to investment, care of public and private space, and general notions of viability. In the 1980s, leaders in Jackson Heights seized upon landmark designation as a way to "break deterioration and crime, as well as a way of preserving the historic features of the neighborhood, which is recognized as the birthplace of the garden apartment and the middle-income cooperative" (Slatin 1994). Leaders sought historic preservation for a variety of reasons, but primarily to ensure that land-use decisions consider the community's aesthetic. However, historic designation has never been simple. While it offers a tool to protect neighborhood structures, preservation can also be used symbolically to express ethnic intolerance.

In 1980, the campaign for historic designation in Jackson Heights began when Community Board 3 asked the New York City Landmarks Preservation Commission to consider landmarking a large portion of the neighborhood. The campaign stalled as a result of bureaucratic hurdles and the progrowth agenda touted by the Queens Democratic machine and late borough president Donald Manes. Although long a popular way of revitalizing urban neighborhoods, the program of historic preservation was not valued in Queens at the time. During the 1970s and 1980s, Manes consistently used his power to block or modify historic landmark designations in Queens (S. Myers 1993b). Advocates in Jackson Heights thus found it difficult to win political support for their landmarking effort. Several events changed the mood toward historic landmark status for Jackson Heights. First, Donald Manes, embroiled in a corruption scandal at the city's Parking Violations Bureau, committed suicide in 1985. His successor as borough president, Claire Shulman, voiced strong support for historic preservation issues. Second, in the late 1980s changes in the city charter granted power to the City Council to ratify and rescind historic designations. Local groups now shifted their political pressure to City Council representatives, who were largely supportive of the designation (Bazzi 1995). Finally, several land-use issues stirred fears of impending development and rallied residents around the historic district proposal. The first involved the demolition of a group of private homes that were replaced with a row of new attached houses. Then a block of two-story neo-Tudor commercial storefronts burned down at the corner of Thirty-seventh Avenue and Eighty-second Street, considered the heart of Jackson Heights. "The fire happened at the crossroads of the entire community," Frank Moon told me on September 23, 1995. "It was this beautiful little building. It had a little bakery that everybody used to go to. And there was this great hole there, kind of like a wound." Shortly after the fire, plans surfaced for the construction of a twelve-story "mirrored-glass box" building. About six months earlier a group of twelve residents had founded the Jackson Heights Beautification Group (JHBG), dedicating themselves to "beautifying the neighborhood" through street cleanups, graffiti removal, and historic walking tours. The plan for the glass office tower galvanized JHBG to develop a vision of the future of Jackson Heights. JHBG called for a neighborhood hearing on the proposed development. As Rudy Greco recalled for me in 1995: "Every group needs an issue to galvanize it, and that did it. We had fifteen hundred people at the meeting. They had proposed a twelve-story building, which would fit in here like a sore thumb. They met a firestorm of opposition. We gave them a design; we gave them criteria. I said what we want is something that will blend into the community and, God willing, maybe enhance the architecture of the neighborhood." JHBG's early efforts over quality-of-life issues were transformed into a greater civic mission to preserve the architectural vision of Jackson Heights. In short order, JHBG emerged as the leading pro-preservation neighborhood voice. JHBG launched a campaign promoting the benefits of landmark designation, sponsoring tours and lectures, and even publishing a book chronicling the architectural history of the neighborhood. "We are the only neighborhood that ever went to [the Landmark Commission]," a former JHBG president told me on November 20, 1995. "We were the first who said we will take an active role in getting ourselves designated. We sought that designation and not only that, we financed a good part of it. Because

there were budgetary constraints, we went out and did the research."
JHBG raised money for one part of the application, including photo-
graphs and researching individual buildings. Leaders considered the volunteer effort involved a labor of love.

In October 1993, after several years of political and bureaucratic hurdles, the New York City Landmarks Preservation Commission designated a significant section of Jackson Heights a historic district (see Map 4.1).
The move was designed to protect the area's buildings from development
or renovations that might change their original character. The district
includes over two hundred buildings and private homes clustered
between Seventy-sixth Street on the west to Eighty-eighth Street on the
east, and Thirty-fourth Avenue south to Roosevelt Avenue (S. Myers
1993). The designation covers a large number of structures built by the
Queensboro Corporation between 1910 and the early 1950s (Slatin 1994).
Landmark districts put significant restrictions on property owners: exte-
riors of landmarked buildings cannot be altered without the commission's approval and owners must obtain permits for even minor work;
notable construction or changes, such as building a garage or porch,
replacing windows, or removing exterior masonry, require a hearing
before members of the commission, and as hearings are open to the public, residents have the opportunity to weigh in on proposed changes
(Bazzi 1994). Landmark status was an important victory for JHBG members, as it offered the group and neighborhood a tool to intervene on
land-use decisions and to preserve distinctive neighborhood features.
According to JHBG members and many nonmember residents, landmark
status and the guidelines it forces owners to follow will create a positive
community identity, enhance property values and economic development, anchor the middle class, and attract home buyers to the distinctive
neighborhood (Holmes 1992).

It is no surprise that groups like JHBG were so active in pursuing the
landmark designation. Many JHBG members own businesses, co-ops,
and private homes in and around the historic district, and so have a significant stake in the physical appearance, image, and quality of life (real
or perceived) in Jackson Heights (Kasinitz, Bazzi, and Doane 1998).
Today, JHBG has approximately two thousand members, and most of its
leaders are middle-aged, middle-class white business owners and professionals. The group's founder is an insurance executive, and over the years
its board of directors has included attorneys, financial analysts, and
small-business owners. Many JHBG leaders active in the historic district
movement saw it as a way to protect the time and money they invested

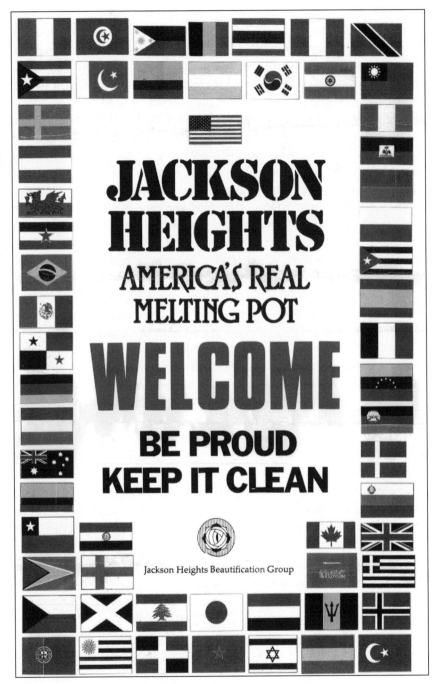

FIGURE 4.4. Jackson Heights Beautification Group Poster.
Courtesy of Rudy Greco of the Jackson Heights Beautification Group

in the neighborhood. And while leaders were aware that landmark designation would improve property values, this was not their only reason for pursuing it. A JHBG member told me on August 21, 1996, that "landmarks" was intended to "balance the community and keep it a livable place where people will not look at [it] as something to come in and in five to six years' time go out. It is a community that children should be raised in." In this sense, JHBG's efforts attempted to control the real estate market and influence who moves into the community. This may sound exclusionary and elitist, yet many ardently defend the landmark status. "[The historic district] is not going to keep you out by virtue of color or anything else, but it will [attract] people who care about where they live and care about that environment and want to preserve it," a JHBG member said in our November 21, 1995, interview. "It is going to attract people who are committed, whether they are purple or green." Given the dramatic changes immigration brought to Jackson Heights—from housing and commercial congestion to cultural norms—landmark status was seen by members as stabilizing the community and attracting middle-class residents.

Undoubtedly, the Jackson Heights buildings, architecture, and community plan have significant historical and architectural merit. Architect Robert A. M. Stern writes that the community was influential in the "development of new urban-suburban multiple-dwelling type, the 'garden apartment,' which functions on the principle that the true unit of planning is the city block rather than the individual building" (quoted in Karatzas 1992). The district includes most of the buildings built by MacDougall's Queensboro Corporation, known for their courtyard gardens, cross-ventilation, and distinctive architectural design. Some leaders see the structures and overall community plan as "irreplaceable," and thus worthy of preservation. As a leader told me on November 21, 1995: "You got something here that is not going to be built today." While it is difficult to argue with such sentiments, the landmark movement was not just about protecting buildings. The movement also sought to preserve certain standards and project a particular neighborhood image. "One of the things that the designation does is that it says, 'Okay, there are norms for this community," noted Jeffrey Saunders in 1996. "Everything is not helter-skelter; we can identify certain norms and they must be respected." Who defines these norms, however, is where things get sticky. Many in the community see the historic preservation effort as an attempt to restore the "old Jackson Heights" symbolized by Edward MacDougall's master plan, interpreted by some new residents as "white Jackson Heights" (Kasinitz, Bazzi, and Doane 1998). This is noticeable in the way JHBG activists have targeted multilingual signage and what some deem improper ways of conducting business, such as street vending and hawking (e.g., yelling at customers as they walk by, leafleting). The tension over Jackson Heights' image was played out dramatically in a debate over commercial signage. In October 1995, the city's Landmarks Preservation Commission proposed guidelines that would restrict the size, type, and color of material that could be used to alter store signage, awnings, light fixtures, and security gates in the historic district. Preservationists, attempting to achieve physical conformity through landmarking, praised these regulations. Jeffrey Saunders, chairman of JHBG's Architecture Committee, argued that these regulations are good for both the owners and the residents: "[Regulations] will ensure that no one can move in next door and engage in predatory tactics by putting awnings or canopies out to the curb, and doing crass things that are going to make [merchants] invisible. There is also less visual clutter." Pro-preservationists hope that the commission's restrictions will eliminate the numerous brightly colored, backlit, translucent, or "gaudy" and "splashy" signs and awnings that have emerged since the 1970s. These restrictions have not, however, sat well with everyone. There has been an undercurrent of opposition from business owners and landlords throughout the historic designation process. Business leaders argue that landmark standards would increase repair costs, restrict their rights, and force them to contend with an extra layer of bureaucracy.

Tension between pro- and antilandmarking groups hit a high point in August 1995, when Action Jackson, an anonymous group, distributed fliers calling for a boycott of eighteen businesses it claimed were not conforming to landmark standards (Cohen 1995). The group, claiming to represent residents of several co-op buildings, distributed its fliers in bank lobbies and at shop doors, angering merchants and residents. Action Jackson urged residents: "Don't shop in the stores listed below! These stores are illegal! Don't give your money to stores that bring the quality of our community down! (McKnight 1995; Cohen 1995). The flier claimed that the businesses "have not complied with landmarking regulations and have impacted negatively on our community" and are violating "our" laws and, oddly, makes an impassioned plea for police assistance. In this case, the police were not being called to deal with property or violent criminal acts, but to stop people from violating landmark law.

FIGURE 4.5. Disputed commercial signage. *Left*, bedroom furniture store, 77th and Roosevelt Avenue; *right*, Esmeralda Travel, 86th and 37th Avenue

Some residents and leaders believed that the Action Jackson campaign was motivated by racism and xenophobia, as immigrants owned many of the targeted stores. "This kind of thing breeds hate in the community," states Joe Reese, president of the Alpine Tenants Association and a landmark-designation critic. "They [Action Jackson] were hiding behind a mask and attacking business people; . . . maybe some of the businesses should be improved, but the way they went about it was wrong" (quoted in Bazzi 1995). The attempt to use landmark law to enforce aesthetic guidelines for storefronts intensified a neighborhood debate "between residents who say they want to preserve the district's beauty and immigrant storeowners who say it is a racist attempt to drive them out of business" (Lii 1995). One storefront that became a symbol of the tension over commercial signage regulations was Esmeralda Travel, a travel agency with a fifteen-foot awning shaped like the front of an airplane that covered the entire sidewalk. The owner, Jorge Moreno, was quoted in the *New York Times* arguing that he and others were being harassed out of racism: "It's some people: They are not happy with us here" (Cohen 1995). Such views are not without foundation. Some JHBG leaders have argued that landmarking was necessary to "speed up the process of civilizing the streets in a historically appropriate way."[24] Why "civilizing" the streets is necessary has not always been clear, but it appears to mean creating an "attractive," "uncluttered," and essentially Anglo commercial area. For example, Jeffrey Saunders (1995) wrote an essay on landmarking published in the Queensborough Preservation League's newsletter in which he lists various physical changes—ranging from landlords subdividing their homes to a homeowner repairing his chimney with black pitch rather than mortar—as signs of negative change affecting communities like Jackson Heights. He writes that these "collective changes cheapen, degrade and coarsen our community. . . . For example, how many can enjoy a stroll along Main Street in Flushing, Broadway in Elmhurst, or Roosevelt Avenue at Seventy-fourth Street?" The streets Saunders names are revealing in that they do not include low-income neighborhoods in Queens or other boroughs beset by disinvestments or abandonment (though he could choose from a long list). Instead, he points to three busy and prosperous business districts associated with Asian and Latin American immigrants—in Jackson Heights, literally the corner of Little India and Little Colombia. Mary Sarro, former district manager for the local community board, used an even less subtle comparison when she told the *New York Times* that she praises Action Jackson's efforts. "I think getting quality businesses back in the community is an admirable pursuit," she said. "Do you want a shopping community like Rodeo Drive or [one] like in Bombay?" (Cohen 1995).

The debate over aesthetic issues—albeit dramatically punctuated by community leaders such as Saunders and Sarro—must be understood in relation to the demographic and cultural changes occurring in Jackson Heights. Many leaders, particularly middle-class whites living in the historic co-ops, appear threatened by the increased immigrant presence and the physical changes accompanying it. Many more lament the lack of neighborhood stores catering to their own needs and wants, and believe that they do not share the economic prosperity being derived from the community's two ethnic-oriented commercial arteries. Ultimately, the debate over signage and enforcing landmark law is an issue of community identity and control. Given the magnitude of changes in Jackson Heights, it is not surprising that residents have sought control of community identity. For many, Jackson Heights is associated with a certain look; understanding this explains why aesthetic issues have been central in recent community struggles. Leaders do not want that look changed, nor do they want the identity changed. Landmark designations are a way to control that image, frame the vision of Jackson Heights, and stamp a collective identity on the community (Zukin 1995). Undoubtedly, the landmark movement mobilized residents around maintaining the neighborhood's aesthetic quality. As such, it illustrates the resolve of community leaders to intervene and sustain Jackson Heights.

The downside to the landmark designation movement is clear in the commercial signage debate. To some residents, landmark status is being used to define the community by mainstream white norms and culture. A leader put it to me this way on November 21, 1995: "Some people oppose [loud storefront displays], because there is an underlying current here that the Anglo kind of lifestyle and exterior appearances should prevail." The rub is that defining what is "crass" or "dignified" is political. "Landmarking is really about one group trying to preserve something that was in the past and you can't go back," said Bart Goft, a community activist, in our 1996 interview. "There is a different aesthetic for Hispanics and for whites." When leaders and residents remark, "We never had that" or "Everything was so dignified back then," there is little recognition that the neighborhood has changed or that ethnic groups may have different, but equally legitimate, values.

Undoubtedly, the historic preservation movement's attempts to impose its vision of community aesthetics have been about more than architecture. Landmark status offers a dwindling white population a method—if only symbolic—of soothing its feelings of displacement. For a faction of the movement, represented by Action Jackson, mandating compliance to aesthetic guidelines or landmark law is really a battle over who will decide what constitutes a proper and civilized community (Kasinitz, Bazzi, and Doane 1998). To this end, these efforts are not inclusive. Leaders spearheading landmark designation expressed little recognition that people outside the co-ops and "historically significant" structures should be involved in discussions over the future of the neighborhood. Mitchell Biderman, an optometrist whose store was listed on Action Jackson's flier, expressed frustration over the lack of input by community members: "The merchants should have a voice in defining what's best for their own interests. . . . That's not happening here. Who defines what's best for the community?" (quoted in Kasinitz, Bazzi, and Doane 1998: 174). The lack of communication among Jackson Heights' diverse interest groups is a source of tension among them and a continuing challenge for community leaders if the landmark designation is to be a positive force for Jackson Heights. One leader, speaking with me in confidence on May 15, 1996, sums up this challenge:

> How do you balance the public statement that we want to turn back the clock and bring back the area to the way it was in the 1920s, when the reality is that the people that are living here are nothing like the people who were living here in the 1920s? And I want to say this really gently, how do you do that without overtly appearing to being either prejudiced or racist? That, I think, was the challenge of the historic district. And what it showed is that you can't, unless you develop communication mechanisms between the different communities so that both understand what it is the other is trying to achieve. And that was something with the historic district that still doesn't exist. The Latino business owners feel very threatened . . . that all of this is an attempt to throw them out of the area.

There are hints, however, that leaders are beginning to identify and address this challenge. For example, in the mid-1990s Jeffrey Saunders made it his mission to go from business to business explaining landmark guidelines. He recounted a story to me in our 1996 interview in which an angry merchant called complaining about landmark regulations, arguing that to get visibility it would cost him $40,000 for a sign. Sitting down with the merchant, Saunders explained that the landmark regulations call for a sign that would cost him only around $8,000. Saunders explained to the man that "after you jump through some hoops for this, you can know that everyone behind you is going to have to jump through the same hoops and . . . this will ensure that no one can move in next door and engage in predatory tactics by putting awnings out to the curb and doing crass things that are going to make you invisible." Efforts like this demonstrate an emerging understanding that dialogue is necessary in Jackson Heights to incorporate the various visions of the community. The key challenge is to broaden the base of residents and merchants who are defining community interests. Without such efforts, landmark status can be a source of elitism and ethnocentric conflict. "The danger in the land-marking concept is if it becomes snobbery, you can defeat what you're doing," noted Rev. Austin Armitstead in our March 13, 1996, interview. "If there is going to be any snobbery, your reason has to be based on something other than color of skin or where you came from. Because there's a tendency toward it and you can't be blind to what's happening. If you get into that kind of thing you perpetuate [racial antagonism] and you don't have the possibility of reducing it."

Redefining Integration and Community Unity

Despite the potential divisive elements of the landmark preservation movement, Jackson Heights is a model of how a community can work to maintain and sustain racial and ethnic integration. To be sure, integration in Jackson Heights was not the result of conscious efforts. Leaders did not profess to promote integration; as one JHBG leader suggested to me on September 23, 1995, "Promoting is such an active term." Instead of self-consciously promoting integration, leaders organized residents around improving neighborhood quality of life and working at creating a positive and civil community image. In many ways, leaders reacted to the effects of significant and swift demographic and cultural changes sweeping over Jackson Heights. Some changes threatened community stability, and thus it is not surprising that most intervention involved issues such as overcrowding and crime, as well as managing symbolic identifiers to project an image of stability and order. All communities require organizations involved in community-building efforts to remain stable and thrive. And in many ways, these organizations work indirectly to promote racial and ethnic integration by preventing neighborhood decline and disinvestment. Yet, as urban history demonstrates, the mere presence of such organizations does not translate into stable integration.

For a neighborhood to remain stably integrated, leaders and organizations must find ways to redefine integration as stable and as a community strength. Jackson Heights' groups are working to reaffirm the value of the area's racial and ethnic mix in a variety of ways, although they are largely symbolic responses to the community's changing composition.

For example, JHBG developed a promotional poster for Jackson Heights displaying the flags of the different countries represented in the community. This symbolic act is a step in the process of creating understanding and dialogue between groups. Leaders are affirming the neighborhood's integration as an attractive feature and element of pride. The poster is curious, however, in that it also seems to read as a directive to newcomers—"Keep It Clean." A more important step involves bringing groups together across racial, ethnic, and cultural divides, and fostering, even at a rudimentary level, interracial or interethnic dialogue. There were attempts—however fleeting—to bridge differences among groups and to create spaces where groups could interact. This is easier said than done, as stable integration diversity requires a strong commitment toward tolerance and inclusion, and leaders willing to initiate such a commitment. Fortunately, Jackson Heights is enriched by a number of leaders committed to these ideals. A JHBG member noted in our November 19, 1995, interview that while the group had "no specific thrust towards promoting diversity," he and others "did attempt to consciously promote tolerance, rather than diversity. The diversity is here; what you try to do is to promote understanding and bring other people in." While this leader speaks of individual-level actions, there were also organizationally sponsored activities to promote interaction and tolerance.

Harmony Day

Attempts aimed at bridging racial and cultural differences trace back to community organizing in the late 1970s, led by Rev. Austin Armitstead and Ivan Lafayette (later elected to the state assembly). Together with other influential members, they founded the Cultural Awareness Council. Eric Jacobs told me on May 15, 1996:

> The group was essentially a multicultural and educational project. Informal—between Jewish people of Jackson Heights, Latino people of Jackson Heights, and a couple of African American groups from East Elmhurst. The sole purpose was just sitting down and getting to know each other, and they did a lot of different types of programs to get to know each other. Then the program was never really institutionalized and fell by the wayside. [However,] it illustrated the fact that you could have an organization that is a true umbrella that could be responsive in terms of providing successful outreach to the community.

These early multicultural organizing efforts were not in vain. Two decades later, several organizations, including the Jackson Heights Community Development Corporation (JHCDC), revived this spirit. "As I walk the streets, more what kept coming back [to] was the cultural divisions, especially among the Spanish-speaking population and the Anglo population, . . . let alone the African American population," notes Jacobs. "And members of my staff came to me and told me that the problem we're having is that people just don't want to talk to each other. So really what we decided to do at that point was to begin thinking about our programs as outreach organizing tools." With this awareness, JHCDC focused on outreach organizing projects that would bring together people from different groups. JHCDC leaders even suggest that maintaining integration in the Jackson Heights area is now an unstated goal of all their activities.

One visible outreach organizational effort led by JHCDC was an interethnic festival dubbed Harmony Day. The festival in 1994 involved ongoing multicultural performances and programs. Two main stages were set up, one at the corner of Thirty-seventh Avenue and Eighty-second Street, and the other at the corner of Roosevelt Avenue and Eighty-second. A range of performers rotated on a half-hour schedule, filling the street with South American folk music, jazz, and other musical styles. A half-dozen smaller stages were set up for quieter activities, such as poetry readings. An estimated 7,500 to 10,000 people were drawn to the event over the day. The importance of this event cannot be downplayed. Unlike many multicultural events where the only sharing involves different food, Harmony Day represents a community-building activity that marshals stronger cultural ties. Jacob notes that Harmony Day "forced, and not in a negative way, different cultures to share, because they were all on the street willing to participate in something." This festival led to a beginning of an area multicultural art collaborative that facilitates cultural sharing, and in this way enriches the overall community.

JHCDC has been particularly involved in facilitating programs—whether they center on culture, housing, or economic issues—that bridge gaps between different racial and ethnic populations. In discussing their programs, a JHCDC leader told me on May 15, 1996: "I think [racial and ethnic integration] is a reality that just has to happen. If it doesn't happen, what you will have is similar to the ethnic camps, where one community doesn't necessarily talk to another community. They meet on the street and they don't necessarily get along." This does not imply that groups must shed their racial and ethnic identities and cultural traditions. In places like Jackson Heights, such identities and cultural backgrounds need to be respected. However, ways to bring people together are also needed, even if they are rudimentary, to form understanding between groups and to reduce the "us" versus "them" dichotomies that can emerge when there are such different populations in the community. While only a start, multicultural festivals offer a step in that direction—sharing food and music can lead to deeper connections.

Community United Methodist Church

The other organization that most community members point to as instrumental in promoting integration is Community United Methodist Church. Since the mid-1970s the Community Church, as residents know it, has been innovative and progressive in fostering racial tolerance and understanding. Many in the community credit the church's role to its now retired pastor, Rev. Austin Armitstead. As pastor of Community United Methodist Church from 1974 to 1995, Armitstead worked tirelessly to ease Jackson Heights' ethnic and cultural transition by implementing inclusive practices and preaching the value of integration. Before coming to Jackson Heights, he was active in a variety of social and philanthropic causes, from leading a clergy effort for open housing in Bay Ridge (Queens) and working on efforts to create New York City's current community-board structure to preserving U.S. Public Health Hospital in Staten Island. These experiences uniquely suited him for his leadership role at the Community Church. After accepting a position in Jackson Heights, Reverend Armitstead restructured the church into four separate ministries, based on language and cultural traditions (Chinese, Korean, Spanish, and English) and opened the church's facilities to a wide variety of community groups, making it a "community center and hub of civic life."[25]

Today, the Community Church is one of the more renowned and recognizable buildings in Jackson Heights. The mass schedule in front of the church lists the four services, and additional signage adorning the church's outer walls is in several languages. Before Armitstead arrived, the church rejected a suggestion to add a Spanish-language service. The previous pastor, soon to retire after twenty-five years of service, resisted any innovation, even though the congregation population declined as whites left. When Armitstead arrived in 1974, he made the controversial decision to restructure the church, even in the face of resistance from some church members. "This church would have died twenty-two years ago when I first came here, if we hadn't [had] a concept that you got to be identified with the total community," noted Reverend Armitstead in our 1996 interview. "You cannot wind up having your own small agenda; a small agenda only appeals to the supporters of your agenda." The

FIGURE 4.6. Community Methodist Church, offering worship in four languages and serving as community center

"total community," according to Armitstead, meant various ethnic and cultural groups. Noting that he divided the church into different congregations to meet a community need, he said: "We are mirroring the community. "That's the church's function, that's our mission" (quoted in Goldman 1989). Although the decision was not greeted with universal acceptance, it not only saved the church, but also created some space for interethnic sharing. Over time, the shift has been positive for the church. In fact, in 1989, after the *New York Times* ran a front-page feature on the Community Church and its diverse mix, even those uncomfortable with the mix began to see it as a source of pride (Goldman 1989). Slowly, the church has been able to define the racial and ethnic mix as a positive institutional and neighborhood quality.

To some, however, the Community Church, with its four separate congregations, is symbolic of integration in Jackson Heights, where "congregations lead essentially parallel lives, coming together occasionally at moments of common interest, but remaining fundamentally distinct"

(Kasinitz, Bazzi, and Doane 1998: 170). Surely, Sunday morning is the most segregated moment of the week even in diverse communities. Yet such a statement ignores the important role the church plays in building community in Jackson Heights. The Community Church is not open only on Sunday, and it draws people from different parts of the community together across a variety of social divisions. For example, Armitstead opened up the church as "common ground" for groups ranging from ethnic associations and gay and lesbian organizations to nonprofits like the JHBG. Armitstead believes that stereotypes can be transcended and goals met "when people are included and people trust you, especially if you draw people together with a greater vision." To Armitstead and others the greater vision involves a belief that diverse groups can share resources and live together. Recalling the philosophy behind his actions at the church, Armitstead told me in 1996: "I believe that there is something unique about this community, . . . but that it falls on deaf ears for many people because they can't see it. It goes back to a statement of a philosopher: 'He drew a circle, it shut me out.' I'd rather not have the victory of one. 'He drew a circle, it took me in.' In other words, the concept is that you should bring people in rather than excluding them. You've got much more opportunity of being a facilitator, an innovator, a catalyst. This is what I believe can happen."

The vision espoused by Armitstead is vital to building bridges between the various racial and ethnic groups. Armitstead is one of several active and vocal leaders who believe that people can be different and still accept and live with one another. By opening the Community Church to more than ninety community groups, Armitstead facilitated interracial and interethnic contact. For example, while the church is not predominantly Spanish speaking, Ecuadorian and Colombian associations meet there frequently. Critics argue that these groups hold meetings in separate rooms, leaving the bathroom facilities as the main space for interaction among groups. However, this misses the larger point. As Armitstead notes, many Spanish-speaking people might have viewed the church as a "WASP-y place" or a "white place." By providing common ground for disparate groups to meet, you begin to break down such stereotypes and encourage tolerance.

Creating common ground for groups is a positive effort in building community among diverse groups. The idea behind such an effort is that over time interaction will sprout, particularly if dialogue is fostered and maintained. Today, Dr. Ronald Tompkins guides the Community Church. Similar to Armitstead, Tompkins views his role at the church as facilitating cross-cultural connections among members of his congregation (Kasinitz, Bazzi, and Doane 1998). His efforts appear successful, as groups continue to see and use the church as a central meeting space. Services continue to be held in four languages. However, this does not mean that groups have little interaction. On a Sunday visit, children and adults from different ethnic backgrounds were interacting in a variety of activities, from helping church leaders prepare for a service to sharing in a prayer circle. While it is difficult to judge the quality of this interaction, it is an important step in building community ties among diverse groups.

Like Uptown, Jackson Heights highlights the complexity of maintaining a racial, ethnic, cultural, and economic mix of residents over several decades. While initially a planned and restrictive community, nothing about Jackson Heights' current integration was planned or directed. Immigration has left its mark on northern Queens over the last three decades, dramatically recasting the character of this once middle-class "suburb in the city." The impact of immigration has presented both opportunities and challenges. Immigrants filled vacancies as whites fled to the suburbs in the 1960s and 1970s. Immigrant entrepreneurs revitalized vacant commercial districts. Racial and ethnic change also brought overcrowding in schools and housing, physical and cultural changes, and debates over community norms and aesthetics. Ethnic conflict exists, as some community members resent newcomers and some immigrants feel that they are treated unfairly. However, the conflict largely gets played out in community debates over abstract issues like aesthetics. Despite this, Jackson Heights is a successful, stable integrated community. Community organizations, leaders, and residents effectively addressed issues threatening the stability and vitality of the neighborhood, negotiated matters of neighborhood identity and norms, and created social space for different racial and ethnic groups to interact or associate with one another. Integration in Jackson Heights appears certain for now, though diverse leaders and groups must continue to work at creating a positive and inclusive identity. Given the existing leadership and social capital, this is an achievable goal.

5   San Antonio–Fruitvale, Oakland

Resident Narrative: Rosalinda Palacios

I was familiar with Fruitvale long before moving there.[1] It was where the Latino community lived. I had been to Fruitvale several times in my youth. I am from Los Angeles and was involved in the Free Angela Davis campaign, so we came up to Oakland because Angela lived there. The Latinos and African Americans involved in her campaign would meet in her Fruitvale house. I just loved it there.

In the 1980s I was working in Sacramento for a health-planning organization when the Reagan administration blue-penciled health planning off the national map. At the time, a doctor friend accepted the position as medical director at La Clínica de la Raza in Fruitvale, the largest community clinic run by Chicanos. After moving to Fruitvale she called me and told me about a health-planner position at La Clínica. She said, "Take the job, it's for you!" And by then, I had not been to Oakland in many years and thought that I would never move to Oakland. All media accounts of Oakland and the black population were negative. By then the crack epidemic had already started and along with that meant a lot of crime. I thought I was going to be mugged or raped or killed, because of being in Fruitvale. So I delayed the interview several times. I finally went and got the job; however, I commuted from Sacramento for a year. I wasn't sure I was going to keep the job. The commute was awful and I decided to move to Oakland.

A friend of mine bought a house in an area called Montclair, north of I-580 and Fruitvale. The house had a unit downstairs and so I moved my son and daughter there. Montclair is an area where few people of color live. My daughter, a teenager at the time, did not like it there. She would come home and say, "Mom, everybody thinks I am the maid's daughter." People would ask her in the store if her mother cleans houses. She was sick and tired of that, and she was like, "No, my mother does not clean houses." She argued with me that we didn't belong in Montclair and we needed to move where there were people of color. So she's the one that convinced me to move to the Fruitvale and we've lived there over fifteen years, in the same house. We rented a three-story Victorian near Twenty-third Street. The house has views of the Bay Bridge and I could see the Oakland Coliseum at night. There are quite a few houses like that here, but you have to rent because the property values are just too high. It was shocking moving to Oakland because the cost of living is amazingly high. I was paying three hundred dollars or less in rent in Sacramento for about fifteen years. When I moved to Oakland my rent went to like eight hundred dollars. Everything is more expensive here in the Bay Area, because there is such a demand of people wanting to live here. They choose to live here and they're willing to pay the price. And renting a house is not easy in the Fruitvale. You will rarely see a For Rent sign. You are competing with people who have money, who work in San Francisco, all these thousands of people who've migrated into the Santa Clara area because of Silicon Valley. You're also competing with students from UC Berkeley. Because you are competing with people with money, . . . you pay a competitive price.

And people tend not to move in the flatlands, because if you do your rent increases twice as much. And not only that, you have first and last month's rent plus the rent to get in. So you have to have at least four thousand dollars to move. Nobody has that kind of money to move. To get into a place, you have to have credit, and you have to have money, and as a result there's a lot of overcrowding. Twelve years ago I left La Clínica and I eventually went to work for the census. They gave me a management job to do a small census before the main census. And my job was to count the homeless in San Antonio and Fruitvale. I could show you some of those hotels where you see a building but you don't see how to get into the building. They have secret doors and everything. It is because owners rent out to men—day laborers—and they charge them forty dollars a night. It is amazing, and people pay it. You will also see families living with families in one room. And they all had to share one little cooking area and they all share one bathroom. We are talking about at least ninety people on a floor.

Fruitvale does have problems. Yet I have never thought about moving or, say, buying a house anywhere else than in the Fruitvale. I like the sense of community and activism in the community. There is always something going on and it is nice. I mean, a lot of people like me could move, but I guess community is important. We like being around people, people that we know, people that we don't know. We like making change. We like looking at making things better. Not so much liberal; . . . Berkeley is liberal. I think people in Oakland are progressive. I mean, if you are progressive you make change. I mean you are out in the street. We are running programs. A lot of people I know in Fruitvale are like me. They are involved, and you see that in the concentration of Latino-run programs. That is one of the reasons why I stay in Fruitvale.

There are also a lot of good things about living in Fruitvale. The mix of people makes it interesting. My kids liked living in the Fruitvale and they had friends from a variety of racial and ethnic groups. There is also a strong sense of community. In the Fruitvale people know one another quite well, especially those that have lived there for a long time. You are used to seeing that Asian man walk to the store every day. You know his patterns; you know him. You might have a casual good-morning conversation, but you know people, by seeing them. You see them on the buses and their kids going to school. I think when you move up into the hills it is just the houses in the area. In the Fruitvale you know everybody. If you go to a restaurant, they know you by name and what you do. You're known. I mean, that is a community. I can pass by and wave and know the kids. You even get to know the immigrants running the taco trucks or selling food on the street corners. You don't see that in a lot of other communities. You leave the Fruitvale, you leave the taco trucks, you leave the street vendors, the people selling corn on the street; . . . you would never see street vendors in Montclair or any of the communities up here [in the hills]. But what you see in Fruitvale is what you are going to see in Los Angeles, Texas, Mexico City.

OAKLAND: THE BAY AREA'S INTEGRATED JEWEL?

The city of Oakland may not be considered as thriving as San Francisco or even San Jose. Yet nestled in the East Bay, surrounded by more affluent suburbs and cities, Oakland is one of most racially and ethnically diverse cities around. And the diversity extends beyond overall numbers to the neighborhood level. "By rating, [Oakland] is the first city in America that has this type of racial and ethnic proximity in the acreage that we know; . . . it is the most integrated city in America," activist David Glover told me in our October 17, 1996, interview. While his is a difficult claim to prove, there is a tremendous mix. And the city and various organizations go out of their way to promote this fact, lauding the diversity in marketing brochures, business-development literature, and public speeches. "I would have said that Oakland has as close to an official ideology about promoting and celebrating diversity as a place could have," noted Victor Rubin of the University of California-Berkeley in our interview on October 19, 1996. "The issue is whether that is carried out in practice." It does not appear that the city makes official policy to promote racial and ethnic integration. Yet in the flatlands of East Oakland lie two contiguous community-development districts (CDDs) that are the city's fastest-growing and most racially and ethnically integrated communities: San Antonio and Fruitvale. Bounded by the bay to the south, McArthur Boulevard (I-580) to the north, Lake Merritt to the west, and High Street to the east, these two communities embody the city's boastful claims of integration.[2]

Yet San Antonio–Fruitvale is not what most likely comes to mind when one thinks about racial and ethnic integration. The two communities are a study in contrasts. Businesses line their main commercial arteries, like International Boulevard (also known as East Fourteenth) and Fruitvale Avenue—from automobile repair shops and grocery stores (selling produce not found in chain supermarkets) to small restaurants and street vendors. The streets are buzzing. Yet garbage clutters the street. Buildings are in disrepair. There are buildings with no front doors—later I am told that many are sweatshops. With shops haphazardly placed, the commercial district lacks a rational pattern. A former bank building is now a rent-a-center surrounded by check-cashing businesses. Customers searching for a quaint shopping area with a Starbucks and national chain stores or boutiques will be disappointed. The housing is similarly haphazard. One block may consist of well-kept bungalow- or Victorian-style housing, the next of rundown housing with two cars parked in every front yard. While not ghettos or slums, neither San Antonio nor Fruitvale has the shine of more affluent areas.

San Antonio–Fruitvale, however, is integrated on a variety of levels. The integration cuts across race, ethnicity, class, and nativity. This part of Oakland is a densely populated, multiethnic, multiracial, multilingual, working-class, and less than economically vibrant community that has been able to maintain integration without any evidence of conscious action on the part of the city or neighborhood organizations. A principal theme of this book is that residential integration is complex; integrated neighborhoods not only find themselves in unique positions, but also take different forms. The demographic, economic, and social character of San Antonio–Fruitvale is a further example of this complexity. These communities may not have invited integration; however, through multiethnic and multiracial collaborations, they have made it work.

GROWTH, DECLINE, AND REBIRTH IN THE FLATLANDS

The Ohlone tribe of Native Americans was the first group to inhabit the San Antonio–Fruitvale area. In the early nineteenth century, Spanish forces displaced the Ohlones and incorporated the area as Rancho de San Antonio, a 44,000-acre land grant given to Don Luis Maria Peralta by the Spanish Crown in 1820 in recognition of his military service (Bagwell 1982). Rancho de San Antonio stretched over thirteen miles of East Bay shoreline from the present city of San Leandro to that of Albany and east to the ridges of the Contra Costa Hills (Snyder 1992). After Don Luis Maria Peralta's death, his son sold various plots of land to local residents, who farmed the land for wheat and barley.

The farms, however, were soon subdivided as settlers flocked to the Bay Area after the Gold Rush of 1849. German, Italian, and Portuguese immigrants settled in the Fruitvale area and either worked in local factories or set up small farms and ranches. In fact, "Fruit Vale" got its name in 1856 from a cherry orchard planted by a German immigrant. Other orchards followed, as the "fertile soil and sunny climate" made the area a major fruit-production center (Counts 1999). Canneries—among them, the Del Monte Cannery—sprouted up south of East Fourteenth, sparking a flurry of housing construction as workers flocked to the area (Alozie 1992). Fruitvale also became known for its mansions and beer gardens, as wealthy San Francisco merchants and business owners built family homes in the area. A streetcar line established along East Fourteenth created a thriving neighborhood that by the early 1900s became known as "Oakland's Second Downtown."[3] The area attracted more residents as shipping and wartime industries created a need for thousands of blue-collar workers (Gust 1988).

In the nineteenth century, San Antonio was a violent and thriving lumber town that relied on harvesting redwoods from the Oakland Hills. Lumber was shipped from San Antonio's shore until the 1860s, when all the redwoods had been felled (Bagwell 1982). Originally, the San Antonio area was divided into three villages: Clinton, San Antonio, and Lynn. The villages were quickly incorporated into the greater township of Brooklyn and eventually annexed into the City of Oakland (Isabel 1984). Transportation improvements made the area popular among prominent business and civic leaders from both Oakland and San Francisco.[4] San Antonio became increasingly popular given its proximity to downtown and the Twelfth Street Dam, which provided access to San Francisco's Thirteenth Avenue Pier. Between 1900 and World War II, San Francisco residents, immigrants, and southern migrants moved to San Antonio for affordable housing and work in places like Alameda's Kaiser Shipyards (Blakely 1988; Chumsai 1992). However, the available housing stock and services often did not meet their needs. As housing construction lagged, large Victorian homes and unused commercial structures were subdivided to create more housing.

The end of World War II brought significant changes to both San Antonio and Fruitvale. The wartime boom altered the housing stock and demographics, transforming each from a quiet suburban residential district to a higher-density neighborhood. To accommodate the housing demand, apartments and temporary housing were built for workers. The war effort had also attracted significant numbers of African American and Latino residents. In the decades following World War II, many factories struggled to adjust to peacetime demands; unemployment, vagrancy, and housing deterioration resulted (Chew 1991). The area's residential character was significantly altered. In 1955, the area of San Antonio known as Clinton Park was chosen as an Urban Renewal Rehabilitation Project. An extensive program of code enforcement resulted in the demolition of approximately 117 structures and the construction of new apartment buildings offering affordable housing (Sugden-Castillo 1996). The program, however, failed to blend the new housing with the existing architecture, as modern apartment buildings were set next to beautiful single-family Victorians (Blakely 1988). Federal housing programs of the 1960s and 1970s continued to encourage the construction of large apartment complexes for low- and moderate-income residents. As a result, a trip to either district today reveals a hodgepodge of housing, ranging from "elegant Queen Annes to utilitarian, box-shaped four-plexes" (Gust 1988:1).

Suburbanization also impacted these Oakland districts. Beginning in the 1950s, white middle-class families began to flee both areas for suburban locales. Federally sponsored highway construction added to the problem in 1949, when the Nimitz Freeway (I-880) was built through Lower San Antonio and Lower Fruitvale, allowing traffic to move freely in and out of Oakland, while opening more suburban areas and creating new subdivisions to the east (Blakely 1988). Before the construction of I-880, East Fourteenth served as the key commercial thoroughfare for both Fruitvale and San Antonio. Now automobile traffic that once moved along the commercial heart of the districts bypassed the area for suburban malls. Relocating residents and a diminishing base of affluent customers undermined local businesses. Numerous banks, including Bank of America, Wells Fargo, and Sanwa Bank, closed their branches, making it difficult for residents and small businesses to bank or even find an ATM (Sugden-Castillo 1996). Montgomery Ward, the heart of the commercial vibrancy of East Fourteenth since 1923, with its one million square feet of commercial space, closed in 1982. The decaying, half-demolished behemoth remains a community eyesore and symbol of the area's past economic strength.[5]

In the 1970s and 1980s the once proud "second downtown" of Oakland fell into disrepair as economic development dwindled and housing deteriorated, while litter, graffiti, and crime increased. The number of houses and buildings with metal bars on their windows and steel front doors in San Antonio–Fruitvale are a reminder of this period. The gates began to appear throughout the area as drug use—heroin and crack cocaine—became prevalent. "There are a lot of heroin addicts and halfway houses that are not managed very well . . . and a lot of people in the halfway houses end up on the street corner," noted Don Davenport, an activist in San Antonio, in our October 15, 1996, interview. "And where drugs are, you are going to have an increase in crime, . . . break-ins and all this other stuff." And while the drug trade still exists in diminished form, the area's past has fostered a lingering sense of fear and a need to keep windows and doors barred.

Fortunately for Fruitvale and San Antonio, in the mid-1960s the area—particularly Fruitvale—became a focal point of activism as Chicano, African American, and Native American leaders worked closely with the civil rights movement.[6] Grassroots organizations were established, rallying the community around such issues as health-care provision, code enforcement, and crime prevention. In the 1960s and 1970s the few federally funded social service or housing programs available served African Americans, not Latinos. The strong and sometimes militant Chicano and Latino organizing produced a number of groups and agencies serving Latinos in Fruitvale and East Oakland. Why Fruitvale? Rosalinda Palacios, former director of a Fruitvale youth center, provided the history in our October 24, 1996, interview:

> The Latino community lived here and Chicanos were for the first time in the 1970s going into universities. You had Chicanos coming from L.A., San Diego, and all these places to UC-Berkeley—a white institution, a white community, liberal, with values very different from ours. So they had to find home. They found home in Fruitvale. Lawyers, medical professionals, social service people, all of them came to the Fruitvale. And what they did is, . . . there was no health services for Latinos. There was no legal services for Latinos. There were no drug services for Latinos. So the students came here [and] they opened a free clinic in the Fruitvale and that clinic is now La Clínica de la Raza, a $13 million health program. No legal services? Centro Legal de la Raza came in. No HUD services. Arabella [Martinez and the Unity Council] came in. No social services. The Spanish Speaking Citizens Foundation came in. No alcohol and drug services. Narcotics Education League. We all developed within five years of each other. We're all celebrating twenty to thirty years of existence. No other community in Oakland has that history.

Many of the seasoned activists remain in Fruitvale leading community organizations that work to stave off neighborhood decline and improve the lives of residents. In 1993, the concentration of community organizations produced the multiracial and multiethnic Fruitvale Community Collaborative (FCC), a consortium of community-based organizations, schools, churches, businesses, homeowners' associations, and research and planning groups to assess and address community needs (Younis 1998). Although the FCC has disbanded, it is testament to Fruitvale as a center for organizing. Emerging over several decades, these organizations are a stabilizing force for the community.

If Fruitvale emerged as a center for the Latino community, sections of San Antonio became a center for Asian culture and commerce in the 1980s. At this time, numerous Asians and Asian-centered businesses found their way to the flatland section of San Antonio, particularly Southeast Asian refugees. In the 1970s and 1980s federal relocation programs resulted in the dispersal of refugees throughout the United States. In the early to mid-1980s a "second migration" occurred as refugees began to migrate to hospitable metropolitan areas and neighborhoods where Asian goods and services were available (Sugden-Castillo 1996).[7] Many immigrants first moved into Chinatown, but overcrowding and high rents pushed this ethnically diverse Asian population toward Lower San Antonio, with its abundance of large, affordable housing and low land values (Lee 1989: 3). Over time, this population not only contributed to the redevelopment of a once bustling commercial strip, but also organized community organizations to provide health, language, employment, and youth services for its population.

INTEGRATION IN SAN ANTONIO–FRUITVALE

San Antonio–Fruitvale is the fastest growing and most racially and ethnically diverse area in Oakland and the East Bay. According to the 2000 census, San Antonio's population had 47,163 residents; Fruitvale had 57,998 residents. The racial and ethnic composition of the combined population of just over 105,000 was 23 percent African American, 30 percent Asian–Pacific Islander, 33 percent Latino, and 11 percent non-Hispanic white (see Figure 5.1). However, this snapshot of the area's demographics is incomplete. Integration in San Antonio–Fruitvale operates at multiple levels and deserves a more textured analysis.

Unlike most neighborhoods undergoing racial change, San Antonio–Fruitvale did not experience population decline. In fact, since

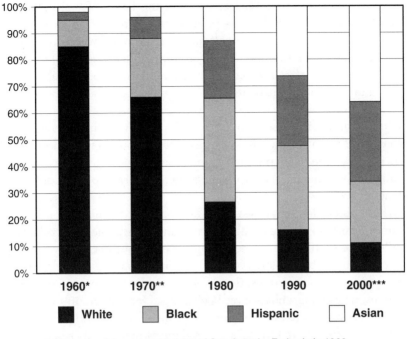

* Other nonwhites comprised 5% of San Antonio–Fruitvale in 1960
** Asians and other nonwhites comprised 12% of San Antonio–Fruitvale in 1970
*** Residents identifying themselves as multiracial comprised 3% of
    San Antonio–Fruitvale in 2000

FIGURE 5.1. Racial composition of San Antonio and Fruitvale, 1960–2000
Source: U.S. Bureau of the Census, STF1

1970, population growth in the two districts outpaced that in every planning district in Oakland. In the 1970s when the city lost population overall, a third of the census tracts that increased in population were located
in San Antonio–Fruitvale (City of Oakland 1994). This growth did not
abate over the next two decades. Between 1980 and 2000, San
Antonio–Fruitvale experienced an unprecedented net increase of 26,652
residents, accounting for nearly half of the 60,153 citywide increase. Thirteen of the eighteen tracts in these two areas experienced growth rates
above 20 percent; eleven tracts grew in excess of 30 percent. Population
increase between 1960 and 2000 ironically followed racial and ethnic
change (see Figure 5.1).

In 1960, over three-quarters of the population in San Antonio–Fruitvale
was white. The percentage of white residents, however, declined in every

subsequent decade, rapidly decreasing in the late 1960s and 1970s—a period in which Oakland's white population was more than halved (Stallone 1993). By 2000, only one-tenth of the population was white. Racial transition, however, did not involve an influx of a single racial or ethnic group. While the African American population grew considerably in the 1960s and 1970s, it declined after 1980. The increase in the number of Latinos and Asians is the real driving force behind the area's racial and ethnic mix. Latinos increased from 8 percent in 1970 to the second-largest group in 1990 (25 percent) to the largest ethnic group of residents (33 percent) in 2000. The Asian population increased in every decade as well and at almost the same pace, comprising approximately 30 percent of the residents in 2000.[8]

These broad demographic trends fail to reflect the nuances necessary to understand the nature of racial change in San Antonio–Fruitvale. First, while white flight has been occurring for over four decades, white residents remain in both districts, albeit for varied reasons. There appear to be two demographic groups. One is older, mostly Italian and Portuguese families, whose households have been around for forty to fifty years. The other is younger, consisting of a mix of professional individuals, couples, and young families. In Fruitvale, you see the former, mainly seniors. "You have pockets of just white people [in Fruitvale]," noted Rosalinda Palacios in our October 24, 1996, interview. "Right behind me there is an entire village of white people. Up here on East Twenty-second Street, right behind me there is a retirement center. They bought up houses, and you know you are going into their block because it says this is not a public road and it is very clean." San Antonio is attractive to the younger group in part because of its proximity to downtown, Lake Merritt, attractive views of the bay, and the presence of large Victorians. Anecdotal and news accounts suggest gentrification by whites is occurring in parts of San Antonio and, to a lesser degree, Fruitvale.[9] However, gentrification is a relative concept. Given the exorbitant cost of housing in the Bay Area, affluent and younger white and minority households have turned to these districts in search of affordable housing. Yet, while housing pressures have brought some whites to San Antonio–Fruitvale, the numbers are neither reversing the decades of white flight nor displacing existing residents.

Racial change in Fruitvale–San Antonio has not been limited to whites. After World War II, Oakland's port expanded for shipbuilding and repair, eventually becoming the Bay Area's most active port. The expansion created a labor shortage that led to active labor recruitment, particularly of southern blacks. As a result, the city's black population grew significantly from 1950 to 1980 (Rhomberg 1996). Blacks found neighborhoods like San Antonio–Fruitvale attractive, and in the 1970s and 1980s African Americans were the largest population groups. This began to change, however, in the 1980s as Latinos and Asians began to move in greater numbers into Fruitvale and San Antonio, respectively. While blacks have undoubtedly migrated out of these districts, a significant number of black families remain.[10] This decline is not altogether surprising, given larger citywide trends of black population loss and out-migration (City of Oakland 1994). The city of Oakland, long considered the center of the "black universe" of the Bay Area, in 2000 experienced black population decrease for the first time since 1860 as job development in neighboring Contra Costa County and other suburban areas drew blacks out of Oakland (Bailey 2001).

Finally, while Latino and Asian growth occurred between 1980 and 2000 in San Antonio–Fruitvale, differences are apparent. For example, the Latino increase was largest in Fruitvale. By 2000, the Fruitvale district was 44 percent Latino, with Lower Fruitvale accounting for most of the growth as immigrants arrived to take advantage of affordable rentals (70 percent of the housing in Lower Fruitvale is rental housing) and social services. By contrast, by 2000 San Antonio's largest racial and ethnic group was Asian (39 percent), as Asian immigrants and refugees migrated from Chinatown. Why did Asians pick San Antonio? "The diversity was in some ways already there, that mix of African American and Hispanics, . . . and they saw that, and I don't know if it was not as fearful than if was into a more black neighborhood," noted Helen Shor in our interview on October 25, 1996. "I think West Oakland may be seen as more of that and I think there might be a little bit of that going on." Also, this influx has been rapid, drawing the attention of residents, organizations, and the media. "Three years ago there were no Asian businesses even as close to across the street from the clinic," Jody Kadimsky, director of La Clínica de la Raza's San Antonio clinic, told me in our November 11, 1996, interview. "Asians have revitalized a lot of the neighborhood by bringing in businesses, buying up the property, building buildings, then bringing in businesses." As in Jackson Heights, the 2000 census reveals that racial change is indeed occurring in Fruitvale–San Antonio. I am skeptical that this will lead to racial transition, given the relatively slow pace of the change and the stake other groups have in the community (as evidenced by the efforts of non-Asian community organizations).

The Geography of Integration

Oakland's physical geography correlates with race and class. The city is geographically divided into the "hills" and "flatlands." Historically, the hills are largely white and affluent, while people of color and low-income households populate the flatlands. The flatlands, or "flats" as they are commonly known, are physically separated from the hills by an imposing stretch of Interstate 580 and, in parts, by MacArthur Boulevard. In many ways, racial and economic disparities are geographically drawn in the dirt. "The tale of the two cities for Oakland is clearly geographical," noted David Glover, a neighborhood activist, in an interview on October 17, 1996. "Some cities talk about the tracks, some cities talk about the freeway, this city talks about its elevation."

This geography of race and class is apparent in San Antonio–Fruitvale. For example, the quality and cost of housing changes significantly as one moves up in elevation. A leader and longtime resident told me in an interview on October 21, 1996: "I looked at homes right here at San Leandro Boulevard and below, and I thought, wow, you can actually get a home for $50,000 to $60,000 down there. They are pretty worn and not well kept. And as you start moving up, you start seeing that pace—it goes [from] 80, 90, 100, 110, 125, and then somewhere between $125,000 and $175,000 is between here [East Fourteenth] and MacArthur Boulevard. Then it just jumps to $200,000, $300,000, . . . and beyond." Also, the closer one gets to East Fourteenth or International Boulevard, the greater the presence of public housing, less desirable property, and impoverished residents.[11] As a result, internal classifications developed. The designations "Upper Fruitvale," "Lower Fruitvale," "Upper San Antonio," and "Lower San Antonio" have emerged to mark socioeconomic differences. And integration in the districts is articulated spatially.

Unlike those in Uptown and Jackson Heights, racial and ethnic groups in San Antonio–Fruitvale are dispersed throughout subareas, with minor exceptions. In 1990, the majority of tracts could be defined as moderately integrated by the Neighborhood Diversity Index, although no single group was a majority. The exceptions include one majority-black tract in Upper San Antonio, two majority-Latino tracts in Lower Fruitvale, and an integrated area bordering MacArthur Boulevard on either side of Fruitvale Avenue. The number of moderately integrated tracts in both communities remained relatively stable during the 1990s (see Map 5.1). Most of San Antonio and the section of Fruitvale above International Boulevard maintained a vibrant multiethnic and multiracial mix. Lower

Fruitvale became decidedly more homogenous in 2000, as recently arrived Latino immigrants entered this area. Fruitvale remains a port of entry for many low-income Latino (particularly Mexican) immigrants. In San Antonio, the predominantly African American section became more diverse with an increase in Asian and Hispanic residents. While most of San Antonio's subareas saw an increase in Asian residents, only one section became majority Asian in the mid- to late 1990s. In fact, Asians largely concentrated in five tracts in Lower San Antonio, extending north to roughly East Twenty-seventh Street and east to Twenty-third Avenue. The area gained 8,045 Asian residents in the 1980s and an additional 2,268 in the 1990s.

While such pockets of homogeneity exist, for the most part integration

MAP 5.1.   San Antonio and Fruitvale districts, Oakland, 2000; Geography of San Antonio and Fruitvale's integration by Census Tract

extends the various subareas of San Antonio–Fruitvale, as census numbers show. For example, in 1980 seven of the combined eighteen tracts were comprised of a clear racial and ethnic majority. By 2000, only four of the eighteen had such a majority. Community leaders confirmed these spatial trends, suggesting that even through a few subareas are dominated by one group, housing in San Antonio–Fruitvale is integrated on a block-by-block basis. "You should see my block," one leader told me in an interview on October 10, 1996. "I live in San Antonio, . . . [and] my side of the street goes Asian, black, white, black, then white, then an Asian-white couple, and then an apartment complex where there is a whole bunch of people. Across the street, there's an apartment complex with all Mexicans and then there's one with blacks and whites." From this one of several testimonials, it is clear that racial and ethnic groups are more evenly spread throughout the community, and some suggest that the diverse housing patterns create a greater opportunity for physical and social integration. As a teacher at Roosevelt Junior High School said in our October 31, 1996, interview: "[Groups] cannot claim the whole area, because you've got everybody living in that area. Every area of Oakland you've got Asians, Hispanics, and blacks." This appears to be a factor in getting groups to work together.

Ethnic Heterogeneity

Like those of Uptown and Jackson Heights, San Antonio–Fruitvale's racial and ethnic composition is a polyglot of ethnic groups and cultural traditions. Immigration has a lot to do with this mix. In the 1990s, Oakland and the East Bay in general were one of the top destinations for legal immigrants to the United States. Indeed, more than half of the 18,000 persons who came from abroad and settled in Oakland since 1985 did so in one of three communities: Chinatown, San Antonio, and Fruitvale (Younis 1998). In 2000, 43 percent of residents of San Antonio–Fruitvale were foreign born (the city average is 27 percent). While Lower San Antonio and Lower Fruitvale had the greatest number of foreign-born residents, every tract had percentages above the city average. Foreign-born residents are new to both Oakland and the United States: a third of those in San Antonio–Fruitvale entered the United States sometime after 1990 and two-thirds are noncitizens. This is not surprising given that immigrants are moving to a community where not only can they speak their language and find stores stocking familiar food, but also they have ready access to affordable housing, low-skill jobs, and social services (Marcucci 2002).

The immigrant influx has created a unique blend of cultures in which broad racial and ethnic categories like Latino and Asian fail to capture the ethnic heterogeneity of the area. For example, Latinos in San Antonio–Fruitvale are an ethnically diverse group. By and large, Oakland, and thus San Antonio–Fruitvale, has a very large Mexican community with strong historical ties to different parts of Mexico. It is not surprising that 80 percent of the 24,000 Latino residents living in the two districts are of Mexican heritage.[12] The two districts also have sizable Puerto Rican, Guatemalan, and Salvadorian communities. This mix is visible in local Catholic churches. Father Ignatius DeGroot, pastor of St. Elizabeth's Church in Lower Fruitvale, notes that while Latino parishioners are predominantly Mexican, there are also members from Cuba, Puerto Rico, and El Salvador. The church serves to unite these diverse ethnic and national groups. "You see, this is another thing that most people who are white don't realize," said Father DeGroot in our October 17, 1996, interview. "There is also a real diversity among the Hispanics. My Cubans and Puerto Ricans don't consider themselves Mexicans or South Americans, and Salvadorians don't consider themselves Mexican. And they would not mix in the same way [outside of the church], but they do mix in the church."

Another important divide in the San Antonio–Fruitvale Latino community is based on immigration status and culture. On the one hand, as mentioned, a significant number of Central American and Mexican immigrants moved into both communities, particularly Lower Fruitvale. Many of the newly arrived immigrants are monolingual and endure an uncertain reality as undocumented residents.[13] On the other hand, Latinos who are distinctly Chicano or Mexican American populate the district. These third- or fourth-generation immigrants are obviously more acculturated than recently arrived Latino immigrants. The census most likely counts this group as Hispanic, yet they maintain a unique place in U.S. culture. "We can move into a white culture and speak the language," noted an informant in our interview on October 24, 1996. "We could move into the Mexican culture and speak the language." There is, however, a cultural divide between Chicanos and the larger Mexican population—differences in the foods each group eats, how they dress, and even how they address people. Many of the Chicanos living in Fruitvale, for example, have ties to Chicano-identity movements that began in the late 1960s and 1970s, and are now running local Latino-based community organizations.

Ethnic heterogeneity is also visible among the Asian population. Currently, there are over 30,000 Asian residents in the districts. The umbrella Asian category masks an internal diversity that is split between Chinese (49 percent), Filipino (15 percent), Vietnamese (14 percent), Cambodian (8 percent), and Laotian (7 percent) residents. Smaller numbers of Japanese and Korean residents round out the Asian population. Also, each district has a different Asian population. In San Antonio, Chinese residents are the largest Asian population group (58 percent), followed by Vietnamese and then smaller numbers of Filipino, Laotian, and Cambodian residents. In Fruitvale, there is no majority ethnic Asian group, although Chinese (35 percent) and Filipino (24 percent) residents are the largest groups. A good number of Asian residents in both districts are refugees from Southeast Asia, most of whom are poor, who settled in the flatlands of both districts, particularly Lower San Antonio (Payton 1999). Given this mix, there is a dizzying array of languages spoken here, estimated at more than twenty, and English is not always one of them. In fact, a quarter of Lower San Antonio residents speak very little English, and most residents speak another language in addition to English.[14]

The multiethnic and integrated character of both districts is visible in local public schools. Figure 5.2 displays the racial breakdown of all public schools within the two CCDs from 1984 to 1999.[15] In the mid-1980s, the majority of students in San Antonio–Fruitvale public schools were African American. In the early 1990s, the number of Latino and Asian students began increasing, and by 1999 the majority of students were Asian (36 percent), Latino (34 percent), or African American (27 percent). The percentage of white students in local schools has been negligible for almost two decades. The districts' schools are internally diverse, as a single racial or ethnic group dominates only six of the fifteen schools. Most schools have a balanced number of students from different racial and ethnic backgrounds, with the exception of white students. The mix creates a unique educational environment, particularly in terms of language. In 2001, 46.4 percent of San Antonio–Fruitvale students were classified as "limited English proficient" compared to 28.5 percent for the district (Oakland Unified School District 2003). In addition, 58.5 percent of area school students are "English Language Learners"; the city average is 42.9 percent.[16] These numbers are brought to life when we consider Garfield Elementary in San Antonio. At this school, of "910 students, 368 are Spanish-speakers, 84 speak Mien, 81 speak Cantonese, 73 speak Khmer, 59 speak Vietnamese, 15 speak Lao, 13 speak Tagalog, six speak Arabic, four speak Tongan, one speaks Farsi and one speaks Bosnian. The

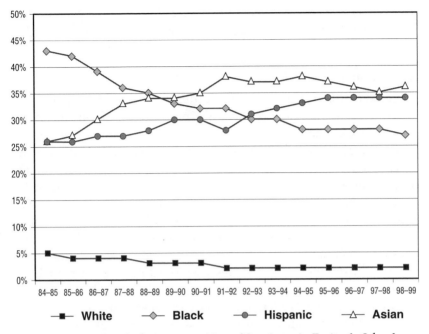

FIGURE 5.2.   Racial and ethnic composition of San Antonio-Fruitvale Schools,
1984–1998
  Source: U.S. Department of Education. 2000. National Center for Education
Statistics. Common Core of Data program. Public Elementary/Secondary School
Universe Survey Data. [http://nces.ed.gov/ccd/]

rest—African Americans, for the most part, and one white student—are
native English speakers" (Marech 2002). Garfield offers bilingual instruc-
tion in nine languages. The ethnic heterogeneity at Garfield illustrates the
complexity of understanding the area's integration.

   While it is common to marvel at the diversity of area schools, there are
obvious costs associated with this mix. Operating nine bilingual programs and having so many students lacking basic language skills can
seriously strain school resources that are used in other schools for other
pedagogical activities. This is a salient issue, given that San
Antonio–Fruitvale students score below average on California Standards
Tests for reading, language, and mathematics. In 2001, 24 percent of students scored above average on the Stanford-9 test for reading, 30 percent
for language, and 39 percent for math (Oakland Unified School District
2001). These scores are significantly below the averages for the state and
the County of Alameda. While many factors figure in to underperform-

ing schools, it seems legitimate to consider the resource pressure that these schools face with such a high percentage of immigrants and English Language Learners.

Economic and Social Diversity

Integration in San Antonio–Fruitvale differs from that in diverse-by-design communities and even that in Uptown and Jackson Heights. In the former communities, a noticeable and usually quite vocal middle-class group of residents is present, shaping land-use decisions and neighborhood identity, and preventing neighborhood destabilization through physical and economic development. Their presence, however, has led at times to class conflict. Such conflict is relatively absent in San Antonio–Fruitvale, as these are "predominantly working class communities with a rich racial and ethnic mix, sharing a reality of limited economic resources" (Younis 1998: 225). The income and housing indicators for San Antonio–Fruitvale support this characterization. Even though the communities have retained some affluent residents and managed to avoid the deprivation suffered in other parts of Oakland, economic and housing disparities make these areas less than glamorous. San Antonio–Fruitvale lacks the middle-class shine of other bastions of racial and ethnic integration. This reality prompted one researcher to remark that "middle-class liberalism as the basis for multicultural/ethnic diversity should not be sought here" (ibid.).

Socioeconomic indicators indeed portray San Antonio–Fruitvale as working-class. The combined median income of the districts was $34,776 in 2000, compared to $96,644 for Oakland Hills and $56,285 for the City of Alameda, the northern and southern communities bordering San Antonio–Fruitvale. And while the median income in both districts has increased since 1980, according to Urban Strategies Council files, other socioeconomic indicators dampen any promise of an economic turn-around for residents. For example, 28 percent of the area households had incomes under $20,000; 21 percent of the residents received some form of public assistance; 44 percent of households had incomes below $30,000; and per capita income is approximately $15,248, well below the city average of $21,936. In addition, education attainment is not high: nearly 60 percent of adults earned no more than a high school diploma. This is significant, as the loss of low-skill manufacturing jobs in Oakland over the last two decades has left many residents scrambling to secure decent-paying jobs (Applied Research Center 1996). Finally, these socioeconomic disparities are reflected in San Antonio–Fruitvale's geography. For example, the per capita income in the area's tracts ranges from a low of $9,730 to a high of $33,604. Tracts with the lowest per capita incomes are in Lower San Antonio and Lower Fruitvale—the flats—and a third of households in Lower San Antonio and Lower Fruitvale earn less than $25,000 (the median for the city is $40,055). A similar trend is found when examining educational attainment and households receiving public assistance.[17]

Homeownership, a popular indicator of socioeconomic status, is considerably lower in San Antonio–Fruitvale (27 percent) than the city average (41 percent). And in 2000 San Antonio's rate of homeownership (21 percent) was much lower than Fruitvale's (35 percent). Within the districts there are also significant differences. Three-quarters of the housing in Lower San Antonio is rental, with some sections approaching 90 percent. Rates of homeownership increase in San Antonio as one nears MacArthur Boulevard to the north. In Fruitvale, homeownership rates are much higher, although the range of homeownership is between 20 and 51 percent. As in San Antonio, homeownership relates to geography. Almost a third of the housing in Lower Fruitvale is rental, while housing in Upper Fruitvale is at least 40 percent homeowner.

Housing market activity confirms San Antonio–Fruitvale's working-class status. In general, the Bay Area housing market is quite strong and housing values, even in places like Fruitvale, are extremely high (Christiansen 1998). Table 5.1 displays the distribution of home-mortgage loans in San Antonio–Fruitvale from 1992 to 1998 by race, income, and subarea. The data reveal real estate expansion in the two districts over the decade, as the volume of originated loans jumped in the early 1990s and again in 1997 and 1998; 89 percent of those loans went toward home purchase. Not surprisingly, the largest percentage of mortgage loans went to Asian home buyers (38 percent), primarily in the San Antonio district. This trend coincides with the rising Asian population in San Antonio and in western Fruitvale. Whites continued to purchase homes at a rate greater than their demographic presence, particularly in the northern section of San Antonio (next to Lake Merritt and below I-580) and around north Fruitvale Avenue. Hispanics and blacks continued to purchase housing in the area, though at lower rates than Asians and whites. Given the size of the Latino population in both districts, the relatively meager share of mortgage loans going to Latinos is surprising. The most plausible explanation is that longtime Latino residents purchased homes much earlier, and the Latinos driving the population increase are newly arrived immigrants, lacking the capital to purchase homes.

TABLE 5.1.   Residential Lending Patterns by Race, Class, and Type—
San Antonio/Fruitvale, 1992–1998: Mortgage Loans Reported from
Home Mortgage Disclosure Act

	Fiscal Year							
	1992	1993	1994	1995	1996	1997	1998	1992–98
Total Loans*	376	406	449	378	444	530	646	3,229
$ of Loans**	$59,757	$65,468	$69,108	$46,236	$61,402	$68,781	$93,363	$464,115
Race								
White	24%	23%	18%	16%	20%	19%	25%	21%
Black	9%	14%	12%	14%	13%	15%	15%	13%
Hispanic	10%	13%	17%	23%	23%	18%	20%	18%
Asian	46%	41%	43%	41%	35%	38%	31%	38%
Income as % of MSA Median Income								
<51%	6%	13%	14%	17%	6%	12%	7%	10%
51–80%	13%	33%	30%	34%	31%	28%	24%	29%
81–95%	14%	10%	12%	11%	13%	7%	9%	11%
96–120%	17%	11%	12%	13%	15%	14%	17%	14%
>120%	23%	17%	16%	17%	21%	27%	32%	23%
% Loans by Subarea								
Lower San Antonio†	9%	9%	13%	15%	13%	12%	9%	11%
Upper San Antonio	31%	32%	30%	25%	27%	29%	32%	30%
Lower Fruitvale††	14%	10%	13%	10%	13%	18%	17%	14%
Upper Fruitvale	45%	50%	43%	51%	46%	40%	42%	45%
Total $ of Loans by Subarea								
Lower San Antonio	$6,234	$6,683	$9,262	$5,923	$7,618	$8,740	$8,892	$53,352
Upper San Antonio	$29,365	$29,113	$33,583	$19,761	$23,681	$31,169	$39,963	$206,635
Lower Fruitvale	$5,756	$7,001	$7,895	$3,551	$6,712	$10,125	$14,266	$55,306
Upper Fruitvale	$19,995	$24,544	$21,386	$19,921	$25,378	$22,186	$31,933	$165,343

*Excludes home improvement or refinancing lending activity.
**In thousands.
†Defined as southwestern half of the district—Lake Merritt to north, 28th Ave. to south; Oakland Estuary to west, E. 22nd St. to east.
††Defined as southeastern half of the district—28th Ave.to north, High St. to south; Oakland Estuary to west, Foothill Blvd. to east.
Source: Right to Know Network (RTK) [http://www.rtk.net]; Federal Financial Institutions Examination Council, Federal Reserve, Washington, D.C.

The data suggest that mortgage money was not simply going to the more affluent San Antonio–Fruitvale residents. Between 1992 and 1998, borrowers with incomes at 51–80 percent of the metropolitan median income ($47,516) received the most mortgage loans in San Antonio–Fruitvale. As a result, some scholars analyzing these trends labeled Fruitvale as a "just-right" community—one that provides low- to moderate-income borrowers a "toehold on homeownership," while maintaining the area as affordable and holding gentrification forces at bay (Wyly et al. 2000).[18] This moniker is not entirely accurate, as affordability is not evenly spread throughout the area. As Table 5.1 illustrates, while three-quarters of loans during the period were originated in Upper San Antonio and Upper Fruitvale, only a quarter went to the flatlands; year in and year out, four-fifths of all mortgage dollars flowed into the upper portions of San Antonio–Fruitvale, where levels of homeownership and income are higher (excluding one flatland tract adjacent to Lake Merritt). In fact, while home buying is increasing and no one group is receiving the majority of loans, few residents and families can afford homes, as property values and rents have increased dramatically.[19] "I have to say that it is not cheap to live in Oakland," one lifelong Fruitvale resident and activist told me on October 21, 1996. "I have a lot of friends that I've gone to school with, many of whom still come and work in the area, who want to be here, but very few can afford to buy a home here. A lot of working couples can't get the house they want, . . . and if you want to make a jump up, it is a real challenge to be able to get a home."

For many working families, incomes did not keep pace with rising property values. For example, 42 percent of Oakland households in 1990 spent more than 30 percent of their income to meet housing needs, either in rent or in costs associated with homeownership (Sugden-Castillo 1996). The burden of high housing costs in San Antonio–Fruitvale is dramatic. In fourteen of the eighteen tracts, 45 percent or more households were spending more than 30 percent of their monthly income on housing (City of Oakland 1994). The situation is particularly stark for renters. Oakland vacancy rates are at their lowest point since 1980, and rents and eviction rates are skyrocketing. In 1996, rents jumped 13.3 percent and most Oakland tenants paid an average of $1,003 per month, the third highest in the nation, creating a rent burden for residents (Thompson 1996). For example, 48 percent of San Antonio renters are paying more than 30 percent of their income on rent. This disproportionately affects the poor, as close to 80 percent of low-income ($20,000 or less) households are rent burdened. Thus, renters find it difficult to transition into homeownership without leaving for East Oakland or outlying suburbs.

With rent and mortgage burdens, low incomes, and low educational attainment, it is not surprising that there is overcrowded housing and schools. Surprisingly, while these are the fastest-growing areas in the city, little construction is occurring. The lament of overcrowded housing conditions in the districts is a persistent theme among community leaders. "You'll find that San Antonio and Fruitvale are the source of the cheapest housing and the most overcrowded parts of the city," one leader told me on October 23, 1996. As a result of overcrowded rental housing, population density, at 9,380 residents per square mile, is the highest in the city (Paoli 2000). In the 1980s, 655 net housing units were added to San Antonio–Fruitvale, while their combined population rose by over 16,000 persons (City of Oakland 1994). No tract gained more than 99 units, while some individual tracts saw population increases in the thousands. Thus, overcrowding is a serious problem.

Since 1980, housing costs, both in terms of rent and home prices, have outpaced income growth. This has led some families to live in very crowded buildings and apartments. Quantitative measures indicate that the area contains disproportionate numbers of overcrowded and severely overcrowded housing.[20] Overcrowded units as a percentage of all rental and ownership units in the two districts in 2000 were twice those found in Oakland (33.2 percent and 17.8 percent respectively). Overcrowding is spread throughout the communities, with some exceptions. Two tracts adjacent to Lake Merritt are not overcrowded, while Lower San Antonio and Lower Fruitvale face the greatest overcrowding, with the percentage of overcrowded units ranging between 37 and 56 percent. Rental housing is the worst, as a third of all units are overcrowded (higher than the city average). The most serious rental overcrowding occurs in the flatland areas—44 percent of units.

Qualitative data illustrate the overcrowding situation. "One of the common phenomena that I hear—of course this is not families, but young guys that come from Mexico—seven or eight will rent an apartment together, you know, will basically have a sleeping bag on the floor," a Catholic priest who serves both districts told me on October 17, 1996. "And most houses here have two or three families living in them, two or three families in the garage, in the apartments." Illegally converted housing contributes to overcrowding and speaks to the economic situation of many San Antonio–Fruitvale residents. A Chicana resident told me on October 24, 1996, of attempting to rent a large four-bedroom, two-bathroom house in Fruitvale for herself and her son. Initially, the landlord was skeptical when she inquired about the house, repeatedly quizzing her to ensure that she would not move another family into the house. Apparently, the last tenant moved eight other people in, placed a phone jack in every room, and rented each room for five hundred dollars, living and dining room included. Equally troublesome stories abound, and not just in residential buildings.

School buildings are just as overcrowded in San Antonio–Fruitvale. These fast-growing districts contain a disproportionate number of young people. Nearly a third of the population is under eighteen years of age, with a large number of teenagers. This puts pressure on public school facilities. In fact, Oakland Unified School District data reveal that all elementary schools in this area exceeded the capacity for which the schools were built. In the late 1980s and early 1990s, the school board responded by converting eleven elementary schools to year-round schedules (Bazeley 1995). The district hoped to ease overcrowding without building any new schools by using the campuses all year, including the summers, and rotating students on staggered schedules. This plan is problematic in that schools are able to accept new students until the campus has again reached overcrowded conditions. Allendale Elementary, built for 580 students, now operates for 780. At Jefferson Elementary, 1,200 students are packed into a campus designed for 750, with the overflow spilling into portable classrooms. As a result, students are forced to share deteriorating bathrooms, a single eating area, and overcrowded and rundown playgrounds; at times, children in the same family do not have the same vacation time because of the staggered schedules (Olszewski 1995). Fortunately, the Oakland Unified School District responded by planning the construction of two new schools and playing fields on the site of the old Montgomery Ward building on International Boulevard (Gammon 1999).

Stable and Accepted but Unplanned Integration

As in other diverse-by-circumstance communities, integration in San Antonio–Fruitvale appears to be stable, accepted, and unplanned. As racial change began, reactions did not involve violent protest or rapid racial transition. White flight occurred in the 1960s and 1970s, while black flight occurred in the 1980s and 1990s. Yet as Latinos and Asians entered, many whites and blacks remained. While the size of the latter groups diminished, there is little evidence that white or black flight was a result of the entry of Latinos and Asians. Integration in San Antonio–Fruitvale developed without conscious or goal-oriented action by leaders to stop racial transition and promote integration. As we will see, maintaining integration has never been a primary goal for community organizations; none has adopted an overt pro-integration stance or mission. In fact, while groups collaborate, most community-based organizations developed around serving particular racial or ethnic groups, for example, Spanish Speaking Citizens Foundation, La Clínica de la Raza, and East Bay Asian Local Community Development Corporation. San Antonio–Fruitvale's multiethnic, multiracial, and mixed-income character resulted from a variety of processes not directly related to community organizing. In other words, integration is more an outcome of these processes. Immigrants, minorities, and low-income residents were attracted to the large supply of affordable housing and necessary social service agencies. In Fruitvale, the presence of Latino organizations and services targeting Spanish-speaking individuals attracted newly arrived immigrants. In San Antonio, the arrival of refugees in the early 1980s and overcrowding in Chinatown found the lower section of the district affordable and a site for the development of organizations and businesses serving a variety of Asian ethnic groups. Working families and even some middle-class residents also found Upper San Antonio's and Upper Fruitvale's housing stock affordable and attractive. And no one group has dominated the districts, though San Antonio has a larger Asian presence and Fruitvale a Latino one. There might be some racial and ethnic reshuffling occurring, but not resegregation. Leaders echo this sentiment.

"This neighborhood will always be diverse, but then I think the demographics will change," Don Davenport, director of the San Antonio Community Development Corporation, told me in our 1996 interview. "The Asian population will probably grow more but . . . it will always be a diverse community." Finally, the unplanned integration in San Antonio–Fruitvale has positively affected social and organizational relations. As noted, the multiethnic-multiracial character of the area extends to the block level, and this is encouraging social integration. The residential proximity of various racial and ethnic groups seems to foster a degree of acceptance and appreciation for the diverse mix of residents, even if it is not on an everyday or overt level. In turn, this dramatically impacts how neighborhood organizing around political and economic issues occurs. "There is a level of basic cultural familiarity that diffuses an awful lot of the typical tension," noted David Glover in our 1996 interview. "You really do see people naturally as neighbors come together around neighborhood concerns. It is not unusual to be at a meeting on East Fourteenth off of Seminary where there's a Portuguese, an Asian, a Latino, a white, and a black person in a room discussing the common problems of the neighborhood." And the extent of the racial and ethnic mix almost forces people to work across racial or ethnic lines to solve neighborhood problems or enhance the quality of life in the area. "I think again that there is so much to learn from each culture and there's such a strength and such richness in the art and the food and the culture, . . . so I think that is a positive thing," Jane Garcia, executive director of La Clínica de la Raza, said in our April 11, 2000, interview. "And not only that, but we have no choice. This is the way it is, and it is going to continue to be more diverse and so we might as well get used to it and see the beauty of it." Thus, these groups are not taking conscious pro-integrative positions, yet the diversity forces them to work together to improve the neighborhood. Various ethnically centered community organizations have taken the lead in meeting shared needs, negotiating competing cultural interests, and improving multicultural understanding. These organizing efforts are vital in stabilizing the racial and ethnic mix in San Antonio–Fruitvale.

SUSTAINING INTEGRATION BY COMMUNITY DEVELOPMENT

The story of maintaining integration in San Antonio–Fruitvale is one of a three-decade effort to strengthen residents' civic capacity. Unlike Uptown or Jackson Heights, where integration maintenance pivoted on balancing the needs of different groups, sustaining integration in these districts involves community-building efforts undertaken by varied local organizations, from advocating for strong institutional supports and building the capacity of residents to participate in local planning and decision making to technical assistance and management of revitalization efforts. Most communities do not have a number of community groups serving disparate segments; thus the challenge involves getting multiethnic-multiracial groups to work together toward neighborhood renewal and keep the "area balanced instead of a swing in the balance," as one resident put it in an October 17, 1996, interview. Such collaborations must be cultivated and require strong leadership. In San Antonio–Fruitvale, organizations of this type exist, although they are not explicitly promoting integration. In less conscious ways, however, groups are involved in preserving the racial and ethnic mix, largely through collaborations with other community groups. Key to San Antonio–Fruitvale's success as stable multiracial and multiethnic communities are local groups reaching across racial and ethnic boundaries to maintain housing, spark and encourage economic development, provide services to immigrants or low-income groups, and create youth programs. These initiatives provide meaningful opportunities for diverse groups to engage in new ways and to become conscious of each other and of the unique character of the community. Such efforts also recast the image of the areas from marginal and transitory to vibrant and attractive places to live and work.

There are two key elements that apply to multicultural collaborations in San Antonio–Fruitvale. First, data indicate that social integration largely occurs among student groups and through conscious attempts at interaction among service providers and community organizers. Second, few organizations are multiracial or multicultural in those they serve. In fact, no group's mission involves promoting integration for integration's sake. Groups are focused around specific issues and serve single racial or ethnic populations, at least in terms of their mission and the grant-funded programs they offer. In our October 23, 1996, interview, Victor Rubin, generally regarded as an expert on Oakland neighborhoods, framed it this way:

> My sense is that organizations get created by particular ethnic groups or racial categories of people and then they run the organizations in a multiethnic, multiracial way; . . . the predominant style of operating is that you start with one ethnic base but you operate in recognition of diversity; . . . for example, the East Bay Asian Local Development Corporation goes out of its way to do joint ventures with organizations in the black community, has a multiracial staff and board of directors. The Native American Health Center, something like 50 to 60 percent of its clients are people who are not Native American. The Spanish Speaking Unity Council is again a multiracial staff, takes on projects that serve multiple races, even though they define themselves as a Latino leadership organization. I would say that there are many—though certainly not all—organizations in those two neighborhoods that are explicitly multiracial in the approach that they take, coming from the starting point of having grown out of the civil rights movement in one ethnic group or another. I would also say a few, like the San Antonio Community Development Corporation or Oakland Community Organizations, are multiethnic or multiracial in their makeup.

Thus, the local organizational structure and focus are similar to Uptown's: local groups developed out of the civil rights movement to serve specific groups. These two districts, particularly Fruitvale, maintain a unique history, as Chicano activists developed organizations in the 1960s and 1970s to serve Latinos. As Asians moved into Lower San Antonio, leaders formed Asian-centered organizations. For African Americans, several large churches and social service agencies serve as anchors. Over time these organizations became well established and quite successful. Yet demographic changes—particularly the growth of the Asian population and the multiethnic/multiracial mix—require organizations to reevaluate their focus and operation to involve multiethnic and multiracial organizing through collaborations.

San Antonio–Fruitvale organizations reach out in a way that one wouldn't necessarily expect, as multicultural coalitions offer services, programs, and advocacy to residents of various backgrounds. If there are conscious attempts at promoting integration, it happens when service providers and community-development people decide to work together, particularly around land-use planning and service provision. "Latino organizations don't work in isolation," noted Jose Arredondo, director of the Spanish Speaking Citizens Foundation, in our interview on November 3, 1999. "We work with several African American groups, Asian groups; we have a joint program with Lao Family. We have another joint training program with Allied Fellowship Services, which serves primarily African Americans. We network quite a bit, . . . La Clínica, Unity Council, the same thing. There's a lot of partnering collaborative joint ventures outside your own group; it is impossible to isolate yourselves." Collaboration became more necessary as Asian migrants, particularly low-income refugees, entered San Antonio and subareas in Fruitvale. Collaboration not only prevents fighting over grant dollars and duplicating services, but also maximizes the effectiveness of action.

Such collaboration is important in a city like Oakland. In the 1970s and 1980s, when white corporate leaders disinvested in Oakland, the tax base eroded, revitalization stalled, and the city's dependence on (dwindling) private investment increased (Rhomberg 2004). As a result, Oakland lags behind other Bay Area cities in investment dollars, economic development, and job creation.[21] Thus, nonprofit agencies drive much of the development and revitalization at the neighborhood level. This is particularly true in San Antonio–Fruitvale, where there is a strong network of nonprofit agencies. This can work well, however, only if there is collaboration among the agencies. As Jane Garcia, executive director of La Clínica de la Raza, noted in our 2000 interview:

> You know the community-based organizations drive a lot of the economic development in both these districts, and so there is a fair amount of collaboration, say, between the East Bay Asian Local Development Corporation and the Spanish Speaking Unity Council. And if you look at the housing development that the Unity Council has done, there's a lot of diversity in the residents. Just recently there was a joint proposal submitted between the two corporations, so there is a lot of synergy that way too. The same with us and Asian Health Services, and part of it has been because they are in Chinatown, but we are in close proximity, . . . and it has been done in a way that it has built upon both of the organizations' strengths and we have also submitted a number of proposals jointly. Asian Health Services has a language bank that we use on a regular basis.

Such collaborations are necessary in a community so desperate for social services. Health care, affordable housing, quality youth services, and economic development are needs shared by all groups. Thus, groups cannot work in isolation on these projects if for no other reason than the people using the services will be multiethnic and multiracial.

The ethnic-specific focus raises questions for organizations about whether to remain narrowly focused or to broaden out to serve multiracial and multiethnic populations living in the area. This is not an easy decision. In our October 14, 1996, interview, David Kakashiba, director of the East Bay Asian Youth Center (EBAYC), explained:

> We don't [make a strong effort to promote integration]. I mean there are different ways of looking at it. I think that some of our advocacy work is along those lines, in trying to really take a look at the big picture and act on the big picture, where I think a lot of organizations similar to us will just simply think of their own narrow organizational and ethnic self-interest. On another level though, we talk about whether this center here and our programs should move beyond just the Asian population. It's not an Asian neighborhood. It is everybody's neighborhood and therefore we should broaden out. We have debates about that internally, and for those who don't want to do that there is a lot of fear . . . that Asians will lose out because when people talk about race and need, they talk about white or black. Asians are not a part of it. Or Latinos.

EBAYC is not the only group raising this concern. La Clínica, a historically Latino-centered health clinic, struggles with a common question, according to a local informant I interviewed on November 11, 1996: "Are we a Latino organization and only serve that, or are we a more health-oriented organization and serve whatever comes in the neighborhood?" Many non-Latino residents do not use La Clínica's services because they do not see it serving them. In the last decade, La Clínica addressed this issue by opening a San Antonio clinic, which serves a multiethnic client base. While half the patients are monolingual Spanish-speaking residents, a third are a diverse group of Asians (Cambodian, Mien, Vietnamese, and Laotian, among others). A trilingual staff runs the clinic for both populations. However, most agencies in Fruitvale–San Antonio have addressed this issue by collaborating with other agencies or by developing the capacity to serve and advocate for multiracial or multiethnic populations while remaining ethnically identified.

Multiethnic collaborations are key to stabilizing San Antonio–Fruitvale, as groups are building residents' civic capacity and engaging in necessary community-development projects. The organizing is more abstract than confrontational. As Helen Shor of East Bay Asian Local Development Corporation (EBALDC) noted in our 1996 interview: "What we do is facilitate different people with different interests to come together and work on a project to the point where it becomes self-sufficient." Collaborations take planning, and they are necessary for integrated communities in order to meet the needs of residents, stem decline, and in the process bring groups together to see their common fate. There are tangible efforts made to improve the community and in the process bring diverse groups together. Community-development efforts are central to challenging not only the image of San Antonio–Fruitvale as less desirable communities, but also the image of integration as temporary and unworkable. The collaborative nature of such efforts also offers a model of multicultural organizing, illustrating that racial and ethnic groups share common needs and can work together to improve the quality of life for everyone.

Youth Development

Understanding youth organizing and development programs in San Antonio–Fruitvale requires an appreciation of larger citywide forces. In the 1980s, Oakland was hit hard by both high employment and crack cocaine. At the neighborhood level most of the problems came not from drug use but from drug dealing. Violent crime rose; by 1990, the city had one of the highest per capita murder rates in the country. Young people were increasingly drawn into the drug business, frequently as victims and perpetrators of the seamy side of the drug trade. Not all young people were involved in the drug business; however, they all suffered from the city's response: increased police activity. Instead of focusing on some of the fundamental issues, such as education, employment, opportunity, or enrichment, the city and its police force turned to punitive actions such as random searches, harassment, crackdowns on cruising, and curfews (Themba 1999: 71). The city put into effect a cruising law under which youths could be cited and fined if they drove past a certain point more than twice in a four-hour period. Two other proposals targeting youths were put before the City Council: an antiloitering and a curfew law. Under the antiloitering law, youths could be arrested for being within six feet of a suspected drug dealer or in an area known for drug dealing, and even for running from a cop. The curfew law, proposed in 1995, would allow police to stop any young persons after 9:00 P.M.; if they couldn't prove they were eighteen years of age or had a valid reason for being out, they could be held in a detention center. Both proposals were defeated through youth organizing (S. Woods 1996). "The City of Oakland, three times, has tried to pass a curfew and we have defeated it," Rosalinda Palacios told me on November 1, 2000. "They [the police] did not want black kids hanging out on the streets of Oakland because it scares people." These practices gave the impression that kids in Oakland were not only living under martial law, but were all-too-often blamed for the outcomes of bad policies. For many youths, there was a feeling of being devalued. "All of these laws do not go toward a better future for the youth," writes Semion Woods, a youth activist with Youth of Oakland United. "Why would you put your future behind bars and make all kinds of laws to send them there?" (S. Woods 1996: 5).

The legacy of police reactions to youth is made worse by the reality that the San Antonio and Fruitvale districts are the fastest-growing areas in the city, contain a disproportionate number of youths, and lack open space, recreational centers, and programs for kids. As noted, roughly one-third of San Antonio–Fruitvale's population is under eighteen years of age. This works out to over thirty thousand adolescents and teenagers in need of programs, open space, and nondeviant alternatives, all of which are lacking. The open space issue is serious. A recent report noted that San Antonio had 0.78 acres of park–school yard area per one thousand residents, one-fifth the city standard (EBALDC 1997). "I have to take my children out of the area to play, . . . and other people do that," said Noel Gallo, lifelong Fruitvale resident and Oakland Unified School District Board member, in our October 19, 1996, interview. "Within Oakland there is certain spaces that we go to play soccer, play baseball, basketball, but they are very limited." In addition, those that exist are in bad shape, forcing youths to find other alternatives. "They [area parks] are nothing; . . . they're small and they're trashed," David Kakashiba of EBAYC told me in our 1996 interview. "Thus, kids play in the alleys and the streets. There is probably a consensus among a lot of different people that there is a real lack." The availability of green and open space for residents, particularly young residents, is a public health indicator. San Antonio–Fruitvale lags behind other parts of the city and behind neighborhoods in other cities.

The dismal state of youth development also centers on child-care concerns and youth programming. First, there is a lack of organized and licensed daycare facilities or programs for preschool children. For example, according to BANANAS, a child-care referral agency, only eighty-nine slots are available for primary-aged children living in San Antonio (EBALDC 1997). This is woefully inadequate given the size of San Antonio's youth population. In addition, according to a recent report on welfare to work, most low-income residents reveal that the lack of accessible, safe, and affordable child care is a significant barrier to their entering the work force and taking advantage of opportunities (Spain 1998). Few residents report using child-care centers; instead they rely on family, neighbors, or other informal networks. With elementary schools operating on year-round schedules, many young people are left unattended and lack a stimulating educational environment. The result is that a large percentage of children is being supervised poorly or through informal networks in less than stimulating environments. "For most kids in the flatlands there are very few day-care centers, so [El Centro] is like where they come because there is nobody at home," Rosalinda Palacios told me in 1996. "I mean, latchkey kids get to go home and watch TV and there's food. In these kids' homes, there is nothing. Nothing!" Groups in the area, such as EBALDC and the San Antonio Community Development Corporation, are pushing for more "opportunities for families to find high-quality day-care for their children," which could range from licensing home-based providers and grandparent training to cooperatively owned and managed day-care facilities (ibid.). At this writing, little headway has been made in this regard.

Second, the presence and funding of youth programs in San Antonio–Fruitvale are limited and cannot possibly serve the needs of the youths in the area. Neither district has a YMCA, Boy's Club, or Girl Scouts, which could provide year-round recreational activities found in other communities. "If you want to find a basketball league or game you could hunt yourself down one, but it is not something that is accessible, . . . that everyone does," said Danny HoSang, former director of People United for a Better Oakland (PUEBLO), in our October 11, 1996, interview. "There isn't one place where you can go." Some agencies may use church or school facilities to run occasional programs, but there are few drop-in centers or after-school programs. With few positive activities for youths, there is a greater potential for kids to engage in deviant behaviors and run afoul of the law. And this is not because kids living in these neighborhoods are bad. The reality is that "young people of color living in certain flatland neighborhoods are far more likely than other youth to know violence, abuse or neglect; . . . for some, danger lurks in nearby streets" (Urban Strategies Council 1996: 11).

Fortunately, community groups are working to increase the amount of physical space and programs available for young people. Recently, groups like the Unity Council partnered with the city to plan and develop Union Point Park. The planned nine-acre park will make significant open space and youth facilities available to San Antonio–Fruitvale residents (the districts with the largest percentage of youths in Oakland). The Unity Council's master plan for the park, developed through an extensive community-design process involving over a thousand residents and fifty community organizations, includes a waterfront trail that connects to the San Francisco Bay Trail, large open recreational fields, picnic and barbeque areas, play areas for children of different ages, a public dock and pier, a public courtyard with outdoor seating, and a new youth center (Unity Council 2002). Union Point Park, under construction at this writing, is the first large open space in Fruitvale–San Antonio with access to the waterfront (Aguirre 2001). Union Point Park is tied to smaller projects also underway to increase the amount of space available and to improve park facilities and activities. For example, one informant told me on October 15, 1996, organizations are also working to improve twelve-acre San Antonio Park, the largest park in the area, advocating more community programs and increased attention to maintenance and renovation. Finally, groups like San Antonio Community Development Corporation and Oakland Community Organizations are partnering with the Oakland Unified School District to maximize use of the facilities at Clinton Park, Franklin and Garfield Elementary, Roosevelt Junior High, and San Antonio Park for after-school and weekend activities and programs. These programs would open schools up to the community after school hours and provide much-needed recreational and program space. While physical and program improvements are vital to these densely populated and working-class districts, flatland youths need alternative programs aimed at enhancing their lives through what are best described as "youth development activities." Such activities go beyond merely adding programs to the existing landscape of youth activities and correcting bad behaviors or preventing risky ones. Youth development for Oakland means "providing quality education, varied and meaningful work opportunities, . . . [as well as] drawing on and developing the assets of youths, their families, and their neighborhoods (Urban Strategies Council 1996: 9). Such activities, important in all communities, are usually not as readily available in working-class and heterogeneous communities. Given the size of the youth population, guided programs are that much more important, not only for the individual youths, but for building strong communities. Organizations, whether based in Fruitvale or San Antonio, are working in this direction.

East Bay Asian Youth Center
The East Bay Asian Youth Center (EBAYC) began in the late 1980s working solely with gang kids or kids on probation. In the beginning, the only funding agencies interested in kids focused on crime and drug prevention. Alameda County's probation department initially funded EBAYC to help prevent kids on probation from getting rearrested. Once

the youths got off probation, EBAYC did not work with them. In theory, the program was a success. The recidivism rate among the kids EBAYC worked with was half that of the county. In practice, however, EBAYC knew it was not successful, as the youths still lacked basic job-readiness skills, and there was not enough time to work toward changing "moral values" or "priorities." In fact, many youths went back in the jail system or graduated to state prisons. EBAYC began offering youth-development programs, working with younger kids, following them through high school graduation. In our 1996 interview, David Kakashiba, the center's director, described EBAYC's work:

> For lack of a better term, people call us a youth development organization. And what that means is that basically we provide services and resources to help young people to grow up to be productive, decent human beings when they become adults. Not unlike what the general mission of the schools is to be. Or should be. We work with a range of young people, whether they walk in the door a straight-A student or they . . . are on parole from the California Youth Authority. It doesn't matter. The bottom line is that at least there is an agreement, a desire on the student's part to want to be committed to their own personal development program. So within that context we provide counseling, we serve as a student's advocate, we do a lot of family work, a lot of home visits, a lot of home support. There is also a lot of academic instruction. People come . . . both after school and during the summer for enrichment and study skills. We do test preparation. And lastly we try to expose young people and get them actually engaged in doing something that is geared towards making social change.

EBAYC does not, however, consciously work at being a catalyst for public school reform. The agenda is bigger and intended to help young people grow, not just inside schools but in their communities. This organization, as well as other community-based organizations and church groups, is vital for the development of youths, strong communities, and schools. EBAYC's focus is on Asian youth, but similar organizations serve the Latino community in San Antonio–Fruitvale.

Spanish Speaking Citizens Foundation
Incorporated as a nonprofit multiservice organization in 1965, the Spanish Speaking Citizens Foundation (SSCF) provides an array of services ranging from information and referral, employment counseling, citizenship and immigrant services, and alcohol and drug-abuse treatment/prevention to life skills, legal aid, and youth development for the Latino community in Fruitvale–San Antonio. SSCF runs numerous programs, even renting space to other Latino-centered agencies. Its youth-

development program, however, is its biggest and most important. Like EBAYC's, SSCF's program initially was "80 percent ex-offenders, kids on probation, truants, gang bangers, and 20 percent or less working on kids who were falling through the cracks," Jose Arredondo, executive director of SSCF, told me in our November 3, 1999, interview. SSCF initially got pulled into high schools, usually as a reaction to problems kids were having (e.g., dropping out, pregnancy, legal problems). The money available to offer programs for this population dried up in the late 1980s. SSCF channeled its energies toward proactive programming, such as tutorial, journalism, employment, Latino history, college prep, and leadership programs. In the mid-1990s, SSCF successfully partnered with the city's Mayor's Summer Jobs Program to find summer jobs and internships for local youths. Youth involved in this program participate in a "rigorous education program," including preemployment workshops, resume writing, interview training, and job-retention skills (Oakland Private Industry Council 2002). With three-quarters of the kids between fourteen and fifteen years old, SSCF stresses labor-market orientation. "It is likely that [most kids] have never had a job, can't cash a check because they don't have ID," Arredondo said. "They don't even carry a wallet. They've never been into a bank; . . . we kind of give our youth a lot of extra help and supervision because it is just needed." The program takes local youths beyond work experience. While youths in the program are placed in downtown office jobs three days a week, they are also involved in seminars on public administration, public speaking, political education, and interviewing skills. This youth-development program is a far cry from merely throwing money at programs for kids involved in gangs, on probation, or considered at-risk.

SSCF also runs a journalism project aimed at reversing how disenfranchised youths feel in the neighborhood. The program involves researching, interviewing sources, and writing stories relevant to the neighborhood. Youths not only learn interviewing and writing skills, but also get a crash course in political education. The journalism project allows youths to learn not just who their local government, school board, and police representatives are, but about important neighborhood issues, how to access information, and how to conduct interviews with leaders. "They need to know that the City Council members have aides, and even though Ignacio [de la Fuente] is the only Latino, Larry Reed is very sensitive to Latino issues in the Seventh District," notes Arredondo. "And so these are things, from speed bumps to lights to police harassment in their neighborhoods, so they learn all this. My goal was [that] they . . . know what community policing is, so they feel like they can take their neighborhoods back." Together with the youth-employment program, SSCF is providing important youth development. Arredondo, for one, believes that over the years SSCF has prevented many kids from falling through the cracks and turned them into productive citizens.

El Centro de Juventud
A third important Fruitvale organization involved in youth development is El Centro de Juventud (the youth center). El Centro, as it is known, is funded by Alameda County through the Narcotics Education League (NEL) to provide alcohol- and drug-free services in recreational settings. Theoretically, it is intended as both a recreational space and a program to help youths stay off the streets by focusing on positive activities. As the *Oakland Tribune* reported in an article titled "Vital Fruitvale Youth Center Celebrates 10th Anniversary" on September 30, 1994, El Centro provides a myriad of services, including youth-advocacy and antiviolence groups, as well as support groups for parents who have lost children to violence. The youth center, under Rosalinda Palacios's directorship, is unstructured and driven by youths' interests. Palacios told me in our 1996 interview:

> I have always felt that kids who are very rebellious don't want structure from society, they want to build their own structures. I am all for that, and so when you try to have a program that is very structured, kids don't go. I mean, it's all right, kids want structure, but those that are being rebellious don't want you to have structure for them. It is okay if they have structure that they've built and you support those structures. So you let them hang out. If they want to listen to the radio for six hours, that is their choice. If they want to sit and talk for six hours, that's their choice. If they want to play pool with each other, that is their choice. If they want to play basketball, that's their choice. If they want to come in here and watch TV and videos, that's their choice. But there is always a peer advisor around with them, because there are certain things that they cannot do. They can't come in here to plot murders, drug deals, and who they are going to kick ass with. They can't do that. There's rules.

This unstructured environment may appear unorthodox for youth development. It is a model, however, that does not simply throw a program at youths, particularly when there is a problem. Palacios's programming does not seek a quick or Band-Aid approach to dealing with youths. "I don't like being an agency where people come to get something and then leave, like a referral. I like establishing community," says Palacios. "The kids are with us are with us for three to four years. I have been with kids now that they're having kids and I'm being asked to go and be at the baptism ceremonies. I think developing long-term relationships is more important than doing job training, . . . a program where you come in and learn computers for two months and then goodbye." For example, instead of job training, El Centro offers tutoring. This model requires day-to-day involvement; it requires listening to what kids want and developing programs for them. Over time, El Centro has developed a reputation as a site where youth leaders and volunteers are known for listening to kids, for understanding the cultural context from which they come to develop community and cultural activities relevant to Fruitvale youths.

El Centro also has a strong record of working with other agencies in a multicultural fashion. In an interview on October 21, 1996, Regina Chavarin, former director of Fruitvale's NEL chapter, told me that Palacios "works a lot with other leaders of other programs. So that's where we get to work with things on a multicultural level, when we bring people together to work on common areas of concern or advocacy issues. Then all of us can come together and say, this is a concern for all of us, and they realize they are not alone. It is not just happening to that particular ethnic group. So we'll work with Asian community, the African American community, and just a real mix, . . . working with programs like PUEBLO or East Bay Asian Youth Group and all, it really helps the diversity."

Kids First!

Historically, El Centro and NEL have developed multiracial and multiethnic alliances, which paid off in a fight to bolster the amount of city funds allocated for youth programs. The effort was guided by the collaborative efforts of EBAYC, El Centro, and PUEBLO, all based in San Antonio–Fruitvale. The effort—known as the Kids First! Coalition—sprang out of a desire to work together toward something concrete for flatland youth development.

The effort started in the early 1990s, as youths and leaders fought back the curfew and antiloitering law proposals. In 1994, the small group of youths and youth-serving agencies pushed a different set of priorities for the city with regard to young people and youth development. They began by asking young people what they thought about the problems in Oakland (Themba 1999). "We organized a group of teenagers to study youth violence and in particular how society responds to it," David Kakashiba told me in 1996. "They did a lot of library research, they read newspapers, watched the news, participated in these town-hall meetings, and then they did surveys of their peers." Youth activists from El Centro and PUEBLO surveyed more than a thousand youths throughout Oakland (Hudson 1996). Most kids surveyed had experienced some aspects of violence and suggested that if there was more support for young people, fewer kids would engage in self-destructive behavior. The youths surveyed were also clear on what to do about the problem: provide safe, supportive places where kids could play, learn, and work (Themba 1999). They also echoed the existing sentiment that the city was overly focused on punishment, while undervaluing youth support and preventative programs. As a result of the research, youths obtained an understanding of the city budget and available youth services. Their research confirmed that little was being invested in youth development. Even the existing resources and programs were underfunded and understaffed, with few places for youths to go after park and recreation centers closed at five PM. "We talked about what the youth were saying," notes Rosalinda Palacios. "And what they want, there is not enough money to fund" (quoted in Hudson 1996).

With this knowledge, three organizers—Rosalinda Palacios, David Kakashiba, and Danny HoSang—met to plan how they might further an agenda to force the city to provide youth-development programs with long-term funding and support. They had a useful model to follow. In 1991, Coleman Advocates for Children and Youth had drafted and San Francisco voters had passed Proposition J, the first initiative in the nation to set aside a percentage of the city's budget for youth programs (Hudson 1996). The organizers now had to decide whether to go to the City Council or to make it a ballot initiative for the voters to decide. "That's when we started thinking, 'We don't want to ask the city council for another penny because it's going to be a battle; always begging for money—for kids!' recalls Palacios. "So we decided, no, we're going to let the voters decide."[22] At this time, city officials and other respected agencies, such as the Urban Strategies Council, developed reports and plans to respond to what the youth researchers found and the problems. For Palacios, HoSang, and Kakashiba, it was time to get past reports and plans, and advance the concept of youth development. This meant several things. First, youth development had to reach beyond plans and proposals from one or two agencies; any money had to be spread evenly across the city. Second, a ballot initiative was necessary that shifted money to programs for young people and involved community input and control over its use. The ballot initiative was deemed necessary because of the dearth of funding for youth programs. While children's programs do get federal funds, they are usually aimed at the youngest age group; little money is available for teenagers, as "Helping Oakland's Harried Youngsters to a Better Life," a February 5, 1996, article in the *Oakland Tribune*, pointed out at the time. The set-aside would ensure long-term youth development program funding. The next step would be to enlist allies citywide.

The core group consulted with groups and youths from across the city, developed a strategic assessment of the political terrain, and explores ways to obtain the necessary financial and human resources. In a short time, the Kids First! campaign initiative—also known as the Oakland Children's Fund, or Measure K—was born. The initiative sought to generate roughly $5 million a year to pay for youth programs. A youth activist writes of the initiative:

> The money will go towards programs such as youth employment and job training, school health clinics, arts and sports camps, neighborhood learning centers, libraries, pre-school programs, and recreation centers. Any program that involves youth ages 0-21 can apply for funding. The best part is it won't raise taxes because the money will come from the existing City of Oakland budget. It redirects 2.5 percent of the city's unrestricted dollars and invests them in our future . . . Oakland's children. In addition, a committee of 21 community members gets to decide where the money goes. Ten of the 21 people must be under the age of 21. This way, we won't have a bunch of adults deciding what youth want and need. (Ealey 1996: 3)

Supporters of Kids First! argued that the measure was necessary to establish a baseline children's budget and create a way for parents, youths, and others to safeguard funds for youth from going to a few politically connected agencies and programs.

Establishing an initiative and getting it passed, however, are two different things. The latter requires an extraordinary effort on the part of many different people. To qualify as a ballot initiative, the Kids First! campaign needed to collect a minimum of thirty thousand signatures—15 percent of the city's registered voters. The small group of non-profit organizations needed support. Each of the core members brought important strengths to the coalition and leveraged the assistance necessary to mount the campaign. The campaign organized in-kind donations from individuals and community groups, a base of more than two hundred volunteers (mostly youths and young adults), pro bono legal help in crafting the initiative's language, and volunteer help from a high-level political consulting firm in shaping the campaign strategy (Themba

1999). To gather the necessary signatures, the Kids First! campaign hired a youth organizer as campaign manager and paid a limited number of professional petition gatherers. Youth and parental volunteers, donning purple T-shirts with the Kids First! name and logo inscribed in bright orange, mounted a massive effort to increase public recognition and awareness. There was no organized opposition to the initiative, so the challenge involved mobilizing resources to get the initiative on the ballot and educating organizations about the measure. Ultimately, the campaign was successful. The coalition turned in fifty thousand signatures to the city clerk. The initiative set aside 2.5 percent of Oakland's General Fund exclusively for youth development and services to children and youths under twenty-one years old. The set-aside was to augment existing funding and stipulated that the city's total support for young people could not fall below the 1995–1996 fiscal year level. The initiative also required a nineteen-member planning and oversight committee to make decisions about how the money would be spent. On November 5, 1996, Oakland voters overwhelmingly passed Measure K (Themba 1999).

Since then, there have been some bumps in the road. Supporters claim that the program was already a success because of the youth involvement in the project. Young people involved in the process got a taste of policy making and advocacy work. Yet there have been political battles over the planning and oversight committee's distribution of funds, staffing, and administration and increased competition for city funds (Bailey 1999; Hudson 1998). These issues aside, the collaborative effort to enhance youth development programs in San Antonio–Fruitvale, and eventually all of Oakland, is an amazing story of community building. The effort involved in getting Measure K passed is in itself successful youth development, as youths were involved from the beginning in the planning, organizing, and implementing policy. This organizing effort was a multiracial and multiethnic endeavor in that not only did it bring together diverse agencies, but also youths from different backgrounds worked together toward a mutually beneficial goal. Kids First! also was not just about implementing programs when problems arise; it was a paradigm shift. "Every time we have a problem with youths, we try to fix it by throwing another program at them," says Rosalinda Palacios. "We need to be developing our youths as a society and asking ourselves what we can do for them" (Bazeley 1996). The programs in San Antonio–Fruitvale are a step in that direction.

Economic Renewal in the Flatlands

Not unlike other nongentrifying inner city communities, San Antonio–Fruitvale has been ignored by private residential and commercial investment for decades. Ethnic entrepreneurs and nonprofits have taken the lead in revitalization. For example, ethnically based small businesses have filled vacancies and revitalized commercial activity through small, family-run businesses targeting the diverse racial and ethnic mix of residents.[23] In San Antonio, Asian entrepreneurs helped revitalize a once vibrant commercial district, which they share now with non-Asian businesses. Along East Fourteenth and Fruitvale Avenue, numerous Latino-owned stores and restaurants coexist with street vendors and multiethnic establishments like Fruitvale Produce. Also, nonprofit organizations are themselves social and economic anchors. "Community-based corporations are an integral part of the economic development of the community, because of all the traffic we generate," noted Jane Garcia, executive director of La Clínica de la Raza, in our 2000 interview. "[We have] patients coming in and patients going out. We are the largest employer in the Fruitvale–San Antonio district, . . . pushing three hundred employees. Every time there is talk of a move, the merchants around us get very nervous about that." Other prominent community-based organizations have offices in and around main commercial centers, also drawing people to the area and generating commercial activity.

While community groups in both districts coordinate an array of social services ranging from Head Start to employment and language-skill programs, a variety of organizations got involved in renewal and revitalization, particularly around commercial development. The recent and impressive strides to enhance community economic and residential capacity reflect an awareness by leaders of the importance of revitalization in improving the community and creating visible signs of community well-being, safety, and stability. The efforts range from local groups assisting ethnic entrepreneurs in organizing merchant associations, obtaining necessary municipal services, and obtaining money for façade upgrades to—most visibly—leveraging funds for the development of commercial projects.

The value of nonprofit groups in San Antonio–Fruitvale's community development deserves notice. First, community groups have initiated and carried out renewal efforts. With local leaders and residents driving most efforts, concern over outside interests coming in and taking over is allayed. Second, the type of development generated does not involve upscale or big-box development, but rather improving the small ethnically based establishments already present. Thus, there is little fear that local

FIGURE 5.3. San Antonio Marketplace on East 14th; affordable housing and retail building developed by San Antonio Community Development Corporation and the East Bay Asian Local Development Corporation

revitalization may spur wide-scale gentrification (and thus displacement). Conflicting class interests are not overt, making revitalization efforts less complicated. Third, nonprofits are joining forces to complete community-development projects. Multiethnic/multiracial collaborations increase the capacity of initiatives and better serve—and assure inclusiveness among—the community's diverse segments (Kuchinskas 1995). All these elements reduce the possibility of tension among groups. Finally, these projects take longer to complete than those directed by private developers, mainly because of the community-driven processes involved. The community benefit of such an inclusive process, however, is worth the slower pace of development. Two major development efforts concern the organization of the Eastlake Merchants Association and the Fruitvale Village project.

Eastlake Merchants Association Organization
In the late 1970s, the influx of Asian residents into Lower San Antonio provided a niche market for small businesses. With rents substantially lower than in Chinatown and residents in need of goods, merchants

quickly set up shop, disregarding the area's reputation for criminal activity. The area is a thirteen-block stretch, running between East Twelfth and East Fourteenth Streets, from Lake Merritt to Fourteenth Avenue (see Map 5.1). The commercial strip has grown in fits and starts since the 1980s. Small ventures tending to the needs of the immediate neighborhood settled along this flatland stretch amid numerous vacant lots, as well as auto-related and industrial businesses (Sugden-Castillo 1996).

In 1982, longtime Oakland businessman Paul Wong put a sign atop his Sun Hop Fat grocery store announcing the area as "New Chinatown." For over a decade, incoming Asian residents and merchants have unofficially adopted this title for the area. "It's the new Chinatown, it actually looks like a Vietnamese town," says Richard Tan Ma, owner of the Pho Hoa Vietnamese restaurant (quoted in Harris 1996). While the moniker is catchy, it fails to fully describe "the multiculturalism of the small businesses and residents there" (Wong 1996). The area is really a hybrid of "Oakland's Chinatown and San Antonio district—a region between the two where Asian and Latino influences overlap" (Wells 1998). It is reported that some twenty languages are spoken in this small commercial center, including Vietnamese, Spanish, Cambodian, English, and Chinese. The area is also home to African American and Yemenite merchants. Thus, the descriptor "New Chinatown" is not an accurate representation of the community. When Wong erected the sign, he did not consult the community or the city, yet the sign began a debate over the future of the area and led to an organizing and revitalization campaign that has stabilized the area and brought the various groups together to solve difficulties, improve the area, and stabilize this part of San Antonio.

In the early 1990s, the East Bay Asian Local Development Corporation (EBALDC) was going through the process of a creating a Neighborhood Planning Council with other community organizations. EBALDC had established a good reputation for providing affordable housing but wished to connect with the community, particularly the business community. EBALDC began to do outreach to local merchants to get their analysis of what was going on in the community and assess their needs. Organizers like Helen Shor and Chuong Nguyen went out and spoke with merchants, with the hope of creating a common vision for the community. And although many merchants were skeptical at first, a small number began to show interest. In fact, through this organizing EBALDC found that merchants were united in their concerns over parking, litter, crime, and most importantly, an unresponsive city government, particularly the Oakland Police Department. "They've had bad experiences with City

Hall not resolving problems," notes John Gruntfest, business manager of the East-West Animal Care Center on East Twelfth. "I just fill up holes in the street myself. Get some concrete, mix it up, fill the hole. The city bureaucracy is just too slow" (quoted in Wong 1996). Vandalism, auto break-ins, shoplifting, and burglaries were also constant irritants to business leaders, and merchants complained of slow police response. These concerns were the impetus for greater action.

With the assistance of EBALDC, the Eastlake Merchants Association (ELMA) was formed in 1994. The next step was to organize a membership base and elect officers. Organizing this diverse group of merchants was not easy. Some of the obstacles included language barriers, cultural misunderstandings, and merchants wary that ELMA was connected with organized crime—seeking protection money (Lerman 1998). EBALDC went store-to-store seeking members, facilitating meetings, and bringing the merchants and police together, but also simply meeting and listening to merchants on their own terms. "Anyone who works with merchants knows the hours they keep," explains Helen Shor, one of EBALDC's key organizers on this project. "You have to bring the meeting to their storefront, listen, and then bringing it to the larger association."[24] While EBALDC has been a catalyst for organizing the area's merchants, business leaders were also active in outreach efforts, even walking the streets and visiting businesses to invite other leaders to join ELMA (Wong 1996). ELMA now has forty-five merchant members, seven or eight of whom serve as board members. The board mirrors the diversity in the community, with Vietnamese, ethnic Chinese from Vietnam, white, Latino, Yemenite, and African Americans representatives. ELMA's current president is Latino.

Since its inception in 1996, ELMA has been quite active. The first pivotal issue confronting ELMA was identity, particularly the "New Chinatown" moniker.[25] Many non-Asian longtime residents and merchants believed the sign and label failed to represent "their" neighborhood. Also, the sentiment from the merchants was that the identity or naming of the area was not a merchant issue, but a community one. Merchants gathered opinions and eventually came to the conclusion that the identity, and thus the signage, should reflect the community's diversity. In the late 1990s, with the city's help, banners were erected throughout the commercial area that read "Eastlake Business District" in four languages. This was an important step towards inclusiveness.

ELMA has also been involved in community-building efforts meant to shore up social and physical elements in the area. These included various

FIGURE 5.4.   Eastlake Marketplace in Eastlake Business District

beautification efforts, including tree planting, streetscaping projects, and adopting and securing better lighting for the area park. In fact, ELMA scraped together $2.2 million from federal sources, EBALDC, and local fund-raising for streetscape projects to improve the look of the commercial district. ELMA's biggest success, however, has come through improved community-police relations. Crime and safety were key issues that Eastlake merchants responded to in the early days of ELMA. EBALDC brought merchants and police together to discuss common concerns. The police responded by increasing their presence in the community, even assigning a beat officer. Tangible results followed, as merchants reported a decline in drug dealing, prostitution, and crime. The increased sense of safety in the Eastlake and Lower San Antonio area has been a stabilizing force.

By the late 1990s, the Eastlake area had become a community strength and asset. ELMA is now operating without EBALDC's assistance and can claim a good measure of success. A mélange of new stores have cropped up and the area's physical appearance is inviting. As a result, the twenty-eight-block strip has outpaced the more affluent Montclair in the Oakland Hills in total sales in recent years (Sugden-Castillo 1996). And with consumer-goods prices much lower than in other areas, Eastlake is attracting people from all ethnic backgrounds. The result is considerable growth. City representatives report that over a ten-year span, the neighborhood has grown 20 percent in economic and employment activity, compared to 10 percent for the city (Harris 1996). This can in no small part be credited to ELMA's work to fashion a safe, clean, prosperous, and inclusive community.

EBALDC's and ELMA's actions can be understood as community development that involves organizing to develop the capacity of local leaders to map their own future and carry out specific tasks to reach goals. The Eastlake area renewal process has involved a slow movement toward inclusiveness. While the area is still in progress, leaders have begun to forge a unified, multicultural vision and plan for this section of San Antonio. The change in signage reflects a larger understanding of ELMA's vision for Eastlake. "As a group, [the Eastlake merchants] seem to be coming around to the idea of diversity, and the neighborhood is saying that is our strength," Shor told me in 1996. "So could we market the area? Could we sell that and really make it our strength?" ELMA and other groups have organized multicultural festivals and are planning a six-month farmers' market that would bring groups together around food. Underlying these efforts is an attempt to "brand" the area as diverse and sell it as a diverse ethnic market and community.

Fruitvale BART Transit Village

For years, the area surrounding East Fourteenth and Fruitvale Avenue, as well as the BART station, has been perceived as unsafe. "Oakland's Second Downtown" included drug-dealing fronts, seedy bars—like the infamous (and now shuttered) Ye Old Inn—and a high number of rooming and halfway houses that gave this commercial strip and Fruitvale a dubious reputation. "When I first started working here in 1977," said Regina Chavarin in our 1996 interview, "those who were out at night once all the workers went home were the people who were hitting the bars and the people on their way home from the bars." Business owners report that for years the strip was a "war zone" that was plagued by "constant gunfire" and a healthy drug trade (Counts 1999). Since the 1980s, public spaces along the commercial strip had been taken over by drug activity and crime. Slowly, Fruitvale developed a national reputation as a dangerous, dilapidated, and crime-centered neighborhood. Data support these perceptions. For example, BART records indicate that the Fruitvale Station ranks in the top seven for reported incidents of crime, ranging from auto theft to assault (Gorman 1997). The area's image is not helped by the large number of dilapidated or boarded-up buildings, as well as businesses advertising check-cashing or pawnshop services. The negative perception has led to a park-and-ride situation for BART riders.

Overcoming these negative perceptions involves a concerted and coordinated effort among many different groups. What plagues Fruitvale are largely economic and infrastructure issues, which any serious effort to effect change must address. In the late 1980s and early 1990s, several factors sparked a unique, multifaceted, and community-led development effort to revitalize the East Fourteenth/Fruitvale commercial district and to foster a positive image for the overall community. The presence of the Unity Council in Fruitvale was central in this regard. The Unity Council, established as a nonprofit in the mid-1960s and known as the Spanish Speaking Unity Council, earned a reputation as a community advocate by not only bringing resources to the community, but also serving as a strong voice for Latino concerns.[26] The Unity Council's first executive director, Arabella Martinez, deserves a good deal of credit for redevelopment efforts in San Antonio–Fruitvale. Martinez left Oakland and the Unity Council in the early 1970s to work for the federal government. She was convinced to return to the Unity Council in 1989 when the organization was in disarray and near bankruptcy. Upon her return, Martinez, aided by strong ties to funders and community members, restructured the group's assets, reorganized its operations, and raised substantial amounts of money. Martinez and the Unity Council board also renewed the council's commitment to building community coalitions to bring about large-scale, comprehensive social, economic, and physical redevelopment. "We knew we were going to have to focus our energy," Martinez notes. "We also knew we had to get involved in large development. We chose to focus on the major commercial district around BART and link it to Fourteenth Street. . . . Originally, we didn't have such a grandiose—some have even said audacious—vision. But we knew we had to do something really big to change the socioeconomic dynamic" (quoted in Counts 1999). The big change was a conscious effort to revitalize the commercial district surrounding the Fruitvale BART station, including International Boulevard and Fruitvale Avenue. This effort led to plans for Fruitvale Transit Village, a multidimensional project aimed at revitalizing the economic, physical, and social character of Lower Fruitvale.

It is overly simplistic to say that the project emerged from Arabella Martinez alone, her staff, or any other outside agency. Several events galvanized the community and focused attention on community-based revitalization of the East Fourteenth and Fruitvale commercial area. In 1991, researchers at UC-Berkeley's University-Oakland Metropolitan Forum produced a report, focusing on Fruitvale and the East Fourteenth Street commercial district. The study group evaluated the area's commercial development potential and assessed resident and leader needs and opinions, identifying the commercial district as a primary development opportunity. The group recommended better integration of the commercial district and the transit station (Chew 1991). The BART station and a huge stretch of surface parking located a block from the East Fourteenth Street shopping district were disconnected from the community and unappealing, replete with litter, crime, and graffiti (Burt 2002). Soon after the study's completion, the BART proposed the construction of a multi-level parking facility adjacent to the Fruitvale BART station.

Residents and leaders contested the proposed parking garage, arguing that it would act as a barrier to the neighborhood and would further economic and environmental decline (L. Olson 1998). The proposal also initiated a conversation among residents and community groups about improved planning for new development and the desire for that planning to reflect community needs. BART wanted to increase ridership by facilitating the transfer of riders from their cars or the bus onto the train. Given that two-thirds of the riders using the Fruitvale Station came from affluent neighboring communities, residents questioned the connection between the garage and community needs such as economic development, safety, and employment opportunities (Hodgdon 1996). Community pressure forced BART to back down from its proposal and to open discussions with community representatives to discuss alternatives. The Unity Council took the lead in organizing residents and leaders, spearheading the effort to redevelop the area around the BART station.

The Unity Council secured $185,000 in city funds to back a sweeping redevelopment plan for the Fruitvale district. The council held numerous community-planning workshops to collect the opinions of residents, merchants, community and environmental groups, and government officials to envision and design the revitalization of Lower Fruitvale's commercial district (Kanigel 1995). What emerged from the discussions was a proposed pedestrian plaza—a "transit village"—that would connect the BART station and the East Fourteenth/Fruitvale commercial district. The Unity Council also set up a "design symposium" to give community members an opportunity to express their needs and wants, and to work with architects in preparing a design that reflected the community (L. Olson 1998). This process was positive in two respects. First, the Unity Council obtained an understanding that the community wanted an attractive design, a mix of housing, parking, traffic flow, safety, and the potential for new businesses. Second, the council gained the trust of the community by reaching out and involving residents. Indeed, the planning process of the Fruitvale Village is unique in that it was from the beginning community driven and supported.

Emerging from this process were the beginnings of an overall plan for commercial revitalization and a specific plan for creating the Fruitvale Village, a "transit-oriented development" that would link the East Fourteenth Street commercial district with the BART station. The Unity Council's revitalization plan, however, does not deal just with economic development. The plan is centered on a variety of community needs.

Arabella Martinez summarized this vision in an op-ed piece in the June 12, 1998, *Oakland Tribune*:

> Its vision was to build a $100 million mixed-use development on 15 acres of land on and surrounding the Fruitvale BART transit station. As envisioned, the Fruitvale BART Transit Village would include new and renovated retail and office space, new community facilities to house child development, senior citizen and health care services, a library and other community service agencies. New family and senior citizen housing would be built. BART and AC Transit facilities would be connected to International Boulevard (East Fourteenth Street) through a pedestrian-friendly plaza and walkway lined with new retail shops.

The Unity Council's vision became reality as ground was broken in the spring of 1998, and construction has moved ahead on the pedestrian plaza, the two mixed-use complexes, and the walkway connecting the plaza to East Fourteenth Street. As Martinez notes, the comprehensive project seeks to combine various aspects to revitalize Fruitvale economically, physically, and socially.

The major phase of the project includes the building of the centerpiece of the Fruitvale Village, a community resource center slated to house the Unity Council's headquarters and Head Start child-care program, the César Chávez branch of the Oakland Public Library, La Clínica de La Raza health-care center, senior housing, and other nonprofit agencies. Various considerations were taken into account when planning the village. First, the plan is attempting to capitalize on the well-developed social services by clustering them in an accessible manner. While Fruitvale (more than San Antonio) has many social services located close to each other, they are not as centralized as they could be. "It [the community] has those services that you need to have a successful community," a former planner with the Unity Council told me on October 18, 1996. "The idea we are trying to use is to kind of cluster them and make them easier to find and hopefully attract more people to it." Anchoring the village with social services will strengthen and improve agencies already in the community. This is not typical revitalization in that "expanding the market" is not the overriding purpose.

Also, given the Unity Council's history, it is easy to view the Transit Village as a Latino-centered project. Unity Council representatives, however, are quick to note that they are attempting to extend the project to other racial and ethnic groups. This is visible in the types of programs (e.g., welfare-to-work, Head Start) and whom the programs serve.[27] The Unity Council's plan is to serve and attract multiple racial and ethnic groups. For example, La Clínica de la Raza plans to relocate its health clinic to the Fruitvale Village. In the process, La Clínica will be able to expand (e.g., to dental and optometry practice), as well as improve access to existing residents and diversify its patient base, which has become important due to managed care.

Developing a pedestrian plaza is important in area like Fruitvale where the rate of automobile ownership is relatively low. On the one hand, affordable senior housing has already been built and more is planned (Rohrig 1998). This population, in need of accessible services, will greatly benefit from centralized services, new retail opportunities, social activities, and increased safety in the area. On the other hand, many area residents, particularly low-income and young ones, walk to obtain services. Local residents that do use public transportation rely largely on AC Transit bus service. AC Transit has connected with the BART near the village for some time. A new intermodal facility is being developed to improve the bus connection not only with the train line, but also with the pedestrian plaza and the commercial strip along International Boulevard. Thus, the Fruitvale Village is situated as a transit hub for various subgroups and is an ideal location for mixed-use development. The idea behind the pedestrian plaza is not just to centralize services for existing residents, but to create activity that does not exist for those using the BART or AC Transit. The plans for mixed-use developments and for connecting East Fourteenth to the Transit Village are the most obvious examples of this.

Mixed-use facilities are an important feature of the project. To create pedestrian traffic at various times of the day, plans are to mix economic development with office space. For example, on the pedestrian plaza there will be three buildings housing the various nonprofits and social services, with the first floor dedicated to retail. The retail is meant to attract area residents as well as to tap into the Bart ridership. "The whole idea is that maybe we'll start attracting people to come in and use the services," Carlos Castellenos, a former city planner working on the project, told me on October 18, 1996. "The idea is to get people to start looking around, to say, 'Hmm, there's an interesting café.' You want to give them something to walk around in and feel comfortable and safe." The Unity Council is attempting to create a pleasant place for pedestrians to visit at different times of the day. If more people are walking around there are more "eyes on the street" and thus a greater sense of safety (Jacobs 1961). "I'll tell you, things shut down around here about six p.m. and things get pretty desolate," one resident said in our October 19, 1996, interview. "Just the people living around here walking back to their homes, then after that there's another informal economy that takes over." Thus, the economic development on the plaza is tied to the centralizing of social services to improve safety and overall perceptions.

The Unity Council's goal, however, is not simply to create new retail space. In fact, new commercial development is only a small part of the project. "The goals were to link the existing commercial strip to the BART station," says Manuela Silva, senior executive officer for the Unity Council and the Fruitvale Development Corporation, owner of the project (quoted in Burt 2002). The plan is to revitalize the larger and existing commercial sector in Lower Fruitvale. In 1995, the Unity Council got involved in the National Trust for Historic Preservation's Main Street program to improve the East Fourteenth commercial district. The Main Street program is about commercial revitalization through community involvement. Organizers and community leaders look at a variety of aspects, including promotion of the commercial sector, business retention, new business attraction, physical improvements (e.g., façade and streetscape projects), and safety and cleanliness upgrades. The Main Street program is connected not only to the Fruitvale Village, but also to the area's overall revitalization. As Jennifer Kassan, the leading Main Street organizer, explained in our interview on September 17, 2002:

> We see the Transit Village as part of Main Street . . . because it is all about preparing the existing market for the opening of the Transit Village, and the Transit Village is all about improving the commercial district and attracting people to the existing commercial district. So Main Street is trying to improve the existing commercial district so that once the Transit Village opens there won't be this stark contrast, where there's this beautiful new building and this kind of ugly, crappy-looking street. Because the whole idea of the Transit Village isn't just to attract people to shop within the Tran-

sit Village, because there aren't going to be a whole lot of shops with the Transit Village, but to attract people to shop in the whole neighborhood. And so the Transit Village has a visual connection to the existing street. That was really tricky, because the BART station is not right there [on East Fourteenth]. So . . . the street that connects you to International Boulevard will become a pedestrian walkway. So people hopefully will be really attracted to walk to see what's going on in the rest of the neighborhood.

The village is not a final destination, but an entryway into the rest of Fruitvale. Main Street is improving the existing commercial district, lowering vacancies, and creating a greater sense of safety.

The Main Street/Fruitvale Village projects are intriguing as atypical forms of economic revitalization. While the projects are attempting to capitalize on the disposable income of affluent residents and visitors, they are not seeking to create an upscale commercial district. "We're happy with what we are, yet we want to improve," Kassan told me in 2002. "People are attracted to what we have, because I think a lot of people are longing for authentic space; everything is a strip mall or really upscale and boring, and not affordable. So people can come here, be around a really diverse group of people, buy food from the street vendors, have a delicious Mexican meal that is really cheap." While the efforts are about revitalization, they are not about "yuppie boutiques" or big-box national chain stores. Leaders hope to attract people to the area,

FIGURE 5.5.   Fruitvale Produce; Fruitvale corridor that Main Street Initiative is targeting

but on their own terms—maintaining the flavor of the district, while improving things. Such a purpose means walking a fine line between improvement for residents and improvement that displaces the good things already present.

Like the diverse social service anchors, the village's commercial aspect will serve multiple groups. A scan of businesses located along International Boulevard and Fruitvale Avenue reveals stores like Fruitvale Produce (serving Latinos and African Americans), as well as other stores and restaurants serving Latinos and Asians. There are plans to attract various groups to the Fruitvale Village through ethnic festivals. "One of the things we are going to do with the pedestrian walkway is to create a festival plaza, where every weekend there would be a different festival," Carlos Castellenos said in our 1996 interview. "It doesn't have to be just Latino culture. It could be African American. It could be Asian. The idea is that every weekend there would be something going on." So while Fruitvale has long been considered a Latino neighborhood, in reality, diverse groups use the area and revitalization plans reflect this. It may even be said that integration is being put into the marketing plan.

The project has involved ten years of planning and has changed somewhat over that time. The core ideas behind the plan, however, have not. "It's about job creation, safety, families, children, adults, employees, and health," says Manuela Silva. "When you put all the ingredients together, you have a project that has the potential for changing the community—not just physically, but mentally" (quoted in Burt 2002). The plan has always focused on centralizing social services, being pedestrian friendly, serving multiple groups, and blending retail development with enhancing existing commercial enterprises. As a community-based and inclusive project, it garnered little opposition and much praise from community, city, and various national urban policy groups.

In sum, the efforts of ELMA and the Unity Council are models of inner city revitalization. These projects are comprehensive attempts at bottom-up revitalization. In both areas, plans focused on safety, commercial revitalization, jobs, and image maintenance. Planners were able to create spaces attractive to multiple groups, improve the physical and commercial structure of the community, and begin to shift the image from dangerous to safe. The nature of the organizing process is distinctive. Collaborative efforts focused on revitalizing the community for existing residents. There was no underlying goal to attract more affluent residents. Equally important, residents and merchants were involved in the planning process. The advocacy of EBALDC and the Unity Council were vital in bringing different racial and ethnic groups together in collaboration, while assisting in obtaining funds and making connections with the city to get these projects off the ground. In the process, leaders, merchants, and residents began to see the diversity as an asset and even something to capitalize on in marketing efforts.

SAN ANTONIO–FRUITVALE highlights the challenge of maintaining integration over time. As in Uptown and Jackson Heights, integration there was neither planned nor directed. Racial and economic change followed by immigration left its mark over the last three decades, recasting the area's character and image. Integration in these flatland communities, however, differs from other diverse-by-circumstance communities in that nearly 90 percent of the population is split between Asian, black, and Latino residents, with a small, geographically isolated, and politically inactive white population. The community is also decidedly working class. Integration in this part of Oakland, then, goes beyond the black and white, and even the middle-class "liberalism," that marks integration in diverse-by-design communities.

Also, because no organization was involved in conscious attempts to promote integration, maintaining the mix meant involving organizations focused on specific ethnic/racial groups to talk and collaborate in order to meet community needs. With the advocacy work of several nonprofits, these collaborative efforts succeeded. This was visible in attempts at improving youth services, as well as improving the social and physical infrastructure. All efforts have stabilizing effects in the community. The tangible results from the efforts create a better environment for area youth and safe, vibrant commercial districts. Community organizations, leaders, and residents also made sure that not only the vision of the community's future emerged from the grassroots, but that residents were involved in any community development project. As a result, San Antonio and Fruitvale are successful, stable integrated communities. Integration is stable for now, though leaders and groups must address other pressing community problems (e.g., affordable housing, employment, overcrowding) and continue to advocate for multiethnic collaborations to maintain the inclusive community identity. With the presence of strong leadership and community organizations, this seems achievable.

Conclusion

DISCERNING RESIDENTIAL settlement patterns by race is not an easy process. Research and news accounts on race and housing tend to focus on the problem of segregation and the failure of integration. This focus has been seen as legitimate, given that thirty-five years after the passage of Title VIII of the 1968 Civil Rights Act it is difficult to say that at the residential level we have moved to a more integrated society. Although levels of segregation have declined and racial change has become more complex, there does not seem to be a widespread movement to create integrated living patterns (R. Smith 1993). Even with the remarkable efforts of pro-integrative communities, racially and ethnically integrated areas continue to be called "fragile." Undoubtedly, this is due in part to how divided the nation is on the desirability of achieving residential integration. As a country, we are morally and legally committed to the ideal of freedom of choice, and public policy cannot legally force anyone to live anywhere.[1] While attitude surveys show a greater acceptance of integrated residential spaces, attitudes do not easily translate into practice. In fact, as Scott Cummings writes: "Busing and open housing are two of the most unpopular liberal policy initiatives of the past three decades" (1998: 201). A scan of the literature on segregation and integration likely gives the impression that little can be done to create shared spaces, either through enlightened public policy or moral and humanistic appeals.

Yet things are not as dour as some would have us believe. While the presence of, and social processes involved in maintaining, racially and ethnically integrated residential spaces have been, until recently, largely ignored, a growing number of studies indicate that the traditional trajectory of racial change to resegregation is more complex than assumed. Urban sociology has a long tradition of examining neighborhood change by focusing on neighborhoods that were "invaded" or "attacked" by outside forces (e.g., urban renewal, gentrification, blockbusting) or groups (e.g., racial change). Scholars are beginning to move beyond this notion to suggest that the "traditional" neighborhood that was attacked by outside forces never existed; that neighborhood life is open-ended and experienced differently by residents. Uptown, Jackson Heights, and San Antonio–Fruitvale surely were never traditional neighborhoods, as residents from varied cultural and economic backgrounds have been part of each community for the better part of forty years. Racial change, a consequence of the restructuring of urban landscapes through global economic changes, immigration, and unchecked sprawl, occurred in each community, although without invasion or transition or a single type of integration. While integration was unplanned, each community managed to remain racially and ethnically integrated over time. These glass-half-full stories offer credible alternative scenarios to historic patterns of segregation and a glimpse into the possibilities and challenges for interracial and interethnic understanding, cooperation, and coexistence.

The careful analysis presented here of the experiences of community leaders working (often indirectly) to sustain integration makes it tempting to offer new or reconsider old policies directed at maintaining residential integration. Politicians, policy makers, and scholars typically seek specific policy initiatives that can be implemented to ameliorate social problems and foster prosperity. Clear and direct policy avenues provide such actors with easy equations to effect change—and possibly with quick successes to claim. In response to this need, many scholars studying segregation and integration end their monographs with policy analysis, such as calls for federal efforts to fight the discriminatory practices that limit the number of integrated neighborhoods. However, the goal of this research was not to create a list of policy recommendations. Its qualitative approach offers insight into the unique neighborhood history and context, the fluidity and complexity of neighborhood life, and the ability of individuals to act as agents of change. The focus is on the social processes involved when local groups are faced with integration. In this sense, this research is about broadening the discussion of racial change, efforts to maintain integrated neighborhoods, and integration itself.

The history of the pro-integration movement and these three case studies illustrate that the social processes at the local level are more complex and fluid than suggested by most policy analysts. There is a long history of community studies—using qualitative designs and methods—that have focused on understanding these local processes. These studies indicate the difficulty in making generalizations about how integration can be, and maybe even should be, maintained. The qualitative approach used here clearly demonstrates that there is no one kind of integrated community. Each community varies in terms of racial demographics, physical character and amenities, class structure, origins of integration, organizational capacity, and even local culture. For example, the character of and social processes experienced by diverse-by-design communities are quite different from those of diverse-by-circumstance ones. Also, the racial and socioeconomic character of each case led to varied social dynamics, community debates, and organizational approaches. This makes it quite difficult to offer simple solutions applicable to all communities working toward stable integration. In sum, a specific set of government policies for urban neighborhoods and suburbs to implement is too simplistic. Instead, consideration must be given to grassroots actions and the context of the neighborhood. The common themes I explore that emerged from the case-study communities are guideposts meant to engender discussion among scholars and activists interested in or working toward maintaining racially and ethnically integrated communities, particularly where integration was not planned.

MULTIETHNIC-MULTIRACIAL INTEGRATION

As illustrated in each case study, racially and ethnically integrated communities indeed exist and can be stabilized. While this is not a new finding, it stands in stark contrast to common understandings of neighborhood racial change, which suggest that as nonwhites move into previously homogenous neighborhoods, various forces conspire to create racial transition and resegregation. The communities presented here did not experience racial violence or the panic selling that occurred in places like East Cleveland or Austin (Chicago), where fear of racial change led to rapid white flight.[2] And although these communities resembled areas experiencing transition, in that initially they lost population when racial change began, their populations have either stabilized or grown. Most importantly, white residents in these communities did not flee, as the bulk of the literature would suggest. With the exception of San Antonio and Fruitvale (where the white population left much earlier), the communities continue to have a white presence as part of the integrated mix. These communities were able to maintain integration over time. And as economist Ingrid Ellen points out, the longer a community is integrated, the greater chance it has for remaining integrated (2000). In sum, the data illustrate that racial change does not inevitably lead to resegregation or racial transition, and that integrated neighborhoods can stabilize in the face of institutional forces encouraging (or enforcing) racial separation.

New Models of Integration

The communities studied here are quite different models of integration when compared to the diverse-by-design communities that emerged out of the urban social conditions of the 1950s and 1960s. The black-white, pro-integrative coalitions that emerged in neighborhoods across the country developed organizations, social networks, and institutions whose purpose was to intervene in racial transition and foster stable integration. Uptown, Jackson Heights, and San Antonio–Fruitvale have both common circumstances and different social dynamics, making for interesting cases. First, these three communities go beyond biracial, black-white models of integration. No single group entered as the community began to experience racial change, and a stable white population remained as racial change occurred. In fact, they are more aptly described as hyperdiverse, mixed on numerous demographic dimensions, yet shifting and complex. How did this happen? The answer is as complex as the mix. On the one hand, external forces brought a disparate mix of residents to these neighborhoods. The arrival of these diverse groups spurred development of advocacy groups and social service agencies, which played a significant role in attracting other residents and shaping the social fabric of the community. On the other hand, the unique local histories and cultural contexts contributed to varied racial and ethnic configurations. For example, the absence of blacks in Jackson Heights appears somewhat related to a legacy of discrimination, while the existence of a small and isolated white population in San Antonio–Fruitvale is related to economic restructuring and less desirable flatland property.[3] Also, amenities (e.g., accessible and far-reaching mass transit lines, necessary social services, affordable housing) in each community attracted racially diverse newcomers and retained longtime residents. Regardless of the context, however, all three communities slowly emerged as integrated.

Second, with the onset of racial change, local organizations arose in response to community needs. Local organizations were not, however, recruiting white residents or developing antidiscriminatory lending or real estate programs to preserve integration. These strategies were not necessary, given that many incumbent white residents stayed in the community and more importantly, no organization articulated the explicit goal of maintaining or promoting integration. In fact, the organization structure in each community was quite different. While ethnically based organizations sprouted up to serve the low-income residents and newly arrived immigrants, more general organizations surfaced to stave off residential and commercial decline through image maintenance and physical improvement. Advocates for the poor toiled to provide low-income residents with affordable housing and to ease overcrowding, while other groups formed to strengthen economic development in stagnant commercial districts. This activism focused on community betterment by targeting disparate community needs. It was not, however, the result of conscious or deliberate attempts to preserve integration, although leaders and residents slowly began to see integration as a marketable community asset, and collaborative attempts (even if small) were made to stabilize the racial mix and foster tolerance and interaction among residents.

Finally, the social, cultural, and economic context of these communities is directly tied to global economic and demographic shifts that alter the racial, ethnic, and social character not only of the nation, but also of urban landscapes. Immigration is a key factor in understanding the complexity of this new model of integration. In each community, a steady flow of immigrants from different parts of the globe entered at various points over the past three decades, reconfiguring the demographic, social, and physical nature of each area. In many respects, immigrant newcomers rebuilt these communities, as street vendors (sometimes lacking proper city permits) and a cadre of small businesses not only filled in vacancies but also created a sense of commercial and social vibrancy. The general global restructuring of cities is on display with the transformation of Argyle Avenue into Asian Village, Seventy-fourth Street into Little India, and the multiethnic Eastlake commercial district. As ethnic entrepreneurs rejuvenate old commercial districts, they not only create new commercial ventures and low-wage, nonprofessional jobs for immigrants, but also demonstrate the reinvention of urban areas through globalization.

Community Development and Image Maintenance

Traditional research on racial segregation or integration has focused on the influence of institutionally structured patterns of inequality (e.g., discrimination) on the racial composition of a community. This focus is legitimate given that neighborhoods "operate always within circumstances given to them by the outside and by others" (Abu-Lughod 1994: 335). In all three cases examined here, immigration and economic shifts altered the racial, ethnic, and social landscapes, creating new challenges for residents and leaders to deal with. Other institutional forces differentially impacted the three communities. For example, the cycle of speculation and movement of capital on Chicago's north lakefront spurred the debate over urban renewal and gentrification in Uptown, while the effect of large numbers of immigrants and the actions of immigrant entrepreneurs galvanized groups in Jackson Heights. External pressures surely impact neighborhood conditions in real and tangible ways. Yet that local groups and individuals always negotiate external forces cannot be understated. When it comes to challenging racial transition and resegregation, pro-integrative efforts are not a simple panacea, as many communities with active pro-integrative organizations and intervention have failed to remain stably integrated (see Molotch 1972; Goodwin 1979; Saltman 1990). However, the one constant finding in studying neighborhoods attempting to stabilize integration is the vital importance of negotiation and intervention on the part of local organizations to challenge institutionalized practices in lending, insurance, real estate, and the media that promote segregated residential spaces. In diverse-by-design communities, the type of strategy matters greatly in determining success (for a review, see Ellen 2000). The research presented here illustrates a new type of integrated neighborhood in which the strategies of the pro-integrative movement do not always apply, as they tend to lack a community group with the articulated goal of maintaining integration. However, local efforts can contribute to stable integration. A key element to this success is a focus on image maintenance and community betterment. Local organizations in all three communities successfully employed community-development strategies to stabilize the area and alter negative perceptions. As noted in Chapter One, neighborhoods are symbolic as well as physical entities, maintaining identities that are continually being shaped and reshaped by perceptions. Thus, the desirability, safety, and vibrancy of a neighborhood is, in part, related to its image. In racially changing areas, neighborhoods develop new identities—usually, these are negative. As Uptown, Jackson Heights, and San Antonio–Fruitvale illustrate, racially changing neighborhoods are often physically and economically declining places when nonwhite residents enter. In addition, outsiders often stereotype integrated neighborhoods as unattractive or risky. And at least initially, some incumbent residents may feel that their integrating neighborhood is being invaded, overrun, or taken over by outsiders (although they do not flee as a result of such feelings). In sum, racially changing neighborhoods find themselves being redefined, and integration becomes part of that redefinition. The direction the redefinition takes is where the efforts of local community organizations come in.

Community-development initiatives were the most common form of locally driven intervention, although these efforts were not directly linked to preserving integration. Instead, they focused on producing assets to improve the quality of life for neighborhood residents.[4] Groups, whether working alone or in collaboration, intervened in the process of racial change by cultivating physical, social, cultural, financial, and political assets, attempting to challenge an area's shortcomings and build upon its strengths. Yet it is important to note that these strategies did not always emerge from an enlightened vision of the moral value of integration. Here I differentiate community-development strategies as indirect or direct, based on their link to stabilizing neighborhood integration. Indirect strategies, the most prominent and common, focus on stabilizing the community without the articulated goal of maintaining integration. Direct strategies focus on bridging gaps between various groups to encourage greater interaction among groups, with some acknowledgement of the value of integration.

Indirect community-development strategies addressed a social need in the community—usually physical or financial—and in the process brought various groups together. These strategies involved improving the commercial, residential, and overall physical character of the area. Whether the work involved improving the character of commercial districts, increasing affordable housing or the availability of youth programming, securing landmark status, or "beautifying" the neighborhood, indirect strategies challenged negative perceptions and stabilized the area. Also, leaders and residents were involved in community-development efforts when they challenged negative media portrayals of the community. For example, Jackson Heights residents challenged news accounts identifying a crime as taking place within its borders; Uptown leaders renamed subsections of the community through historic district status to manipulate the area's image; and San Antonio–Fruitvale leaders touted commercial projects as indications of neighborhood vitality. Behind these efforts is a desire to restructure the symbolic identifiers of each community and, in the process, to fend off physical and economic decline. And while such community-development efforts produced tension in some cases, they were vital to stabilizing the community and gradually led some leaders to work toward maintaining integration.

As residents and leaders involved themselves in indirect community-development strategies to improve and stabilize the community, they began to see the value of integration, and a few organizations were even involved in pro-integrative projects—albeit without an explicit embrace of integration. These direct community-development strategies centered on building the neighborhood's social and cultural assets, rather than its physical, financial, or political assets. Direct strategies involved collaborating to foster dialogue and trust among groups, building multiethnic coalitions, creating multicultural spaces, and even marketing the diversity. In these diverse-by-circumstance communities, these strategies require drawing on disparate and untapped leaders to negotiate an integration that was "thrust upon them." Leaders' actions were not attempts to ensure that everyone gets along, but rather efforts to build community among different racial groups and different visions of what makes a good community.

An important aspect of direct community-development strategies was the attempt to build bridges among the various racial and ethnic groups. For example, attempts were made to bring racial, ethnic, and cultural groups together through neighborhood festivals.[5] Harmony Day in Jackson Heights, the Organization of the Northeast's (ONE) annual meeting, and the multicultural festivals in Eastlake and near the Fruitvale Transit Village were signs of community-building activities that serve as symbols of a commitment to integration, while also encouraging interracial and interethnic contact. However, direct community-development efforts to bring groups together were not always intentional. For example, the struggle over signage and aesthetics in Jackson Heights and over land use in Uptown forced leaders and residents to talk to one another about community concerns. Although a consensus was not always reached, groups were at least reaching out to one another. When the issues crossed racial and ethnic lines, groups did form multiethnic coalitions to achieve goals. The battles over affordable housing in Uptown and obtaining youth services in San Antonio–Fruitvale illustrate how leaders representing different interest groups within the community can join together to accomplish goals. Involvement in these coalitions enabled leaders and residents to see their shared concerns and interests. This realization lays the groundwork for future collaborations. Finally, these efforts may seem less relevant than other community-development activities in terms of neighborhood stabilization, but they are just as vital for altering a community's identity. In conjunction with indirect community-development strategies, these efforts reshaped the community's image as organized, diverse, and viable.

Over time, as leaders and residents worked together to stabilize and strengthen their community, stable integration became a matter of pride and distinction. For example, it was quite common for the number of languages and countries represented in a community to be held up as symbols of distinction and pride. This sense of pride was not just about the number of different groups, but about the way the groups were able to interact in relative peace. For example, I.S. 145 in Jackson Heights celebrated the number of countries represented, while proudly proclaiming on almost all school literature that the school had "one race, the human race." ONE celebrated the area's integration proudly on its postcards with the motto: "We are many, we are ONE." These proclamations are important, given that such neighborhoods are ahead of the curve in a globalizing world. Such claims of distinction are not just symbolic gestures that are less likely to hold the forces of segregation at bay. They are necessary in the formation of a new, attractive community identity that counters the negative stereotypes of integrated neighborhoods.

Finally, in each community, leaders—ranging from businesspersons to political representatives to community groups—attempted to market the diversity and integration, particularly by heralding the ethnically or multiethnically identified commercial districts as community assets. Whether it was Argyle Avenue in Uptown, Seventy-fourth Street in Jackson Heights, or the Eastlake or East Fourteenth and Fruitvale Avenue areas in San Antonio–Fruitvale, leaders pointed to these areas as the embodiment of the integration in the community. This effort can be seen as an attempt to brand the area as diverse, attracting people by bringing people together initially around food. The selling of these areas is a form of affirmative marketing, without necessarily trying to bring whites back to the community. Instead, the goal is to sell the diversity and integration as community strengths, rather than as risks. The idea is that it is possible to sell stable multiethnic/multiracial neighborhoods in the same way that homogeneous residential areas create demand through the presence of high-priced condos and chain stores.

In sum, areas like Uptown, Jackson Heights, and San Antonio–Fruitvale represent positive alternatives to segregated communities. Each community became multiethnic and multiracial without a planned strategy to promote integration. No government or private sector support necessarily brought the mix of racial, ethnic, and cultural groups to each community. Once these were present, however, local interventions helped maintain the integration. Both indirect and direct community-development initiatives represented positive investments in time, energy, and money for improving the community and maintaining integration. These communities offer us an important lesson about the importance of community organizations in stabilizing communities, particularly integrated ones. As Shabecoff and Brophy (1996) write: "Community-based organizations have a rightful place as a carrier and articulator of values. Like many Americans, community developers may think that values are strictly individual and value-setting is solely the job of families and religious institutions, . . . [but] the ability of a community to set its own shared moral values is central to its strength. A public life empty of moral meanings and shared ideals does not secure freedom but offers an open invitation to intolerance. If the neighborhood does not have a clarity of values, others will impose it."

While Uptown, Jackson Heights, and San Antonio–Fruitvale did not "clarify" their values toward integration early on, as the racial mix became more prominent, organizations and leaders became active first in stabilizing the community, then in promoting integration. Over time, there were organizations and leaders who began to articulate new community values of inclusion, tolerance, and integration. Explicitly stressing the value of integrated communities in an otherwise largely segregated metropolis is a particularly useful strategy not only for maintaining integration, but also for attracting needed investment and improved services. Without these investments, maintaining integration is extremely difficult.

BEYOND SEGREGATION

One goal of this research was to go beyond discussions of segregation to focus on the prospect and processes involved in maintaining integration. The cases of Uptown, Jackson Heights, and San Antonio–Fruitvale provide a glimpse into a few key issues surrounding residential integration in the post–civil rights era. It should be clear by this point that there are important exceptions to the rule of segregation and separation. Stable integrated neighborhoods do exist and remain attractive residential choices for many individuals and households. It is also important to avoid romanticizing integration as something simple and easy, for it is neither. Whether planned or unplanned, integration requires a good deal of work on the part of local organizations. This study does illustrate, however, that the way the integration emerges and the local reaction to it play a large role in determining the potential of stable integration. For example, the efforts by the pro-integration movement illustrate that certain strategies (e.g., race-neutral and, to a lesser extent, race-conscious ones) and factors (e.g., absence of public housing, amenities) can contribute to maintaining racial integration. Diverse-by-circumstance communities, as illustrated in Chapters Three through Five, have used some of these same strategies—albeit in very different social settings and with varying levels of commitment to integration—to help stabilize the area and even promote integration. However, the diverse-by-circumstance communities chronicled here faced a different road on the way to maintaining integration. Class and cultural issues as well as immigration posed significant challenges in organizing to preserve integration. These factors, reflections of shifting global economic and social trends, also force us to rethink our notions of integration. I address each in turn.

The Intersection of Race, Ethnicity, and Class

The pro-integrative communities emerging in the civil rights era were largely economically homogeneous. The early leaders of the pro-integration movement were homeowners who formed pro-integrative organizations and were motivated by a mixture of postwar liberalism and concern over neighborhood decline. Not surprisingly, the policies of such local organizations were largely based on maintaining property values or eliminating threats to property values. Leaders saw integration maintenance as tied to fighting fears that integration would lower property values, trigger white flight, and lead to resegregation. The strategies, ranging from banning For Sale signs to equity insurance to testing for discrimination in lending, targeted the middle-class homeowner. During the civil rights movement and the waning years of the second Great Migration of southern blacks to cities, such tactics appeared appropriate, as rapid racial transition was occurring in thousands of neighborhoods across the country. As Andrew Wiese (1995) correctly points out, it was this rapid racial transition that mobilized whites and upwardly mobile African Americans to fight for open housing and intervene in the forces working toward resegregation. While community groups continue to use these strategies with varying degrees of success, several factors have altered the social and demographic landscape. On the one hand, as the Great Migration ended and racial transition slowed, as Wiese points out, so did active and vocal support for the open housing movement and the strategies of organizations in diverse-by-design communities.

On the other hand, global restructuring of the economy and increased immigration have not only recast the country's demographics, but also altered the pattern of racial and ethnic settlement. In the process, the issues that face neighborhoods have changed. Immigrants, largely lower income, have flooded major cities, taking the low-end jobs of the new global economy and searching for affordable housing, usually in declining neighborhoods. Nonimmigrants and nonwhites seeking the same bundle of amenities (e.g., affordable housing, access to transportation, better schools, and safer streets) find these neighborhoods attractive. At the same time, the number of middle-class or upwardly mobile residents increased as jobs in the economy's primary sector started concentrating in cities. As a result, cities across the country began to contend with the pressures of gentrification fueled by the presence of high-end workers. At the neighborhood level, middle-class residents may either find new housing opportunities in "renewed" neighborhoods or scramble to secure affordable housing and work to protect their investment (and "their" community) as immigrant newcomers enter. Both trends reflect the changing social and racial geography of urban areas and neighborhoods. Stable, multiethnic, and multiracial integrated communities are one result of these forces, as are varied class dynamics in stable integrated spaces.

   As a consequence, community leaders seeking to stabilize places like Uptown, Jackson Heights, and San Antonio–Fruitvale do not find the majority of the pro-integration movement strategies as relevant as in previous decades. For example, residents do not see claims for increased enforcement of fair-housing laws as a primary concern—even though it may still be necessary, as it was in Jackson Heights with its small black population—as families and households of color are not having difficulty renting or buying housing based on their race or ethnicity. Banning For Sale signs or providing equity insurance also seems out of place, particularly since property values are increasing in each community. What these communities share with diverse-by-design communities are community-development efforts to reestablish a positive image of the area. However, given the class and racial dynamics, how that image is defined becomes political and a source of conflict among residents and leaders. This is particularly true in places like Uptown and Jackson Heights where there is both a racial and an economic mix. Not surprisingly, an increase in economic and racial integration can foster conflict, usually as a result of the presence of heterogeneous values (Robinson 1989). In these places, the intersections of race and class are on display; both variables are intertwined in such a way that it is impossible to view them separately.

   In Uptown and Jackson Heights, the lack of class solidarity fostered conflict in determining how to improve the community and who to improve it for. For example, in both communities identity and image were flashpoints. Residents and organizations with varying agendas sought to promote different images of the neighborhood through their community-development efforts. In Uptown, the debate over gentrification involved quite different visions of who would benefit. The UCC and the progentrification movement argued that it would benefit the entire community, while others were not so convinced, fearful that such development would displace the poor. In Jackson Heights, debate over preservation versus development was contentious, as beautification and preservation efforts were not as inclusive as they could have been. In some ways, both Uptown and Jackson Heights appear to be "defended" communities. Incumbent residents are not defending the neighborhood from racially and ethnically different newcomers but appear to be defending cultural and class signifiers. This was not the case, however, in San Antonio–Fruitvale. Such cleavages were noticeably absent, as the class composition in San Antonio–Fruitvale was largely lower-middle to working class and the more affluent residents were residentially isolated and relatively absent from community affairs. Unlike Uptown and Jackson Heights, class solidarity was a unifying factor for San Antonio–Fruitvale leaders and residents. Whatever the project, no group coming to the table was threatened by another in terms of taking over or displacing current residents.

Class cleavages appeared to make organizing in Uptown and Jackson Heights more difficult. It is useful to compare these communities to the diverse-by-design model of integration. Diverse-by-design communities have tended to be more homogenous in terms of class. When class backgrounds are fairly similar, the goals and methods for development and neighborhood improvement are usually agreed upon (i.e., most residents want growth and development in order to alter negative perceptions). Diverse-by-circumstance communities, on the other hand, tend to be racially integrated and class-heterogeneous environments. As illustrated in Uptown and Jackson Heights, not everyone agrees on the goals and methods of neighborhood improvement. In Uptown, lower-income residents feared that condo development would push (and to some extent already pushed) them out of the community by driving up housing values (both rental and owner occupied). Middle-class residents in Uptown viewed such development as necessary for stabilizing the community. In Jackson Heights, race and class intersect again as the immigrants moving into the community and seeking an economic foothold view development as good (even if haphazard looking), while middle-class whites tend to view certain types of development as harmful. These issues make discussions over land use less straightforward than in other places. In essence, they require residents to confront their class biases, as well as any racial biases.

The issues of class conflict and cultural conflict are often left out of the research literature on integrated communities, yet class and cultural differences must be taken seriously. Left unaddressed, class cleavages can create a sense of intolerance and exclusiveness as destructive to stable integration as racial conflict. However, when managed correctly, conflict can be functional for community stability, by strengthening bonds between loosely structured groups and increasing community cohesion (Coser 1971; Erasmus 1968; Alinsky 1972). In diverse-by-circumstance communities, a vital strategy for maintaining integration involves cultivating leaders who are both sensitive to the link between race and class and willing to facilitate negotiations among the varying views and outlooks before these become divisive and destructive. Without leaders paying close attention to community dialogue, it is easy to miss the underlying issues or concerns of residents and leaders. Cultivating social and political capital within the community thus becomes more important than controlling the real estate market or testing for discrimination. Fortunately, leaders in all three case-study communities found ways to use the conflict to bring various groups together to consider common needs and desires. Yet the point should be clear: leaders face unique challenges to stabilizing integration when the mix is racial, ethnic, cultural, and economic. This is made more difficult given that racial and class interests are so interconnected, making it hard to deal with either separately.

Bridging racial, cultural, and class differences in diverse-by-design communities involves breaking down both racial stereotypes and the assimilation model of race relations. It is important to distinguish between two types of social integration: one-way and two-way. One-way integration suggests that nonwhite newcomers assimilate into mainstream white (middle-class) culture without sharing power. In Jackson Heights and Uptown, many long-term white residents regularly avoided talking directly about race, instead referring to various social problems (e.g., garbage, people hanging out on the street, crime) resulting from the emergence of newcomers. These discussions appeared rooted in misconceptions of different racial and ethnic groups, as well as in fears that nonwhite newcomers would not assimilate into "their" community, or at least their vision of the future of the community. Tied to this is an unspoken assumption that integration is okay as long as nonwhites accept white middle-class culture. Such a view creates division, resentment, and diminished desire for integration.

What is needed is two-way integration. As John Calmore notes: "Real integration is a two-way street. Whites must somehow come to see themselves not merely as the gracious hosts of integration, but, rather, as the hardworking, risk-taking joint agents of integration. They must push for it more, assume some of the risks, and carry a heavier load. They, too, will have go through some changes" (2001: 50). This approach requires not only an end to demands that people of color acclimatize to "universal expectations" of what is deemed proper, but also the formation of coalitions to create social conditions where the "meaningful contact" and "cultural sharing" go both ways. Or put another way, two-way integration occurs when the values, beliefs, traditions, and even language of each group are equally valued and power is shared. This implies more than a "tasting of cultures," but transcending boundaries to interact as equal members in an overall culture. This move has proven to be the elusive next step in efforts to bring about racial justice. Careful examination of the organizations of the pro-integration movement, at least in the early stages, shows movement in that direction. Also, the cases presented indicate that leaders struggled to foster this equality, with greater and lesser degrees of success.

Integration and Racial Justice

While this study is about the processes involved in stabilizing multiethnic and multiracial integration, some reflection on the how successful these communities were in achieving racial justice is in order. Indeed, a principal justification for residential integration by race is to alleviate racial inequality. It has been assumed that the life chances for people of color would improve in integrated settings. Acknowledging that assessing the impact integration has in this regard is complex, looking at school quality and the regional context provides some insight. On the one hand, this study shows that many people of color living in or moving into the three neighborhoods improved their quality of life. In each case, the incoming residents found affordable and better-quality housing, safer streets, improved access to transportation, and greater neighborhood stability than could be found in other parts of the city. However, are these really enough? The answer is obviously no. Other factors have to be considered.

Indicators of school quality are one way to address this issue, as education is considered a strong predictor of social mobility. For the most part, the schools in the three neighborhoods are similar. They have large percentages of English Language Learners (i.e., students whose first language is not English), students with limited English proficiency, and students classified by the districts as low income. Test scores indicate that while students at these schools are achieving at higher levels than students at other (more segregated) city neighborhood schools, they are still below the state average. San Antonio–Fruitvale, decidedly lower in income than Uptown or Jackson Heights, is the exception, as students are testing well below both county and state averages.

These findings have various implications. On the one hand, the results indicate that such schools face barriers that more homogeneous (race and class) neighborhoods do not. Undoubtedly, such "resource pressure" negatively impacts perceptions of neighborhood-school quality and will prevent many middle-class families, particularly already underrepresented whites, from sending their children to neighborhood public schools. (This effect is supported by anecdotal evidence in each neighborhood.) The fact remains that while these schools are incredibly diverse and multicultural (often viewed as an asset), white and other middle-class families seem to avoid them, particularly when there is a charter or magnet option available. On the other hand, in Uptown and Jackson Heights, test scores are not that bad. While several local schools are underperforming, overall the schools appear to be doing a better job than those in other city neighborhoods. So, at least for students of color, integrated schools seem to be providing better educational opportunities than more segregated ones. However, it should be noted that although the schools are, for the most part, performing at acceptable levels, they are not on a par with schools in wealthier and suburban districts. Thus, this model of integration is limited in its ability to provide access to improved life chances for people of color. The Gautreaux or Move to Opportunity model of integration, by sending students of color to resource-rich and higher-performing schools, may do better at improving the life chances of these students (Rubinowitz and Rosenbaum 2000).

Another way to look at the opportunities and limitations of this model of integration for achieving racial justice is to consider the metropolitan context in which these communities exist. While this study focused on how individuals and community groups worked to maintain racial integration and a better quality of life, there is always a larger context to consider. For example, these neighborhoods were indeed shaped by global economic and immigration shifts. However, regional shifts that have been occurring since the 1970s are also relevant. For example, employment has largely moved to the suburbs. The proportion of manufacturing jobs has risen in the suburbs, while substantially declining in central cities (W. Wilson 1997; Ranney 2002). In addition, approximately 60 percent of the nation's offices are now located in the suburbs (Pierce 1993).

The lack of jobs in central cities has led to an increase of concentrated poverty, which impacts not only the lives of families but also inner city schools. The result is that better opportunities for jobs and schools become concentrated in the suburbs. Thus, the positives created by the community-empowerment efforts in these cases are counterbalanced by regional disparities. This is one reason racially integrated neighborhoods have long been considered "fragile." Local efforts are necessary and vital, but without regional attempts to reduce racial disparities, the long-term success of maintaining neighborhood integration, and thus of achieving racial justice, will always remain incomplete.

Immigration and Defining Integration

Understanding diverse-by-circumstance communities requires addressing immigration and how it alters discussions of integration. Immigration played a significant role in slowing the pace of racial change in the three communities studied, even contributing to stable integration. Leaders in each community noted that the presence of multiple groups reduces fears of rapid racial transition or of one group "taking over" the area. This is important, given that the history of racial transition and resegregation involved a fear that if too many blacks moved in, property values would decline, resegregation would begin, and the neighborhood would collapse. The presence of more than one group appears to soothe such fears and results in a slowing of racial change. It is reasonable to argue that Latino and Asian immigrants serve as a buffer between whites and blacks. In other words, when there are Latinos and Asians also moving into a community, white residents are not as threatened by incoming blacks. As a leader in Uptown suggested in our August 22, 1996, interview: "If you had the kind of white flight [in Uptown] that the city or the north side has had and you didn't have immigrants to fill the vacuum, maybe Uptown would be 100 percent black by now." A leader in Jackson Heights echoed this view. The multiethnic and multiracial composition of the area makes it difficult for any one group to claim ownership or to identify it as, for example, a "white" or "black" or "Latino" neighborhood.

That the Latino and Asian newcomers were newly arrived immigrants adds to this reality. Immigrants generally have differences of outlook, of a sense of public life in their new home, and of needs. Whites often feel less threatened by Latino and Asians than by African Americans. Also, immigrants are attractive as neighbors because, as Robert Suro notes in *Strangers among Us*: "They seem unsullied by familiar conflicts, especially the conflict between native-born blacks and whites" (1998: 44). To some

Americans, immigrants and even native-born Latinos and Asians do not carry the baggage of the civil rights movement and in some ways are the embodiment of traditional virtues, such as strong families and hard work. This is not to suggest that if we include multiple groups the chance for stable integration increases. If anything, it suggests that the color line between blacks and whites remains as relevant as ever in U.S. culture and housing markets. Race clearly matters in these contexts, as leaders seem quite aware of the negative racial attitudes that go along with neighborhoods that are either predominantly black or mixed among blacks and whites. While this view is nothing new, it does suggest that we continue to pay attention to why whites remain so fearful of living with blacks. What is new is the increasing number of multiethnic and multiracial neighborhoods. Close examinations of such places provide unique insight into the nature of integration.

In addition, the current wave of immigrants to central city neighborhoods differs from the turn-of-the-century flood of European immigrants. The availability of inexpensive air travel, cheap telephone service, and the Internet "encourage immigrants and their offspring to remain tied to their ancestral homeland" (Lindsay and Singer 2003: 230). As Michael Jones-Correa notes: "Latin American immigrants . . . are not fully part of the immediate neighborhood communities. Latin American immigrants, for their part, do not see themselves as being bound to a territorial community that is physically present, but to one that exists mostly in memory" (1998: 21). In other words, the allegiances of many recently arrived immigrants are not simply to their current neighborhood, but to their home countries and the social ties they have to such places. The character of recently arriving immigrants is more fluid and, as such, hinders organizational efforts and political participation. Community leaders have to find ways to bring such groups into the integration project of each neighborhood.

Finally, these changes require us to broaden our definition of integration. The changing demographic, social, and economic patterns in our cities require us to move beyond the notion that integration involves simply bringing middle-class blacks and whites together. Multiethnic and multiracial communities, even ones that are neither solidly middle income nor predominantly white (e.g., Jackson Heights, San Antonio–Fruitvale), constitute a form of integration. The idea is not to find a way to attract more whites—suggested by some in the pro-integration movement and recent literature—but, rather, to understand the process in these spaces in order to maintain integration. It is not enough to find spaces where numerical integration is occurring. Just having people of different races or classes is not enough. Helen Shiller, alderman of the Forty-sixth Ward in Uptown, captured this notion very well in our July 15, 1996, interview:

> The truth of the matter is that the stability of the community is not defined by what percentage of people are different ethnic or racial or socioeconomic backgrounds. The real test of the strength of the community is its own process of struggle, its own collective struggle to define itself. To what extent . . . do people join together on the basis of respect? With respect being a key part of it, that we are respecting people as human beings. So that if there are collective structures in the community that allow [people] to be able to struggle to change the basic things that are not fair or not functional in terms of the development of their children, their development of their families, et cetera. It is when you have the opportunity to realize the potential in the community.

Shiller is suggesting that demographics are not enough. Racial diversity is not integration if you never talk to your neighbors. Thus, the test of stable integration is not in the percentages of groups, but in the community's process to join different groups in such a way that there is respect and a sharing of power. This is difficult to measure. And this difficulty illustrates the complexity of integration and the need to broaden our discussion of integration.

THE CHANGING realities of our nation's mosaic are inescapable. Given that these changes promise to continue for decades to come, they will test the forces that knit the country together. As James Lindsay and Audrey Singer recently noted:

> Two decades of intensive immigration are rapidly remaking our racial and ethnic mix. The American mosaic—which has always been complex—is becoming even more intricate; . . . the rapid growth in the size of America's Latino and Asian communities as a result of immigration means that our national narrative on diversity will no longer be only, or perhaps even primarily, about whites and blacks. . . . Diversity in the twenty-first century will still be about race, but it will involve more hues. How well America succeeds in weaving its newcomers into the social fabric will do much to determine whether the American experiment with diversity continues to be a success. (2003: 217–218)

However, these trends do not exist in the abstract. In our nation's largest cities, they are engraved in urban space. Travel to any city—particularly any large metropolitan area—and these changes are on display on the streets and in the shops and parks. Uptown, Jackson Heights, and San Antonio–Fruitvale are visible reminders of these larger national and cultural trends. And while these quite remarkable places reflect the potential for multiethnic and multiracial integration, they should not be romanticized. Racial change and integration cause stress. These three communities are important to understand because they magnify the issues and potential lines of division that will occur in the larger society as a result of demographic changes. These issues are multifaceted and far-reaching. They range from cultural and class conflict to debates over the relevance of assimilation. The efforts by community groups give some insight into the challenges that emerge as multiethnic and multiracial populations mix, as well as the role of agency in the process of negotiating the impact of larger and often institutional forces.

The rapidly changing racial and ethnic mix in the United States has engendered predictions of greater racial balkanization or integration. Balkanization implies that the growing diversity is not being felt uniformly across the country and that it is leading to greater racial and ethnic polarization. Integration counters this fear by offering the possibility of a more inclusive, tolerant, and even multicultural society. The cases studies examined here demonstrate that the situation is more complex than we think. For example, balkanization and integration appear to be occurring at the same time. The conflict that has resulted in multiethnic and multiracial integrated areas illustrates the potential for polarization; the efforts to bring groups together to work on community issues shows the promise of integration. While it is tempting to fall into either/or thinking when it comes to polarization and integration, this dichotomy is false and keeps us from understanding the processes involved in creating either. The challenge for community leaders and policy makers is to find ways to reduce polarization and generate greater recognition of the value of integrated spaces.

Notes

PREFACE

1. In Uptown, I supplemented the open-ended interviews I conducted with interview data collected for a collaborative research project on Uptown by researchers from Loyola University of Chicago and the Organization of the North East (ONE). Although these interviews were based on a different set of research questions, they proved to be an invaluable source for understanding community dynamics. I acknowledge Phil Nyden, Joanne Adams, Maryann Mason, Josh Hoyt, and ONE staff and member representatives who conducted the research.

2. Living on the northern edge of Uptown provided me great access to the community. In 1996, I spent more than a month in Jackson Heights. During the same year, I rented an apartment in Fruitvale for two months. I made return trips to each community in the years that followed.

INTRODUCTION

1. For a good discussion of the complexity of integration, see Hartman 2001, which includes a symposium entitled "Is Integration Possible" (33–90).

2. I acknowledge that the literature in this area has been quite mixed. See Rosenbaum et al. 1991 and Sigelman et al. 1996 for a more detailed discussion of the contact hypothesis.

CHAPTER ONE

1. David Gordon suggests that manufacturers initially located their factories in cities to capitalize on an urban environment that gave them the upper hand in labor disputes. Because both heavy manufacturing and residential areas for its employees were located away from the central core, and individuals in nonindustrial or light industrial work were packed in or near the central business district, there was little opportunity for the two groups of workers to see themselves as potential allies (1984: 32–40). Industrialization segmented social and urban space in this way to prevent interaction among various groups.

2. Between 1910 and 1930, approximately 1.4 million African Americans left southern farms and cities to move north (Farley and Allen 1987).

3. Before 1900, the main way to restrict blacks from buying property was through deed restrictions on single land parcels. Restrictive covenants were devised to allow local real estate boards or neighborhood organizations to establish rules forbidding real estate agents from selling to blacks or anyone else whose presence was deemed "detrimental to property values in that neighborhood" (Massey and Denton 1993; Helper 1969; Trotter 1985).

4. The second wave of southern migrants, greater than the post–World War I wave, brought a net flow north of approximately three million blacks between 1950 and 1960 (Farley and Allen 1987; Massey and Denton 1993).

5. For example, in 1942, 84 percent of white Americans polled answered affirmatively to the question "Do you think there should be separate sections in towns and cities for Negroes to live in?" and in 1962, 61 percent of whites surveyed agreed that "white people have the right to keep blacks out of their neighborhood if they want to, and blacks should respect that right" (Allport 1958; Schuman, Steeh, and Bobo 1985).

6. Blockbusting has been described as a practice of real estate agents to exploit the color line for profit (Massey and Denton 1993: 37–38). Blockbusting agents would select a promising area for racial turnover, one that often bordered the black ghetto and contained older housing, poorer families, aging households, and some apartment buildings. Agents would quietly purchase a small number of homes and apartments in the area, renting or selling them to carefully chosen black families. Whites inevitably reacted with violence and resistance. Agents countered this with deliberate attempts to increase white fears and spur black demand, often going door-to-door warning white residents of the impending "invasion" and offering to purchase or rent homes on generous terms. As the number of panicking whites increased, realtors would advertise widely within the black community, quickly expanding black demand. Realtors would then inflate the price when selling to blacks. Given that most blacks were more than eager to escape the overcrowding and deplorable conditions of the ghetto, they succumbed to inflated prices, ensuring tremendous profits for real estate agents.

7. Both FHA and VA programs, by insuring up to 80 percent of the value of a property, lowered a lending institution's risk and allowed the borrower to pay a low down payment, with the remaining principal and interest spread out over a twenty-five- or thirty-year period, making it possible for millions of white families to realize the "suburban dream."

8. Between 1935 and 1975, the FHA insured about 9.5 million housing units representing a face value of more than $109 billion (Bureau of National Affairs 1976).

9. Between 1946 and 1959, blacks purchased less than 2 percent of all housing financed with the assistance of federal mortgage insurance (Gelfand 1975).

10. Taeuber and Taeuber report examples such as Chicago's south and west sides, Cleveland's east side, Philadelphia's north and west sides, and most of central city Newark, Detroit, Baltimore, and Washington, D.C. (1965).

11. Segregation levels among whites and blacks in the suburbs (an index of dissimilarity score of 70) were not dramatically lower than in central cities (77) (Massey and Denton 1993). In addition, suburbs accepting black residents were older, lower in socioeconomic status, and densely populated (Clay 1979; Lake 1981; Logan and Schneider 1984).

12. For example, studies indicate that areas with small or declining black populations receive a greater share of mortgage money and that mortgage credit is reduced in areas where black population growth is occurring (Dane 1991; Hula 1981; Squires, Velez, and Taeuber 1991; Yinger 1999).

13. Ernest Burgess, a prominent scholar at the University of Chicago, used this phrase to refer to the cycle through which the character and composition of urban land areas changed as cities grew. Burgess noted that invasion-succession occurred through four stages, not clearly distinguished, but overlapping and blending into one another. The stages included: (a) first entry of newcomers or new land uses (i.e., invasion); (b) reaction to the entry by existing inhabitants; (c) continued entry by newcomers and abandonment of the area by original inhabitants; and (d) complete displacement of the original inhabitants or land uses by the new ones (i.e., succession) (1928). Racial change, however, was just one example of the invasion-succession model. The model has been used broadly to explain how cities grow and develop (see Keating and Smith 1996).

14. Real estate brokers, standing to reap tremendous profits, unscrupulously promoted rapid racial transition. Brokers would attempt to exploit white fears of living in a black area and losing the value of their housing investment by spreading rumors that the neighborhood was declining and changing. A vicious cycle would be created—as more white homeowners put their houses up for sale, others were frightened and encouraged to sell. White fear and desire to leave the neighborhood rapidly allowed brokers and speculators to purchase these homes cheaply. Brokers and speculators would then sell these houses at inflated prices to middle-income blacks (most of whom were eager to escape the current conditions of the ghetto), creating a dual housing market, one for whites and one for blacks.

15. Chicago's Hyde Park–Kenwood Community Conference, organized in 1949, was the first (Saltman 1990).

16. For instance, in the 1960s and early 1970s, community groups emerged in the following areas: Oak Park and Park Forest, Illinois; Shaker Heights, Ohio; Butler-Tarkington in Indianapolis; Sherman Park in Milwaukee; Crenshaw in Los Angeles; Volluntine-Evergreen in Memphis; Rochester New York's Nineteenth Ward; Blue Hills in Hartford; the west side of Akron; and Belmont-Hillsboro in Nashville.

17. A fair-housing audit is a survey technique designed to isolate the impact of a person's minority status on the way he or she is treated when inquiring of either a landlord or real estate agent about available housing. Audits consist of "successive visits to the same housing agent by two audit teammates who are equally qualified for housing but who differ in minority status" (Yinger 1996: 22). Each teammate then independently fills out a detailed audit survey form, describing what he or she has been told and how he or she was treated (see Yinger 1996).

18. Incentives may include "deal sweeteners" such as low-cost appraisals and closing fees, or even low-interest mortgage loans for those making pro-integrative moves (Keating 1994; DeMarco and Galster 1993).

Chapter Two

1. This statement itself represents white privilege. Whites *are* equally segregated and isolated from racial minorities. Whites, however, have greater access to power and privilege, diluting the deleterious effects of their segregation.

2. The Hart-Cellar Immigration Act abolished previous country-of-origin immigration quotas, which designated small quotas to southern and eastern Europe and even smaller quotas to Asia. The immigration act allowed more immigrants to ether the United States and created two criteria for admission: family ties to citizens or permanent residents or possession of scarce and needed skills. As a result, there was a dramatic increase in immigration from Asia, Latin America, and the Caribbean (Bureau of Citizenship and Immigration Services 2003).

3. This is particularly true in a dozen or so "gateway" immigration magnets (e.g., the counties in the New York, San Francisco, Chicago, and Los Angeles regions) (Frey 2000).

4. Several studies reveal that the diversification of cities is spreading to suburbs as well (Frey 2000; Myers 1999).

5. The index of dissimilarity is a measure of evenness; it detects how evenly two racial groups (usually majority and minority) are distributed across a geographical area. Evenness is defined in relation to the racial composition of the overall area. For example, "if a city is 10 percent black, then an even residential pattern requires that every neighborhood be 10 percent black and 90 percent white" (Massey and Denton 1993: 20). For a neighborhood that is 20 percent black to reach a racially even distribution, 10 percent of blacks must move to a neighborhood where black percentage is less than 10 percent. Thus, the measure indicates the percentage of blacks that would have to move to achieve an even racial residential structure. It is considered a "macro" measure of residential settlement, as it adds up the dissimilarity scores of tracts or blocks into a score for the city or metropolitan region. Researchers are thus able to compare segregate scores across time and space, although the measure limits their ability to understand intraregional trends.

6. Metropolitan areas were selected for this study if they had a total population of over one million, black population shares of greater than 5 percent in 1990, and Latino population shares of less than 30 percent (Ellen 2000).

7. The Chicago, New York, and Oakland neighborhoods selected for this analysis had to have a minimum of 100 residents and small percentages of individuals living in group quarters (e.g., jails, mental institutions, homeless shelters, and other institutional shelters).

8. The ND index considers how numerically close a subarea (e.g., census tract) is to the overall racial composition of an area and allows for the presence of multiple groups (i.e., more than two) in a single measure. Integration, then, is quantitatively defined as the population distribution of each group in a given city. Thus, considering four racial categories (white, black, Latino, and Asian), an integrated neighborhood is one with percentages of the four groups roughly similar to those found in the city overall. For example, in New York in 1990, an integrated neighborhood would be 42 percent white, 26 percent black, 24 percent Latino, and 7 percent Asian. The ND index detects where a neighborhood lies along the continuum of heterogeneous and homogenous. A stable integrated (or segregated) neighborhood is one that was categorized as integrated for more than ten years.

9. The categories white, black, and Latino include all individuals who did not identify themselves as non-Hispanic. Individuals identifying themselves as American Indian or "other" are included in the "white" category in order to include all groups. This clearly creates a problematic umbrella group, masking cultural traditions and diversity. While this assumption is arguably problematic, the relative size of these population groups justifies the move.

10. Overall, Oakland is actually a more multiethnic and multiracial city than Chicago or New York. Scholars have explained this by noting that Oakland never experienced the historically harsh racism and discrimination that marked northern rust-belt cities (Lee and Wood 1991). This might explain the high levels of integration in 1980. Second, the mean ND Index score for Oakland neighborhoods in all three census years is close to 20 points lower than that of Chicago or New York. Third, in 58 percent of Oakland's moderately integrated tracts in 2000, no single racial group constituted a majority of the population. This implies two things: (a) Oakland neighborhoods are already more multiethnic and multiracial than other areas; and (b) based on the index's assumptions, Oakland's neighborhoods are more difficult to categorize as integrated (even though they are more mixed than integrated neighborhoods in the other cities)—this is a limitation of the ND Index. Finally, Oakland is a much smaller city (less than 400,000 residents) than Chicago or New York. And although immigration has altered the demographics in each city, Oakland has been disproportionately impacted (e.g., over 128,000 immigrants between 1992 and 2000). Increases in immigration drive up levels of segregation. In sum, the numerical picture of integration in Oakland is not entirely accurate, as there are contextual factors that mask the extent of the city's multiethnic and multiracial neighborhoods.

11. Studies by Frey and Farley (1996) and McKinney and Schnare (1989) also contribute to this conclusion.

12. Almost 40 percent of the nation's Asian population gains in the 1990s were in Los Angeles, New York City, and San Francisco; 43 percent of all U.S. Asians live in these three metros (Frey 1998).

CHAPTER THREE

1. Andrea Lowry, interview by author, Chicago, June 1999. Lowry is a twenty-seven-year-old African American college student.

2. Courtyard structures are large structures arranged in a horseshoe with the open end facing the street.

3. These building types were spatially separate, with mansions near the lake, apartment buildings east of Broadway, and more inconspicuous single-family homes and three-flat buildings west of Broadway.

4. Conversation with Timothy Larkin, Uptown Baptist Church, December 2000.

5. Loyola/ONE interview by Maryann Mason, Uptown, June 11, 1991.

6. Chicago Fact Book Consortium 1995; U.S. Bureau of the Census 1980, 1990, 2000.

7. The schools included are Arai Middle School, and Brennemann, Goudy, McCutcheon, Peirce, Stewart, Stockton, and Swift elementary schools. Several

schools on the border of Uptown and Edgewater are included because of their proximity to Uptown.

8. According to the Chicago Public Schools Web site, "low-income students are pupils, aged 3 through 17, from families receiving public aid, living in institutions for neglected or delinquent children, being supported in foster homes with public funds, and/or eligible to receive free or reduced-price lunch" (www.cps.k12.il.us).

9. The mobility rate is based on the number of students who enroll in or leave school during the school year. Students may be counted more than once. Students in schools with high mobility rates can be negatively affected due to the continual readjustments school staffs must make to accommodate the influx of new students. Ibid.

10. The Overall Student Performance ("all state tests") and overall Illinois Standards Achievement Test (ISAT) measures were used here as indicators of school quality. "Illinois State School Report Cards" 2001 (www.statereportcards.cps.k12.il.us/), accessed January 4, 2004.

11. The Neighborhood Diversity Index was used here (see Chapter Two).

12. For example, while Eritreans are usually referred to as Ethiopians, a long history of tension separates these groups. Eritreans are among the most distressed people in Ethiopia. Eritrea, a province of the coast of the Red Sea, was once part of Italian East Africa. The province then came under British rule, after which the United Nations placed it under Ethiopian rule. Since the 1960s, Eritreans have been engaged in a brutal battle for independence. This history is not forgotten once Eritreans and Ethiopians arrive on U.S. soil. On the other hand, black Americans often treat both groups with disdain upon discovering that they are "foreign" (Cross 1985).

13. Loyola/ONE interview by Joanne Adams, Uptown, June 18, 1991.

14. Loyola/ONE interview by Maryann Mason, Uptown, June 11, 1991.

15. In the early 1960s, Students for Democratic Society (SDS) initiated Jobs or Income Now (JOIN) in an effort to push the student social movement beyond campuses and to build ties with the urban working class. JOIN found a home in Uptown, seeing its Appalachian white population as a potential ally for the civil rights movement.

16. See chapter 3 of Bennett's *Neighborhood Politics* (1997) for a detailed discussion of the urban renewal battle.

17. Slim Coleman was a founder of the Intercommunal Survival Committee (later the Heart of Uptown Coalition—HOUC). Coleman, a former member of SDS with ties to the Black Panther party, represented a political coalition described by some as notorious and enigmatic. He expressed their agenda: "We're interested in keeping the poor together as a power base. When you scatter people into isolated pockets they remain isolated" (in Bennett 1991: 46).

18. Chicago is divided into fifty wards, each electing a representative to the city council. Uptown is served by the Forty-eighth (Alderman Maryann Smith) and Forty-sixth (Alderman Helen Shiller).

19. I employ Neil Smith's definition of gentrification: "Gentrification is a process by which the poor and working-class neighborhoods in the inner city are refurbished via an influx of private capital and middle-class home-buyers and

renters—in neighborhoods that had previously experienced disinvestment and a middle-class exodus" (1996: 32). Those sympathetic to the process use more anodyne language, such as "neighborhood recycling" or "renaissance."

20. As the designation passed, key organizations protested and formed an antidisplacement coalition. Although, not surprisingly, residents (most low-income) were displaced, the coalition was organized enough to secure commitments for affordable housing units from the city.

21. In 1990, only 24 percent of Uptown's occupied housing structures had between two and nine units. Over 60 percent had twenty or more units.

22. Home Mortgage Disclosure Act data are intended to provide the public with loan data, useful in determining whether financial institutions are serving the housing needs of their communities and to aid in identifying possible discriminatory actions. Banks, savings associations, credit unions, and other mortgage-lending institutions must report data about home purchase and home improvement to various regulatory agencies (Right-to-Know Network 1999).

23. The median income for families in the Chicago metropolitan area is considerably higher than that of the city ($30,707). The median income for Uptown families is very close to the city median.

24. Langer was instrumental in obtaining the Sheridan Park historic designation. Also, during the mid-1980s, Langer rehabilitated twenty-two buildings in the Heart of Uptown/Sheridan Park area, creating over five hundred units of housing, including many condominium conversions (Juárez Robles 1988).

25. Sheridan Park is not the only part of Uptown that has been renamed for the sake of distancing it from the community. Ted Kleine, a reporter for the *Chicago Reader*, suggests that the new names are an "effective marketing tool" until people find out the area is located in Uptown (1998a). In many of the areas that have received bad publicity in the past, marketers try to sell potential buyers the areas by calling them something else.

26. Several informants noted this event and news accounts also chronicled it (Juárez Robles 1988).

27. Loyola/ONE interview by Maryann Mason, Uptown, June 11, 1991.

28. Loyola/ONE interview by Joanne Adams, Uptown, April 3, 1991.

29. The associations represented American Indian, Vietnamese, Chinese, Ethiopian, Laotian, and Cambodian residents.

30. Nyden and Adams report in one building approximately 60 percent of tenants are foreign born and many are recent immigrants from Russia, Romania, Central America, and the Philippines (1996: 16).

31. Low-interest mortgages allowed developers to make money and private involvement permitted the government to provide affordable housing different from a "housing project." Prepayment is clearly beneficial to landlords. Many buildings are near the lakefront and low-interest mortgages position owners to substantially profit.

32. Loyola/ONE interview by Joanne Adams, Uptown, April 3, 1991.

33. I draw here on Lewis Coser's (1971) classic theory of the functions of conflict. In addition, my thoughts are informed by Robinson's (1989) suggested conflict approach to community development.

34. Loyola/ONE interview by Maryann Mason, Uptown, August 11, 1991.

35. According to these authors, signs of incivility include public drinking, abandoned buildings, graffiti, litter, poorly kept-up parks, and children out of control.

36. See "A World of Healing in the Babel That Is Uptown" for the full story on this amazing clinic (Condor 2000).

37. Loyola/ONE interview by Maryann Mason, Uptown, June 11, 1991.

38. Ibid.

39. Ibid.

40. Ibid.

41. Here I am indebted to Larry Bennett, who suggested the term.

42. Quoted from Alderman Shiller's Web site, www.cityofchicago.org/Ward46/BroadwayLawrenceTIF.html, accessed June 10, 2001.

CHAPTER FOUR

1. John Nicholson, interview by author, Jackson Heights, November 1998. Nicholson is a forty-year-old white co-op owner and corporate professional.

2. Jackson Heights was no different from many restrictive and elite suburbs that developed during this time (Jackson 1985). MacDougall's plan was similar to those of other "garden cities" built in Queens around the same time: Robert Law Olmstead's more upscale Forest Hills Gardens and Sunnyside Gardens (see Goldberger 1983).

3. A cooperative is a form of real estate ownership common to apartment buildings. Unlike condominium owners, who purchase individual units outright, co-op owners are shareholders in a corporation. The corporation's purpose is to own and operate the property. In return for their investment, co-op owners receive a proprietary lease to their apartment.

4. Community boards are decentralized planning units introduced by the city in 1973 in an effort to bring government more in touch with neighborhood concerns (Sanjek 1998). Ironically, although most of Jackson Heights' residents are members of minority groups, its political and community board representatives are mostly white (see Jones-Correa 1998).

5. In the 1990s Queens experienced a net increase of 269,000 immigrants and a net decrease of 346,000 domestic residents. The influx of immigrants along with positive birth-death rates led to an overall population increase (Pindell 2000).

6. When Rocker was a pitcher for major-league baseball's Atlanta Braves, he commented about New York and the Number 7 line that passes through Jackson Heights on its way to Shea Stadium: "Imagine having to take the [Number] 7 train to the ballpark, looking like you're [riding through] Beirut next to some kid with purple hair next to some queer with AIDS right next to some dude who just got out of jail for the fourth time right next to some 20-year-old mom with four kids. It's depressing." He also stated: "The biggest thing I don't like about New York are the foreigners. I'm not a very big fan of foreigners. You can walk an entire block in Times Square and not hear anybody speaking English. Asians and Koreans and Vietnamese and Indians and Russians and Spanish people and everything up there. How the hell did they get in this country?" (Pearlman 1999).

7. The community was described as a "microcosm of the world" in many of my interviews. Giovanna Reid, Community Board 3 district manager, later said of the 2000 census: "The census has confirmed what we've already known. Community Board 3 is a small 'microcosm of the world'" (quoted in Cheng 2001).

8. A top official of the city's planning commission remarked that "we did a better job of counting addresses in Queens. There are all sorts of units that we found that the Census Bureau didn't know about" (quoted in Lowe 2001).

9. In 1980 Queens's white population constituted 71 percent; by 2000 a third of the residents were white (Lowe 2001).

10. The schools included are three elementary schools (PS 2, PS 69, PS 149), one middle school (IS 145), and a charter school (the Renaissance School). Since the Renaissance School did not open until the 1996–1997 school year, earlier data were unavailable.

11. New York City Department of Education 2000, *1999–2000 Annual School Reports*, Jackson Heights School/P.S. 69: District 30, www.nycenet.edu/daa, accessed July 22, 2001.

12. Ibid., 2003, *2001–2002 Annual School Reports*, www.nycenet.edu/daa/SchoolReports, accessed December 30, 2003.

13. Ibid.

14. The historic district and north of Northern Boulevard are the most obvious areas. However, the historic district cuts a jagged line through the community, leaving parts of the community distinct. The upper Nineties includes those streets close to Junction Boulevard between Northern Boulevard and Roosevelt Avenue. The low Seventies includes those streets around Seventy-first Street to the Bronx-Queens Expressway, between Northern and Roosevelt.

15. These data are from the 1990 census. Immigration data from the 1990s suggest that these patterns have continued.

16. These figures have changed very little from 1990. In fact, the ratio of Hispanic renters to owners increased in 2000.

17. The U.S. Department of Housing and Urban Development defines overcrowding as occurring when a housing unit contains more than one person per room. Severe overcrowding exists when a unit contains more than 1.5 persons per room.

18. Jackson Heights residents, interviews by the author, May 15, 1996, and November 21, 1995.

19. Sanjek (1998) reports a similar trend in the adjacent and equally diverse neighborhood of Elmhurst.

20. Resident, interview by the author, May 15, 1996. The groups included the Jackson Heights Community Development Corporation (JHCDC), Jackson Heights Beautification Group, and various other neighborhood associations from Jackson Heights, East Elmhurst, and North Corona.

21. Rudy Greco, telephone interview by author, July 1996. This sentiment was common among community leaders.

22. While the claim that most Indian shoppers and merchants are not Jackson Heights residents is confirmed by interviews with Indian merchants and by census data, anecdotal evidence suggests the numbers are changing.

23. This quote, attributable to fieldwork by Mohammed Bazzi, a *Newsday* reporter, also appears in Kasinitz, Bazzi, and Doane, 1998:170.

24. This quote is attributed to Jeffrey Saunders in Kasinitz, Bazzi, and Doane, 1998:173.

25. This information comes from a Community United Methodist Church pamphlet commemorating Reverend Armitstead's retirement (June 4, 1995).

CHAPTER FIVE

1. Rosalina Palacios, interviews by author, Oakland, May 2002 and January 2003. Palacios is a Latino activist.

2. San Antonio and Fruitvale, two of Oakland's nine CDDs, are not traditionally defined communities but administrative creations. Yet residents in both "districts" identify each by its administrative name. (Subareas are identifiable, but for simplicity I use the overall name.) Also, while each community could be examined separately, they blend in many ways. They share commercial areas, social service agencies, a City Council representative, schools, and a multicultural identity. The racial and ethnic trends, as well as shared local activism surrounding the racial mix, necessitate examining them together. I will refer to them as "San Antonio–Fruitvale" when referring to the combined districts.

3. "History of Fruitvale," César E. Chávez Branch Library, 2001. [www.oaklandlibrary.org/branches/CCB/history/fruitvalehistory] Accessed June 4, 2002.

4. In the later nineteenth century, San Antonio residents included a state senator, two California Supreme Court justices, Gertrude Stein, Jack London, Robert Louis Stevenson, and Francis "Borax" Smith (Snyder 1992).

5. Debate persisted over the future of the Ward building. Preservationists fought various plans to improve the site through the construction of either condominiums or schools. At the time of this writing, the plan being supported by the City Council involves demolishing the structure and building two new schools on the site, complete with soccer fields and playgrounds (Gammon 1999; DeFao 2001).

6. In the early 1970s Oakland's Hell's Angels and Black Panther Party also maintained headquarters in Fruitvale (Alozie 1992).

7. In 1983, the U.S. Department of Health and Human Services identified eighteen counties across the nation as "highly impacted" by refugees, those with high refugee-per-population ratios and refugees collecting welfare; not surprisingly, half of the counties were located in California, and three were Bay Area counties, including Oakland's Alameda County. See "18 Counties Listed As Too 'Impacted' to Take More Refugees," *New York Times*, December 12, 1983.

8. During the last two decades, the Asian population in the districts expanded by over 16,000 residents.

9. Isabel, 1984; Snyder, 1992; personal communication from Laura Counts, *Oakland Tribune* reporter, May 2002.

10. The absolute number of black residents dropped from 29,783 in 1980 to 24,005 in 2000.

11. In the mid-1990s, through a series of community meetings, residents and business leaders generated the concept of changing the name of East Fourteenth to International Boulevard, in an attempt to capitalize on the perceived strength of the cultural and ethnic diversity of the strip. Leaders in the different communities along East Fourteenth viewed the name as a unifying theme and even a catalyst to support economic development and revitalization.

12. U.S. Census Bureau 1990. Immigration data from the 1990s and fieldwork confirm the continuation of these trends.

13. Data indicate that among residents who speak Spanish at home, 22 percent speak English "not well" or "not very well."

14. East Bay Asian Local Development Corporation, 1996:7 (hereafter cited in text as EBALDC).

15. The schools included are eleven elementary schools (Allendale, Bella Vista, Cleveland, Franklin, Fruitvale, Garfield, Hawthorne, Jefferson, La Escuelita, Lazear, and Manzanita), two junior high schools (Calvin Simmons and Roosevelt), and two high schools (Oakland and Dewey/Baymart). Nine of the elementary schools are on year-round schedules.

16. An "English Language Learner" is a student whose primary language is other than English and who also has limited English proficiency.

17. The percentage of households receiving public assistance ranges from a low of 7 to a high of 32 percent. Tracts with a greater number of households receiving public assistance are in the flatlands. The range of residents with less than a high school degree is between 42 and 53 percent in seven tracts in the flatlands of San Antonio and Fruitvale.

18. The report by Wyly and colleagues based its findings on the examination of one tract in the Fruitvale district, ignoring the larger district.

19. In the mid-1990s a national survey of professionally managed apartment complexes ranked the Bay Area at the top of the list of both occupancy and rental costs (Thompson 1996).

20. According to the U.S. Department of Housing and Urban Development, overcrowding occurs when a housing unit contains more than one person per room. Severe overcrowding exists when a unit contains more than 1.5 persons per room (City of Oakland 1994).

21. It does not help that one of the strongest political voices in Oakland is the police officers union. Almost two-thirds of the city's budget goes for law enforcement.

22. This quote and a detailed history of the Kids First! initiative can be found in Themba 1999.

23. One exception is the shopping center called Fruitvale Station. Not to be confused with the Fruitvale BART Transit Village, this shopping area located east of the freeway and near the waterfront contains several national chains, including Starbucks and Hollywood Video.

24. Helen Shor, personal correspondence with the author, April 2003.

25. The infamous "New Chinatown" sign was destroyed when a string of arson-related fires swept through the Eastlake business district between 1997 and 1999. While anxiety producing, the fires did not dampen the resolve of merchants. Most, including Paul Wong, decided to stay and rebuild. While it is speculated

that the fires were the result of gangs persuading merchants to pay protection money, no definitive answers have been forthcoming (Drudis 1999).

26. Community Development Corporation Oral History Project, "Spanish Speaking Unity Council (SSUC)," Pratt Institute Center for Community and Environmental Development, 1997.

27. For example, the Unity Council runs an employment program that mainly serves immigrants. The population includes Latinos and six different Asian groups. The Unity Council also collaborates with Laotian, Vietnamese, and Cambodian agencies.

Conclusion

1. See Cummings 1998 and Ellen 2000 for a more elaborate discussion of freedom-of-choice arguments.

2. Dennis Keating's 1994 study reports that between 1960 and 1965, 159 out of 172 real estate parcels changed hands at least once in East Cleveland. Without any leadership to deal with the issues confronting East Cleveland, the area quickly became resegregated.

3. The legacy of past housing discrimination could contribute to a sense that Jackson Heights is not open to blacks, whether or not current residents feel this way or act in discriminatory ways. I found no evidence of antiblack discrimination; however, perceptions can have the same effect.

4. Ferguson and Dickens suggest that assets in community development take five basic forms: (1) physical capital (e.g., buildings, tools); (2) human capital (e.g., skills, knowledge, confidence); (3) social capital (e.g., norms, understandings, trust); (4) financial capital; and (5) political capital (e.g., capacity to exert political influence) (1999:4–5).

5. The Gay and Lesbian Pride Parade in Jackson Heights is a similar community-building event. While all members of the community may not attend such an event, it represents a commitment to tolerance and diversity.

References

Abrams, Charles. 1955. *Forbidden Neighbors*. New York: Harper and Brothers.

Abu-Lughod, Janet. 1994. *From Urban Village to East Village*. Oxford: Blackwell.

Aguirre, Ben. 2001. "Oakland's Union Point Park Clears Another Hurdle of Red Tape." *Oakland Tribune*. June 10.

Alba, Richard, Nancy Denton, Shu-yin Leung, and John Logan. 1995. "Neighborhood Change under Conditions of Mass Immigration: The New York City Region, 1970–1990." *International Migration Review*. 24(3): 625–656.

Aldrich, Henry. 1975. "Ecological Succession in Racially Changing Neighborhoods: A Review of the Literature." *Urban Affairs Quarterly*. 10(3): 327–348.

Alinsky, Saul. 1972. *Rules for Radicals*. New York: Random House.Allee, Shawn. 2000. "TIF Proposals Put New Urgency in ONE Appeal." *Inside*. Posted August 8. [www.insideonline.com/archives/0802/tif.html] Site accessed June 8, 2001.

Allport, Gordon. 1958. *The Nature of Prejudice*. Garden City, N.Y.: Doubleday Anchor.

Alozie, Emmanuel C. 1992. "City of Change: Fruitvale District: Ripe for Small Business." *Oakland Tribune*. October 5.

Anderson, Martin. 1964. *The Federal Bulldozer: A Critical Analysis of Urban Renewal, 1949–1962*. Cambridge: MIT Press.

Applied Research Center. 1996. *Deliberate Disadvantage: A Case Study of Race Relations in the San Francisco Bay Area*. Oakland, Calif.: Applied Research Center.

Backes, Clarus. 1968. "We Call Them Hillbillies." *Chicago Tribune Magazine*. September 22: 26–27.

Bagwell, Beth. 1982. *Oakland: The Story of a City*. Oakland, Calif.: Oakland Heritage Alliance.

Bailey, Chauncey. 1999. "Fewer Oakland Youth Programs Are Competing for More City Funds." *Oakland Tribune*. May 9.

———. 2001. "U.S. Census: Number of Blacks in Oakland Falling." *ANG Newspapers*. May 18. [www.visitron.com] Accessed May 29, 2001.

Balu, Rekha. 1996. "White Flight Ebbs While Minorities Rise." *Chicago Reporter*. 25(1): 1–15.

Barry, Dan, and Mirta Ojito. 1997. "In Many New York Neighborhoods, Tensions Rise over Immigrant Housing." *New York Times*. July 29.

Bauman, John. 1987. *Public Housing, Race, and Renewal*. Philadelphia: Temple University Press.

Bazeley, Michael. 1995. "Oakland Year-Round Schooling: Stopped in Its Tracks." *ANG Newspapers*. November 20. [www.visitron.com]. Accessed May 21, 2002.

———. 1996. "Advocates for Kids Push Plan: Coalition's Ballot Initiative Would Set Aside Funds for Youth." *Oakland Tribune*. January 14.

Bazzi, Mohamed. 1994. "Jackson Heights: 'Historic' in Making: Community Looks Forward to Past with Landmark Status." *Newsday*. January 30.

———. 1995. "Overlooked Treasures: Landmark Designations Are on the Rise in the 'Forgotten Borough.'" *Newsday*. March 26.

———. 1996. "Brothels Busted: Cops Set Up Raids on Prostitution Houses." *Newsday*. September 2.

———. 1997. "Building on Education: Board Unveils Its Plans for a New Middle School." *Newsday*. May 20.

"Benign Steering and Benign Quotas: The Validity of Race-Conscious Government Policies to Promote Residential Integration." 1980. Comment. *Harvard Law Review*. 93:938–965.

Bennett, Larry. 1991. "Uptown: Port of Entry, Hotbed of Movements, Contested Territory." Report submitted to the Policy Research Action Group. Chicago.

———. 1993. "Rethinking Neighborhoods, Neighborhood Research, and Neighborhood Policy: Lessons from Uptown." *Journal of Urban Affairs*. 15(3): 245–257.

———. 1997. *Neighborhood Politics: Chicago and Sheffield*. New York: Garland.

———. 1999. "The Shifting Terrain of Neighborhood Politics." *Research in Politics and Society*. 7:21–41.

Bernstein, Gail. 1987. "Margate Park—Boom Town in Uptown." *Chicago Tribune*. May 3.

Berry, Brian, Carol Goodwin, R. Lake, and K. Smith. 1976. "Attitudes toward Integration: The Role of Status in Community Response to Racial Change," in Barry Schwartz (ed.), *The Changing Face of the Suburbs*. Chicago: University of Chicago Press.

Binder, Frederick, and David Reimers. 1995. *All the Nations under Heaven*. New York: Columbia University Press.

Blakely, Edward. 1988. A *Community Development Plan for the San Antonio Neighborhoods of East Oakland*. Studio Report: 007b. University of California at Berkeley: Community Development Studio of the Department of City and Regional Planning.

———. 1990. *Fruitvale Community Development Plan*. Oakland Forum Publication: SR-020. University of California at Berkeley: University-Oakland Metropolitan Forum.

Bobo, Lawrence, James Kluegel, and Ryan Smith. 1997. "Laissez-Faire Racism: The Crystallization of a Kinder, Gentler, Antiblack Ideology," in Steven Tuch and Jack Martin (eds.), *Racial Attitudes in the 1990s: Continuity and Change*. Westport, Conn.: Praeger.

Bradburn, Norman, Seymour Sudman, and Galen Gockel. 1971. *Side by Side: Integrated Neighborhoods in America*. Chicago: Quadrangle Books.

Bradbury, Katherine, Karl Case, and Constance Dunham. 1989. "Geographic Patterns of Mortgage Lending in Boston: 1982–1987." *New England Economic Review*. September/October: 3–30.

Bratt, Rachel. 1983. "People and Their Neighborhoods: Attitudes and Policy Implications," in Phillip Clay and Robert Hollister (eds.), *Neighborhood Policy and Planning*. Lexington, Mass.: Lexington Books.

Breslin, Jimmy. 2001. "New York's New Majority." *Newsday*. March 18.

Bruni, Frank, and Deborah Sontag. 1996. "Behind a Suburban Facade in Queens, a Teeming, Angry Urban Arithmetic." *New York Times*. October 8.

Bureau of Citizenship and Immigration Affairs. 2003. *Immigration and Naturalization Legislation from the Statistical Yearbook*. [www.bcis.gov/graphics/shared/aboutus/statistics/legishist/index.htm] Accessed June 26, 2003.

Bureau of National Affairs. 1976. *The Housing and Development Reporter*. Washington, D.C.: Bureau of National Affairs.

Burgess, Ernest. 1928. "Residential Segregation in American Cities." *Annals of the American Academy of Political and Social Science*. 140 (November): 105–115.

Burt, Cecily. 2001. "Census Report Says Latino Population up More Than 69%." *Oakland Tribune*. April 15.

———. 2002. "Fruitvale Village Gets Under Way: BART Development Will Cater to Shoppers." *Oakland Tribune*. May 13.

Butler, Patrick. 1999. "Buena Park Group to Work with Alderman Shiller on Permit Parking." *News-Star/Booster*. October 20. [www.intheloop.net/newsstand/newsstar/102099/BUENA.htm] Accessed June 6, 2001.

Calmore, John. 1995. "Racialized Space and the Culture of Segregation: Hewing a Stone of Hope from a Mountain of Despair." *University of Pennsylvania Law Review*. 143:1233–1273.

———. 2001. "Viable Integration Must Reject the Ideology of 'Assimilation,'" in Chester Hartman (ed.), *Challenges to Equality: Poverty and Race in America*. New York: M. E. Sharpe.

Carter, Dan. 1995. *The Politics of Rage: George Wallace, the Origins of the New Conservatism, and the Transformation of American Politics*. New York: Simon and Schuster.

Cater, Darryl. 2002. "Not Just Black and White: Oak Park, Illinois Grapples with Questions of Diversity." *In These Times*. March 18: 18–20.

Chandler, Mittie Olion. 1992. "Obstacles to Housing Integration Program Efforts," in George Galster and Edward Hill (eds.), *The Metropolis in Black and White: Place, Power, and Polarization*. New Brunswick, N.J.: Rutgers University Press.

Cheng, Mae M. 2001. "In Queens, 'Microcosm of the World'; Areas among Most Diverse in the City." *Newsday*. March 20.

Chew, Jeff. 1991. *Fruitvale: A Neighborhood Commercial Revitalization Plan*. Oakland Forum Publication: SR-021. University of California at Berkeley: University-Oakland Metropolitan Forum.

Chicago Fact Book Consortium. 1984. *Local Community Fact Book: Chicago Metropolitan Area*. Chicago: University of Illinois.

———. 1995. *Local Community Fact Book: Chicago Metropolitan Area, 1990*. Chicago: University of Illinois.

Christiansen, Lynn. 1998. "East Bay Renters at Mercy of Landlords." *ANG Newspapers*. June 28. [www.visitron.com/archives] Accessed June 2, 2002.

Chumsai, Areeya. 1992. "City of Change: San Antonio District: A True Blend of Cultures." *Oakland Tribune*. September 14.

Chung, Andre. 1995. "Low-Income Housing Stirs Debate in Uptown." *Chicago Sun-Times*. March 10.

City of Oakland. 1994. *Population and Housing Trends, 1980–1990*. Working Paper #1. Office of Planning and Building. July.

Clark, William A.V. 1986. "Residential Segregation in American Cities." *Population Research and Policy Review*. 5:95–127.

———. 1993. "Neighborhood Transitions in Multiethnic/Racial Contexts." *Journal of Urban Affairs*. 15(2): 161–172.

Clark, William A.V., and Julian Ware. 1997. "Trends in Residential Integration by Socioeconomic Status in Southern California." *Urban Affairs Review*. 32(6): 825–843.

Clay, Phillip. 1979. "The Processes of Black Suburbanization." *Urban Affairs Quarterly*. 14:405–424.

Cohen, Mark Francis. 1995. "Conformity and Commerce Collide." *New York Times*. September 3.

Condor, Bob. 2000. "A World of Healing in the Babel That Is Uptown: A Children's Clinic Speaks a Universal Language." *Chicago Tribune Magazine*. January 2: 12.

Connolly, Harold X. 1977. *A Ghetto Grows in Brooklyn*. New York: New York University Press.

Coser, Lewis. 1971. *The Functions of Social Conflict*. Glencoe, Ill.: Free Press.

Counts, Laura. 1999. "The Rise, Fall, and Rise Again of an East Bay Neighborhood." *Oakland Tribune*. July 27.

Cross, Robert. 1985. "Famine Gives Chicago's Ethiopians a Hunger for Unity." *Chicago Tribune*. January 6.

Cummings, Scott. 1998. *Left Behind in Rosedale: Race Relations and the Collapse of Neighborhood Institutions*. Boulder, Colo.: Westview Press.

Cutler, David, Edward Glaeser, and Jacob Vigdor. 1999. "The Rise and Decline of the American Ghetto." *Journal of Political Economy*. 107(3): 455–490.

Cuza, Bobby. 2000. "Both a Blessing and Curse: Prosperity Floods Jackson Heights with Traffic and Trash." *Newsday*. December 10.

Dailey, Pat. 1993. "Street of Dreams." *Chicago Tribune*. May 20.

Dane, Stephen. 1991. *A History of Mortgage Lending Discrimination in the United States*. Toledo, Ohio: Dane, Cooper, Straub, Walinski, and Cramer.

DeBat, Don. 1993. "Upscale Rehabs Give Uptown an Uplift." *Chicago Sun Times*. April 9.

DeFao, Janine. 2001. "Ward Demolition Begins Anew: School to Replace Historic Building." *San Francisco Chronicle*. February 6.

DeMarco, Don, and George Galster. 1993. "Prointegrative Policy: Theory and Practice." *Journal of Urban Affairs*. 15:141–160.

Denney, Valerie. 1989. "Neighborhoods: The Gay Factor." *Chicago Enterprise*. December.

Denton, Nancy. 1999. "Half Empty or Half Full: Segregation and Segregated Neighborhoods 30 Years after the Fair Housing Act." *Cityscape: A Journal of Policy Development and Research*. 4(3): 107–122.

Denton, Nancy, and Douglas Massey. 1991. "Patterns of Neighborhood Transition in a Multiethnic World: U.S. Metropolitan Areas, 1970–1980." *Demography*. 28(1): 41–63.

Deutsch, Claudia. 1994. "Commercial Property/Flushing's Chinatown: A Chinatown with a Polyglot Accent." *New York Times*. October 2.

Dobmeyer, Doug. 1996. "Events and Groups Worth Noting." *Poverty Issues . . . Date-*

line Illinois. October 7. 1(17). [www.civic.net/civic-values.archive/199610/msg00160.html] Accessed February 2, 2001.

Drake, St. Clair, and Horace Cayton. 1945. *Black Metropolis.* New York: Harcourt, Brace.

Drudis, Eric. 1999. "Oakland Arsonist Still on the Loose: New Chinatown Merchants Impatient for Answers." *San Francisco Examiner.* April 19.

Duncan, Otis, and Beverly Duncan. 1957. *The Negro Population of Chicago.* Chicago: University of Chicago Press.

Ealey, Lakisha. 1996. "Kids First!" *Power.* Oakland: Youth of Oakland United.

East Bay Asian Local Development Corporation [EBALDC]. 1996. *Lower San Antonio Community Profile.* Oakland: EBALDC.

———. 1997. *Make It Happen: Lower San Antonio Neighborhood Plan.* Oakland: EBALDC.

Eisendrath, John. 1983. "Slim Coleman: The Poet, the Politician, and the Punk." *Chicago Reader.* December 2.

Eisinger, Peter. 2000. "The Politics of Bread and Circuses: Building the City for the Visitor Class." *Urban Affairs Quarterly.* 35(3): 316–334.

Ellen, Ingrid. 1998. "Stable Racial Integration in the Contemporary United States: An Empirical Overview." *Journal of Urban Affairs.* 20(1): 27–42.

———. 2000. *Sharing America's Neighborhoods: The Prospects for Stable Racial Integration.* Cambridge: Harvard University Press.

Ellison, Christopher, and Daniel Powers. 1994. "The Contact Hypothesis and Racial Attitudes among Black Americans." *Social Science Quarterly.* 75(2): 385–400.

Erasmus, C. 1968. "Community Development and the Encogido Syndrome." *Human Organization.* 27(1): 65–74.

Farley, Reynolds, and Walter Allen. 1987. *The Color Line and the Quality of Life in America.* New York: Russell Sage.

Farley, Reynolds, and William Frey. 1994. "Changes in Segregation of Whites from Blacks during the 1980s." *American Sociological Review.* 59(1): 23–45.

Farley, Reynolds, Howard Schuman, Suzanne Bianchi, Diane Colasanto, and Shirley Hatchett. 1978. "Chocolate City, Vanilla Suburbs: Will the Trend toward Racially Separate Communities Continue?" *Social Science Research.* 7: 319–44.

Farley, Reynolds, Charlotte Steeh, Tara Jackson, Maria Krysan, and Keith Reeves. 1994. "Stereotypes and Segregation: Neighborhoods in the Detroit Area." *American Journal of Sociology.* 100(3): 750–780.

Ferguson, Ronald, and William Dickens (eds.). 1999. *Urban Problems and Community Development.* Washington, D.C.: Brookings Institution.

Ferman, Barbara, Theresa Singleton, and Don DeMarco. 1998. "West Mount Airy, Philadelphia." *Cityscape: A Journal of Policy Development and Research.* 4(2): 29–59.

Fischer, Claude. 1984. *The Urban Experience.* 2d edition. New York: Harcourt Brace Jovanovich.

Fisher, Ian. 1993. "Jackson Heights Streets Familiar to Drug Cartels." *New York Times.* May 11.

Fisher, Robert. 1994. *Let the People Decide: Neighborhood Organizing in America.* New York: Twayne.

Fix, Michael, and Jeffrey Passel. 1994. *Immigration and Immigrants: Setting the Record Straight.* Washington, D.C.: Urban Institute.

Franczyk, Jean. 1989. "Southeast Asians Pay the Price for Success Image of Other Asians." *Chicago Reporter.* January: 3–6.

Fremon, David. 1990. "Chicago's Uptown: Struggling or Thriving on Diversity?" *Illinois Issues.* November: 25.

Frey, William. 1979. "Central City White Flight: Racial and Nonracial Causes." *American Sociological Review.* 44:425–448.

———. 1980. "Black In-Migration, White Flight, and the Changing Economic Base of the Central City." *American Journal of Sociology.* 85:1396–1417.

———. 1991. "Are Two Americas Emerging?" *Population Today* 19(1): 6–8.

———. 1998. "The Diversity Myth." *American Demographics.* 20(6): 38–43.

———. 2000. "The New Urban Demographics: Race, Space, and Boomer Aging." *Brookings Review.* 18(3): 18–21.

Frey, William, and Ross DeVol. 2000. *America's Demography in the New Century: Aging Baby Boomers and New Immigrants as Major Players.* Policy Brief No. 9. Santa Monica, Calif.: Milken Institute. March 8.

Frey, William, and Reynolds Farley. 1996. "Latino, Asian, and Black Segregation in U.S. Metropolitan Areas: Are Multiethnic Metros Different?" *Demography.* 33(1): 35–50.

Fund for an Open Society. 2003. *About Us.* [www.opensoc.org/] Accessed January 8, 2004.

Galster, George. 1987. "Federal Fair Housing Policy in the 1980s." Working Paper No. 5. Cambridge: MIT Center for Real Estate Development.

———. 1990. "Racial Discrimination in Housing Markets during the 1980s: A Review of the Audit Evidence." *Journal of Planning Education and Research.* 9:165–175.

———. 1992. "The Case for Residential Integration," in George Galster and Edward Hill (eds.), *The Metropolis in Black and White.* New Brunswick, N.J.: Rutgers University Press.

———. 1998. "A Stock/Flow Model of Defining Racially Integrated Neighborhoods." *Journal of Urban Affairs.* 20(1): 43–51.

Galster, George, and Mark Keeney. 1988. "Race, Residence, Discrimination, and Economic Opportunity." *Urban Affairs Quarterly.* 24:87–117.

Gammon, Robert. 1999. "Ward's Site for School Solidified: School's Needs Topple Wards." *ANG Newspapers.* November 26. [www.visitron.com] Accessed May 29, 2002.

Gans, Herbert. 1967. *The Levittowners.* New York: Pantheon.

Gardiner, Sean. 1998. "Prostitution Raids Nab 100." *Newsday.* October 30.

Gelfand, Mark. 1975. *A Nation of Cities: The Federal Government and Urban America, 1933–1965.* New York: Oxford University Press.

Gitlin, Todd, and Nanci Hollander. 1970. *Uptown: Poor Whites in Chicago.* New York: Harper and Row.

Glaeser, Edward, and Jacob Vigdor. 2001. *Racial Segregation in the 2000 Census: Promising News.* Brookings Institution. April. [www.brook.edu/dybdocroot/es/urban/census/glaeser.pdf] Accessed June 23, 2002.

Goering, John. 1978. "Neighborhood Tipping and Racial Transition: A Review of

Social Science Evidence." *Journal of the American Institute of Planners*. 44(1): 68–78.

Goetze, Rolf. 1979. *Understanding Neighborhood Change: The Role of Expectations in Urban Revitalization*. Cambridge, Mass.: Ballinger.

Goldberger, Paul. 1983. "Utopia by Bus and Subway," in Goldberger (ed.), *On the Rise*. New York: Times Books.

Goldman, Ari. 1989. "For Immigrants, a Four-Language Church." *New York Times*. November 23.

Goodwin, Carole. 1979. *The Oak Park Strategy*. Chicago: University of Chicago Press.

Gordon, David. 1978. "Capitalist Development and the History of American Cities," in William Tabb and Larry Sawyers (eds.), *Marxism and the Metropolis*. 2d edition. New York: Oxford University Press.

Gordy, Molly. 1996. "Stomping the Launder Trail: Funnel Pinched Off thru Crackdown on Cash-Wiring Outlets." *New York Daily News*. December 23.

Gorman, Anna. 1997. "Fruitvale BART Transit Village Plan Complete: Restaurants, Stores Aim to Revitalize Area's Future." *Oakland Tribune*. August 24.

Graber, Alice. 1968. "Hank Williams 'Lives' in Uptown." *North Town*. October 1.

Gray, Thomas. 1970. "Planned Razing to Displace Unknown Number in Uptown." *Chicago Sun-Times*. June 23.

Greenberg, Stephanie. 1981. "Industrial Location and Ethnic Residential Patterns in an Industrializing City," in T. Hershberg (ed.), *Philadelphia: Work, Space, Family, and Group Experience in the Nineteenth Century*. New York: Oxford University Press.

Gregory, Steven. 1998. *Black Corona*. Princeton, N.J.: Princeton University Press.

Grossman, James. 1989. *Land of Hope: Chicago, Black Southerners, and the Great Migration*. Chicago: University of Chicago Press.

Gust, Kelly. 1988. "Fruitvale." *Oakland Tribune*. November 11.

Harris, Sandra Ann. 1996. "The New Chinatown: Along Oakland's East 14th, Asian Entrepreneurs Set Up Shop, Reviving a Once-Rundown Area." *San Francisco Examiner*. July 22.

Harrison, Bennett, and Barry Bluestone. 1988. *The Great U-Turn*. New York: Basic Books.

Harrison, Roderick, and Claudette Bennett. 1995. "Racial and Ethnic Diversity," in R. Farley (ed.), *State of the Union: America in the 1990s*. Volume 2: *Social Trends*. New York: Russell Sage.

Hartman, Chester. 2001. *Challenges to Equality: Poverty and Race in America*. New York: M. E. Sharpe.

Hartstein, Larry. 1996. "Check Out the Many Faces of Uptown: An International Neighborhood—No Passports Needed." *Chicago Tribune*. April 6.

Hawley, Amos. 1950. *Human Ecology: A Theory of Community Structure*. New York: Roland Press.

———. 1986. *Human Ecology: A Theoretical Essay*. Chicago: University of Chicago Press.

Haymes, Stephen. 1995. *Race, Culture, and the City*. New York: SUNY Press.

Hein, Rich. 1995. "Uptown Revival: This Neighborhood Wants a Remake. Can It Please All the Players?" *Chicago Sun-Times*. March 12.

Hein, Rich, and Ellen Domke. 1999. "Valkommen to Andersonville: Swedish Culture—and the Housing Market—Thrive in This Chicago Neighborhood." *Chicago Sun-Times*. October 3.

Helper, Rose. 1969. *Racial Policies and Practices of Real Estate Brokers*. Minneapolis: University of Minnesota Press.

———. 1986. "Success and Resistance Factors in the Maintenance of Racially Mixed Neighborhoods," in John Goering (ed.), *Housing Desegregation and Federal Policy*. Chapel Hill: University of North Carolina Press.

Hepp, Rick. 2001. "Some Uptown Residents Feeling the Pinch." *Chicago Tribune*. June 10.

Hershberg, Theodore. 1981. "Free Blacks in Antebellum Philadelphia: A Study of Ex-Slaves, Freeborn, and Socioeconomic Decline," in Hershberg (ed.), *Philadelphia: Work, Space, Family, and Group Experience in the Nineteenth Century*. New York: Oxford University Press.

Hirsch, Arnold. 1983. *Making the Second Ghetto*. Chicago: University of Chicago Press.

Hodgdon, Peter. 1996. "Visions of a Fruitvale Plaza: Spanish Council Sees Big Potential." *Oakland Tribune*. March 27.

Holmes, Stanley. 1992. "Garden Delights: Move to Preserve Historic Area." *Newsday*. July 5.

Horton, John. 1995. *The Politics of Diversity*. Philadelphia: Temple University Press.

Howell, Ron. 1999a. "The Faces of Tomorrow: A Widening Flow of Immigrants and Ethnic Groups Is Transforming the Borough into a Global Society." *Newsday*. January 3.

———. 1999b. "Immigrant Housing: The Stories of 35-50." *Newsday*. November 29.

Hudson, Victoria. 1996. "Measure for Kids Closer to Ballot." *Oakland Tribune*. June 11.

———. 1998. "With Kids First Locked in Limbo, Who's to Blame? $4.2 Million Left, Let the Accusations Fly." *Oakland Tribune*. April 15.

Hula, Richard. 1981. "Public Needs and Private Investment: The Case of Home Credit." *Social Science Quarterly*. 62:685–703.

Hunter, Albert. 1978. "Symbols of Incivility: Social Disorder and Fear of Crime in Urban Neighborhoods." Paper presented at the annual meeting of the American Society of Criminology, Dallas, Texas. November.

Isabel, Lonnie. 1984. "Brooklyn: An Oakland Neighborhood's Rebirth." *Oakland Tribune*. November 25.

Jackman, Mary, and Marie Crane. 1986. "Some of My Best Friends Are Black: Interracial Friendship and Whites' Racial Attitudes." *Public Opinion Quarterly*. 50:459–486.

Jackson, Kenneth. 1985. *Crabgrass Frontier*. New York: Oxford University Press.

Jacobs, Jane. 1961. *The Death and Life of Great American Cities*. New York: Vintage.

Jacoby, Tamar. 2000. *Someone Else's House: America's Unfinished Struggle for Integration*. New York: Basic Books.

Jakubs, John. 1986. "Recent Racial Segregation in the U.S. SMSAs." *Urban Geography*. 7:146–163.

Janowitz, Morris. 1967. *The Community Press in an Urban Setting*. 2d. edition. Chicago: University of Chicago Press.

"January Home Sales Soar in Cook County." 1996. *Lerner Booster*. March 13: 14.

Jargowsky, Paul. 1997. *Poverty and Place: Ghettos, Barrios, and the American City*. New York: Russell Sage.

Jones-Correa, Michael. 1998. *Between Two Nations: The Political Predicament of Latinos in New York City*. Ithaca: Cornell University Press.

Joravsky, Ben. 1989. "Low-Income Housing: A Big Deal in Uptown. *Chicago Reader*. December 8.

———. 1999. "Bad for Business: As TIFs Blossom across the City, Small Merchants Are Dying on the Vine." *Chicago Reader*. September 7: 5–7.

Juárez Robles, Jennifer. 1988. "The Uptown Gamble." *Chicago Reporter*. Special Issue. 17(11): 1–11.

Judd, Dennis, and Todd Swanstrom. 1998. *City Politics: Private Power and Public Policy*. 2d edition. New York: Longman.

Kalita, S. Mitra. 2000a. "Crusader's Lasting Impression: de Dios' Death 8 Years Ago Led to Improvements in Jackson Heights." *Newsday*. March 28.

———. 2000b. "A Time to Celebrate: Religion, Commerce Bring Groups Together." *Newsday*. October 26.

Kanigel, Rachele. 1995. "Group Aims to Renew Fruitvale." *Oakland Tribune*. May 21.

Karatzas, Daniel. 1992. *Jackson Heights: A Garden in the City*. New York: Jackson Heights Beautification Group.

Kasher, Steven. 1996. *Civil Rights Movement: A Photographic History, 1954–68*. New York: Abbeyville Press.

Kasinitz, Philip, Mohamad Bazzi, and Randal Doane. 1998. "Jackson Heights, New York." *Cityscape: A Journal of Policy Development and Research*. 4(2): 161–177.

Kearney-King, J., and H. Marquis. 1989. "Freedom of Choice versus Integration Maintenance." *Trends in Housing*. 28:16–17.

Keating, Dennis. 1994. *The Suburban Racial Dilemma*. Philadelphia: Temple University Press.

Keating, Dennis, and Janet Smith. 1996. "Neighborhoods in Transition," in Dennis Keating, Norman Krumholtz, and Philip Star (eds.), *Revitalizing Urban Neighborhoods*. Lawrence: University of Kansas Press.

Kennedy, Randall. 1996. "On Racial Integration." *Dissent*. 43 (Summer): 47–52.

Khandewal, Madhulika S. 1994. "Spatial Dimensions of Indian Immigrants in New York City, 1965–1990," in Peter van der Veer (ed.), *Nation and Migration: The Politics of Space in the South Asia Diaspora*. Philadelphia: University of Pennsylvania Press.

Killorin, Jessica. 1995. "San Antonio Eyesore Now Pristine Housing." *Oakland Tribune*. March 13.

Kim, Jungwon. 1997. "A Heavy Toll: Out-Call Sex Industry a Nightmare for Women." *Newsday*. September 19.

Kirby, Michael. 1998. "Vollintine-Evergreen, Memphis." *Cityscape: A Journal of Policy Development and Research*. 4(2): 61–87.

Kleine, Ted. 1998a. "Down on Uptown: Inside the Mysterious Shrinking Neighborhood." *Chicago Reader*. April 3.

———. 1998b. "Moving Plea: Tenants Forced Out by Rehabbing Are Given Little Notice." *Chicago Reader*. June 26.

————. 1999. "Radical Chick." *Chicago Reader*. April 2.

Krivo, Lauren, and Robert Kaufman. 1999. "How Low Can It Go: Declining Black-White Segregation in a Multiethnic Context." *Demography*. 36(1): 93–109.

Kuchinskas, Susan. 1995. "Transforming Neighborhoods: Nonprofit, Community-based Developers Plan for the Future." *San Francisco Examiner*. November 26.

Kusmer, Kenneth. 1976. *A Ghetto Takes Shape: Black Cleveland, 1870–1930*. Urbana: University of Illinois Press.

Lake, Robert. 1981. *The New Suburbanites*. New Brunswick, N.J.: Rutgers University Center for Urban Policy Research.

Lauber, Daniel. 1991. "Racially Diverse Communities: A National Necessity," in Philip Nyden and Wim Wiewel (eds.), *Challenging Uneven Development: An Urban Agenda for the 1990s*. New Brunswick, N.J.: Rutgers University Press.

Lauerman, Connie. 1999. "Taste of Asia." *Chicago Tribune*. July 25.

LeDuff, Charlie. 1998. "Cruising the Corridor." *New York Times*. February 1.

Lee, Barrett, and Peter Wood. 1990. "The Fate of Residential Integration in American Cities: Evidence from Racially Mixed Neighborhoods, 1970–1980." *Journal of Urban Affairs*. 12(4): 425–436.

————. 1991. "Is Neighborhood Succession Place Specific?" *Demography*. 28(1): 21–40.

Lee, Mi Yeong. 1989. *Southeast Asian Small Businesses and Community Economic Development*. Working Paper No. 1989-09. University of California at Berkeley: University-Oakland Metropolitan Forum.

Leigh, Wilhelmina, and James McGhee. 1986. "A Minority Perspective on Residential Racial Integration," in John Goering (ed.), *Housing Desegregation and Federal Policy*. Chapel Hill: University of North Carolina Press.

Lemann, Nicholas. 1992. *The Promised Land*. New York: Vintage Books.

Lerman, Sharon. 1998. "East Lake Markets Mirror Area's Diverse Population." *Oakland Tribune*. May 23.

Levavi, Peter. 1996. "Citywide CDCs: Chicago's CDCs Increase Efficiency." *Shelterforce*. May/June.

Lewis, Dan, and Michael Maxfield. 1980. "Fear in the Neighborhoods." *Journal of Research in Crime and Delinquency*. 17:160–189.

Lieberson, Stanley. 1963. *Ethnic Patterns in American Cities*. New York: Free Press.

————. 1980. *A Piece of the Pie*. Berkeley: University of California Press.

Lifson, Edward. 1995. "Middle-Class Recruiting." *All Things Considered*. National Public Radio. May 13.

Lii, Jane H. 1995. "Landmark Proposal Intensifies Debate over Store Facades." *New York Times*. September 29.

Lin, Jan. 1998. *Reconstructing Chinatown*. Minneapolis: University of Minnesota Press.

Lindsay, James, and Audrey Singer. 2003. "Changing Faces: Immigrants and Diversity in the Twenty-First Century," in Henry Aaron, James Lindsay, and Pietro Nivola (eds.), *Agenda for the Nation*. Washington, D.C.: Brookings Institution Press.

"Living in Greater Chicago." 2000. *The Buyers and Renters Guide!* Chicago: GAMS Publishing.

Logan, John, and Mark Schneider. 1984. "Segregation and Racial Change in American Suburbs." *American Journal of Sociology* 89(4): 875–888.

Lowe, Herbert. 2001. "A Population Jump: Borough's Residents Rose Much Faster Than City's Overall." *Newsday*. March 16.

Machleder, Elaine. 1998. "A 74th Street Boom: Thriving Indian Shops Bring Traffic and Noise." *Newsday*. April 7.

Maly, Michael. 1998. "Racial and Ethnic Diversity in Select U.S. Urban Neighborhoods, 1980 to 1990." Ph.D. dissertation. Loyola University, Chicago.

———. 2000. "The Neighborhood Diversity Index: A Complementary Measure of Racial Residential Settlement." *Journal of Urban Affairs*. 22(1): 37–44.

Marable, Manning. 1992. *The Crisis of Color and Democracy*. Monroe, Maine: Common Courage Press.

Marciniak, Ed. 1981. *Reversing Urban Decline: The Winthrop-Kenmore Corridor in the Edgewater and Uptown Communities of Chicago*. Washington, D.C.: National Center for Urban Ethnic Affairs.

Marcucci, Michelle. 2002. "Why Immigrants Select Oakland—Common Language, Familiar Foods Draw New Citizens." *Oakland Tribune*. March 25.

Marech, Rona. 2002. "San Antonio, Oakland: Flavors Meld in Community East of Lake." *San Francisco Chronicle*. May 31.

Martinez, Michael. 2000. "Another Bad Year for City Schools: More Fail Than in '99 but Not All Lost." *Chicago Tribune*. November 1.

Massey, Douglas. 1996. "The Age of Extremes: Concentrated Affluence and Poverty in the Twenty-first Century." *Demography*. 33(4): 395–412.

———. 1998. "The Social Organization of Mexican Migration to the United States," in David Jacobson (ed.), *The Immigrant Reader*. Oxford: Blackwell.

Massey, Douglas, and Nancy Denton. 1988. "Suburbanization and Segregation in U.S. Metropolitan Areas." *American Journal of Sociology*. 94(3): 592–626.

———. 1993. *American Apartheid*. Cambridge: Harvard University Press.McKinney, Scott, and Ann Schnare. 1989. "Trends in Residential Segregation by Race: 1960–1980." *Journal of Urban Economics*. 26(3): 269–280.

McKnight, Tom. 1995. "Mystery Group Calls for Jackson Hts. Biz Boycott." *Queens Chronicle*. August 31.

Molotch, Harvey. 1972. *Managed Integration*. Berkeley: University of California Press.

Moss, Mitchell, Anthony Townsend, and Emanuel Tobier. 1997. *Immigration Is Transforming New York City*. New York: Taub Urban Research Center, New York University. December.

Mozumder, Suman Guha. 2000. "Jackson Heights Residents Upset over Growing Problems in Shoppers' Heaven." *India in New York*. October 20. [www.indiainnewyork.com/inyk1020/Chronicle/Jacksonhgts] Accessed August 7, 2001.

Murphy, Paul. 1992. "Much Ado over 'Little India' Plan." *India Abroad*. August 14: 28.

Myers, Dowell. 1999. "Immigration: Fundamental Force in the American City." *Housing Facts and Findings*. Washington, D.C.: Fannie Mae Foundation.

Myers, Steven Lee. 1993a. "Bazaar with the Feel of Bombay, Right in Queens." *New York Times*. January 4.

————. 1993b. "Historic Preservation Comes of Age in Queens: Scarcity of Landmarks Reflects Distrust within the Borough and Snobbery outside It." *New York Times*. February 3.

National Advisory Commission on Civil Disorders. 1968. *Report of the National Advisory Commission on Civil Disorders*. Washington, D.C.: U.S. Government Printing Office.

Nelson, Kathryn, Jill Khadduri, Marge Martin, Mark Shroder, Barry Steffen, and David Hardiman. 2000. *Rental Housing Assistance—The Worsening Crisis*. Office of Policy Development and Research. Washington, D.C.: U.S. Department of Housing and Urban Development.

Nyden, Philip, and Joanne Adams. 1996. *Saving Our Homes: The Lessons of Community Struggles to Preserve Affordable Housing in Chicago's Uptown*. A report completed by researchers at Loyola University Chicago in collaboration with the Organization of the NorthEast. Chicago: Loyola University Center for Urban Research and Learning.

Nyden, Philip, Larry Bennett, and Joanne Adams. 1993. *Diversity and Opportunity in a Local Economy: Community Business in Edgewater and Uptown*. A report completed by researchers at Loyola University Chicago in collaboration with the Organization of the NorthEast. Chicago: Loyola University Center for Urban Research and Learning.

Nyden, Philip, John Lukehart, Michael Maly, and William Peterman. 1998. "Neighborhood Racial and Ethnic Diversity in U.S. Cities." *Cityscape: A Journal of Policy Development and Research*. 4(2): 1–17.

Nyden, Philip, Michael Maly, and John Lukehart. 1997. "The Emergence of Stable Racially and Ethnically Diverse Urban Communities: A Case Study of Nine U.S. Cities." *Housing and Policy Debate*. 8(2): 491–534.

Oakland Private Industry Council. 2002. "Developing a World-Class Workforce: Oakland Career Center." [www.oaklandpic.org/Oakland_Career_Center.htm] Accessed August 12, 2002.

Oakland Unified School District. 2001. *District Public Information Data Portal*. [www.dataportal.ousd.k12.ca.us/dataservices/default.asp]. "Site Plans: Key Results and School Report Cards, 2000–2001." Accessed December 30, 2003

————. 2003. *District Public Information Data Portal*. [www.209.77.220.74/portal/profile.asp?curyear=2003] Accessed December 30, 2003.

Obejas, Achy. 1999. "Wilsonian Democracy: Haves and Have-Nots Coexist Warily along Wilson Avenue as Uptown Turns Seriously Upscale." *Chicago Tribune*. December 27.

Olson, David. 2001. "Fruitvale Transit Village Is on Track: Developers Hope to Revitalize a Beleaguered Commercial Zone without Changing Its Character." *East Bay Express*. November 28.

Olson, Laura. 1998. *Mobility Partners Case Study: Fruitvale BART Community Redevelopment Project*. Surface Transportation Policy Project. [www.transact.org/case/fruit.htm] Accessed January 1, 1998.

Olszewski, Lori. 1995. "Oakland Wrestles with Problems in Its Public Schools: Overcrowding in Classrooms Is a Big Issue." *San Francisco Chronicle*. August 7.

Onderdonk, Dudley, Donald DeMarco, and Kathy Cardona. 1977. *Integration in Housing: A Plan for Racial Diversity*. Park Forest, Ill.: Planning Division.

Onishi, Norimitsu. 1996. "In Polyglot Queens, Overflowing Melting Pot Adds to Pupils' Obstacles." *New York Times*. September 6.

Oppenheim, Carol. 1974. "City's Newest Skid Row—Uptown." *Chicago Tribune*. September 29. Osofsky, Gilbert. 1968. *Harlem: The Making of a Ghetto*. New York: Harper Torchbooks.

Ottensmann, John. 1995. "Requiem for the Tipping-Point Hypothesis." *Journal of Planning Literature*. 10(2): 131–141.

Ottensmann, John, and Michael Gleason. 1991. "The Movement of Whites and Blacks into Racially-Mixed Neighborhoods in Nine Metropolitan Areas, 1980." Paper presented at the North American Conference of the Regional Science Association, New Orleans, Louisiana. November 8–10.

———. 1992. "The Movement of Whites and Blacks into Racially Mixed Neighborhoods: Chicago, 1960–1980." *Social Science Quarterly*. 73(3): 645–662.

Ottensmann, John, David Good, and Michael Gleason. 1990. "The Impact of Net Migration on Neighborhood Racial Composition." *Urban Studies*. 27(5): 705–716.

Paoli, Richard. 2000. "It Takes a Village: Financing Incentives, Big Housing Plans in Oakland's Fruitvale District." *San Francisco Chronicle*. November 26.

Patterson, Orlando. 1997. *The Ordeal of Integration*. Washington, D.C.: Civitas.

Payton, Brenda. 1999. "Developing New Voices for Social Change." *Oakland Tribune*. March 4.

Pearlman, Jeffrey. 1999. "At Full Blast: Shooting Outrageously from the Lip, Braves Closer John Rocker Bangs Away at His Favorite Targets: The Mets, Their Fans, Their City and Just About Everyone in It." *SI Online*. December 23. [www.sportsillustrated.cnn.com/features/cover/news/1999/12/22/rocker/] Accessed July 3, 2003.

Petersen, Pier. 2000. "Developer Reveals Plan to Renovate Glodblatt's in Uptown." *Inside*. 33(41): June 21–27.

———. 2001. "Proposed TIF Seeks to Revitalize Uptown without Remaking It." *Inside*. [www.insideonline.com/0110/tif.html] Accessed June 8, 2001.

Phillips, Richard. 1976. "Chinatown North: Can It Revive Area." *Chicago Tribune*. December 12.

Philpott, Thomas. 1978. *The Slum and the Ghetto: Neighborhood Deterioration and Middle-Class Reform, Chicago, 1880–1930*. New York: Oxford University Press.

Pierce, Neal R. 1993. *Citistates*. Washington, D.C.: Seven Locks Press.

Pierre-Pierre, Garry. 1997. "Immigration Fosters Surge in Subway Use." *New York Times*. February 11.

Pindell, James W. 2000. *Immigration Report*. [www.Colombia.edu/~jwp/immigration] Accessed August 1, 2001.

Podgorski, Al. 1993. "Uptown Is Melting Pot for New Family Homes." *Chicago Sun-Times*. July 5.

Polikoff, Alexander. 1985. "What's in a Name?—The Diversity of Racial Diversity Programs." *Issues in Housing Discrimination*. Consultation/Hearing of the U.S. Commission on Civil Rights. Washington, D.C. November 12–13.

———. 1986. "Sustainable Integration or Inevitable Resegregation: The Troubling

Questions," in John Goering (ed.), *Housing Desegregation and Federal Policy*. Chapel Hill: University of North Carolina Press.

Pollard, Kelvin, and William O'Hare. 1999. "America's Racial and Ethnic Minorities." *Population Bulletin*. 54(3): 3–48.

Powledge, Fred. 1964. "'Mason-Dixon Line' in Queens." *New York Times Magazine*. May 10: 12, 94–98.

Rainwater, Lee. 1970. *Behind Ghetto Walls: Black Life in a Federal Slum*. Chicago: Aldine.

Ranney, David. 2002. *Global Decisions, Local Collisions*. Philadelphia: Temple University Press.

Rapkin, Chester, and William Grigsby. 1960. *The Demand for Housing in Racially Mixed Areas*. Berkeley: University of California Press.

Reed, Danielle. 2000. "Housing Boom in New Hot Nabes." *New York Daily News*. March 16. Reider, Jonathan. 1985. *Canarsie: The Jews and Italians of Brooklyn against Liberalism*. Cambridge: Harvard University Press.

Rhomberg, Christopher. 1996. "The Consequences of Collective Action: Ethnicity, Class, Race, and Social Movements in Oakland, California, 1930–1970." Ph.D. dissertation. University of California–Berkeley.

———. 2004. *No There There: Race, Class, and the Struggle for Political Community in Oakland*. Berkeley: University of California Press.

Richie, Winston. 1990. "Pro-Integrative Policy and Incentives." Paper presented at the National Conference of the National Federation for Neighborhood Diversity. Cleveland. June 15.

Right-to-Know Network. 1999. A Copy of the Federal Financial Institutions Examination Council's Home Mortgage Disclosure Act (HMDA) database, 1992–1996. Washington, D.C.: OMB Watch and Unison Institute. [www.rtk.com] Accessed July 20, 1999.

Robinson, Jerry. 1989. "The Conflict Approach," in James Christenson and Jerry Robinson (eds.), *Community Development in Perspective*. Ames: Iowa State University Press.

Rohrig, Carolyne. 1998. "Las Bougainvilleas Offers Quiet Senior Living in Fruitvale's Heart." *ANG Newspapers*. April 30 [www.206.169.18.209/ Ang1998\ Ang1998_data\30apr98\ANG\bouganvi.htm] Accessed August 8, 2002.

Rosenbaum, James, Susan J. Popkin, Julie E. Kaufman, and Jennifer Rusin. 1991. "Social Integration of Low-Income Black Adults in Middle-Class White Suburbs." *Social Problems*. 38(4): 448–461.

Rozhon, Tracie, and N. Kleinfield. 1995. "Getting into Co-ops: The Money Bias." *New York Times*. October 31.

Rubinowitz, Leonard, and James Rosenbaum. 2000. *Crossing the Class and Color Lines*. Chicago: University of Chicago Press.

Rudwick, Elliot. 1964. *Race Riot in East St. Louis: July 2, 1917*. Urbana: University of Illinois Press.

Saltman, Juliet. 1990. *A Fragile Movement: The Struggle for Neighborhood Stabilization*. New York: Greenwood Press.

Sanders, Marion. 1970. *The Professional Radical: Conversations with Saul Alinsky*. New York: Harper and Row.

Sanjek, Roger. 1998. *The Future of Us All: Race and Neighborhood Politics in New York City*. Ithaca: Cornell University Press.

Santiago, Anne. 1991. "The Spatial Dimensions of Ethnic and Racial Stratification." Research Report No. 91-230. Ann Arbor: University of Michigan Population Studies Center.

Sassen, Saskia. 1992. *The Global City: New York, London, and Toyko*. Princeton, N.J.: Princeton University Press.

———. 1998a. *Globalization and Its Discontents*. New York: New Press.

———. 1998b. *The Mobility of Capital*. Cambridge: Cambridge University Press.

———. 2000. *Cities in a World Economy*. 2d edition. Thousand Oaks, Calif.: Pine Forge Press.

Saunders, Jeffrey. 1995. "Why Landmarking Is Good for You." *The Telegraph: The Newsletter of the Queensborough Preservation League*. 1(2).

Schelling, Thomas. 1971. "Dynamic Models of Segregation." *Journal of Mathematical Sociology*. 1:143–186.

———. 1972. "A Process of Residential Segregation: Neighborhood Tipping," in Anthony Pascal (ed), *Racial Discrimination in Economic Life*. Lexington, Mass.: Lexington.

Schmidley, Dianne. 2001. *Profile of the Foreign-born Population in the United States: 2000*. U.S. Census Bureau, Current Population Reports, Series P23–206. Washington, D.C.: U.S. Government Printing Office.

Schmidley, Dianne, and Campbell Gibson. 1999. *Profile of the Foreign-born Population in the United States: 1997*. U.S. Census Bureau, Current Population Reports, Series P23–195. Washington, D.C.: U.S. Government Printing Office.

Schorr, Mark. 1978. "Gunfights in the Cocaine Corral." *New York*. September 25: 48–54.

Schuman, Howard, Charlotte Steeh, and Lawrence Bobo. 1985. *Racial Attitudes in America*. Cambridge: Harvard University Press.

Serant, Claire. 1996. "Heightened Crime Awareness: Group Takes Aim at Violence in Gay World of Jackson Heights." *New York Daily News*. July 21.

Shabecoff, Alice, and Paul Brophy. 1996. "The Soul of the Neighborhood." *Shelterforce*. May/June. [www.nhi.org/online/issues/87/slneighbhd.html] Accessed August 4, 2003.

Shlay, Ann. 1989. "Financing Community: Methods for Assessing Residential Credit Disparities, Market Barriers, and Institutional Reinvestment." *Journal of Urban Affairs*. 11(3): 201–223.

Shulka, Sandhya. 1999. "New Immigrants, New Forms of Transnational Community: Post-1965 Indian Migrations." *Amerasia Journal*. 25(3): 19–36.

Sigelman, Lee, Timothy Bledsoe, Susan Welch, and Michael Combs. 1996. "Making Contact? Black-White Social Interaction in an Urban Setting." *American Journal of Sociology*. 101(5): 1306–1332.

Skogan, Wesley, and Michael Maxfield. 1981. *Coping with Crime*. Beverly Hills, Calif.: Sage.

Slatin, Peter. 1994. "A Landmark Agreement: Many Merchants Back Preservation." *Newsday*. March 26.

Smith, Janet. 1996. "Interpreting Neighborhood Change." Ph.D. dissertation. Cleveland State University.

Smith, Neil. 1996. *The New Urban Frontier: Gentrification and the Revanchist City.* New York: Routledge.

Smith, Richard. 1993. "Creating Stable Racially Integrated Communities." *Journal of Urban Affairs.* 15(2): 115–140.

———. 1998. "Discovering Stable Racial Integration." *Journal of Urban Affairs.* 20(1): 1–25.

Snyder, Bill. 1992. "City of Change: Newcomers Transforming the City of Oakland Economically, Socially, Culturally, and Politically." *Oakland Tribune.* September 13.

Sontag, Deborah. 1997. "Captive in Queens: Dozens of Deaf Immigrants Discovered in Forced Labor." *New York Times.* July 20.

Sørenson, Annemette, Karl Taeuber, and Leslie Hollingsworth. 1975. "Indexes of Residential Segregation for 109 Cities in the United States, 1940 to 1970." *Sociological Focus.* 8:125–142.

Spain, Selena. 1998. *Lower San Antonio Welfare to Work Partnership: Focus Group Results.* Oakland, Calif.: National Economic Development and Law Center.

Spear, Allan. 1967. *Black Chicago: The Making of the Negro Ghetto, 1890–1920.* Chicago: University of Chicago Press.

Squires, Greg. 1994. *Capital and Communities in Black and White.* New York: SUNY Press.

———. 1996. "Friend or Foe? The Federal Government and Community Reinvestment," in Dennis Keating, Norman Krumholz, and Philip Star (eds.), *Revitalizing Urban Neighborhoods.* Lawrence: University Press of Kansas.

Squires, Greg, William Velez, and Karl Taeuber. 1991. "Insurance Redlining, Agency Location, and the Process of Urban Disinvestment." *Urban Affairs Quarterly.* 26:567–588.

Stallone, Steve. 1993. "Clout without Bite." *San Francisco Bay Guardian.* October 6.

Steinhorn, Leonard, and Barbara Diggs-Brown. 1999. *By the Color of Our Skin.* New York: E. P. Dutton.

Stuenkel, Nancy. 1993. "HUD Helps Tenants to Buy Their Building." *Chicago Sun-Times.* October 7.

Sugden-Castillo, Michelle. 1996. *San Antonio Neighborhood Analysis: Community Information, Resources, and Recommendations.* Working Paper No. 33. University of California at Berkeley: University-Oakland Metropolitan Forum. Spring.

Suro, Roberto. 1998. *Strangers among Us: Latino Lives in a Changing America.* New York: Vintage.

Suttles, Gerald. 1968. *The Social Order of the Slum.* Chicago: University of Chicago Press.

———. 1972. *The Social Construction of Communities.* Chicago: University of Chicago Press.

Taeuber, Karl, and Alma Taeuber. 1965. *Negroes in Cities.* Chicago: Aldine.

Tardy, Marcella. 2000. "Wilson TIF Gets OK from Panel." *Chicago News-Star.* December 20.

"Task Force Tackles Social, Economic Issues along Lawrence Avenue." 1996. *Lerner Booster.* April 16: 15.

Taub, Richard, Garth Taylor, and Jan Dunham. 1984. *Paths of Neighborhood Change.* Chicago: University of Chicago Press.

Themba, Makani. 1999. *Making Policy, Making Change: How Communities Are Taking Law into Their Own Hands.* Berkeley, Calif.: Chardon Press.

Theodorson, George (ed). 1982. *Urban Patterns.* University Park: Pennsylvania State University Press.

Thernstrom, Stephen, and Abigail Thernstrom. 1997. *America in Black and White.* New York: Simon and Schuster.

Thompson, Chris. 1996. "Tough Times for Oakland Tenants: Vacancy Rates Are Low and Evictions Are at Record Highs While the Possibility of Effective New Tenant Protection Legislation Remains Remote." *East Bay Express.* October 18.

Trotter, Joe William. 1985. *Black Milwaukee.* Urbana: University of Illinois Press.

Turner, Margery Austin, Raymond Struyk, and John Yinger. 1991. *Housing Discrimination Study.* Washington, D.C.: Department of Housing and Urban Development.

U.S. Bureau of the Census. 1980. *1980 Census of Population: General Population Characteristics for Metropolitan Areas.* Washington, D.C.: Government Printing Office.

———. 1990. *1990 Census of Population: General Population Characteristics for Metropolitan Areas.* Washington, D.C.: Government Printing Office.

———. 2000. *Census 2000 Summary File STF 1.* [www.census.gov] Accessed December 1, 2002.

U.S. Department of Education. 2000. National Center for Education Statistics. Common Core of Data Program. Public Elementary/Secondary School Universe Survey Data. [nces.ed.gov/ccd/] Accessed June 11, 2000.

U.S. Department of Housing and Urban Development. 2000. *The State of the Cities 2000: Megaforces Shaping the Future of the Nation's Cities.* Washington, D.C.: Department of Housing and Urban Development.

Unity Council. 2000. "History of the Unity Council." [www.unitycouncil.org] Accessed November 11, 2001.

———. 2002. "Union Point Park Master Plan." [www.unitycouncil.org/html/masterplantext.html] Accessed August 8, 2002.

Urban Institute. 1991. *Housing Discrimination Study: Methodology and Data Documentation.* Washington, D.C.: Department of Housing and Urban Development, Office of Policy Development and Research.

Urban Strategies Council. 1996. *Call to Action: An Oakland Blueprint for Youth Development.* Oakland, Calif.: Urban Strategies Council.

Valent, Edward, and Gregory Squires. 1998. "Sherman Park, Milwaukee." *Cityscape: A Journal of Policy Development and Research.* 4(2): 105–130.

Varghese, Romy. 2001. "Thousands Watch Gay Pride Parade." *Newsday.* June 4.

Vecsey, George. 1994. "India Casts Its Subtle Spell on Queens." *New York Times.* August 19.

Waldinger, Roger. 1996. *Still the Promised City.* Cambridge: Harvard University Press.

Washington, James Melvin (ed.). 1986. *A Testament of Hope: The Essential Writings and Speeches of Martin Luther King, Jr.* San Francisco: HarperCollins.

Wells, Stacy. 1998. "East Lake Area Celebrates Unity: Merchants' Efforts Pay Off." *ANG Newspapers.* June 11. [www.visitron.com] Accessed July 11, 2002.

White, Michael. 1980. *Urban Renewal and the Residential Structure of the City*. Chicago: Community and Family Studies Center.

———. 1986. "Segregation and Diversity: Measures in Population Distribution." *Population Index*. 88:1008–1019.

Wicker, Thomas. 1996. *Tragic Failure*. New York: Morrow.

Wiese, Andrew. 1995. "Neighborhood Diversity: Social Change, Ambiguity, and Fair Housing." *Journal of Urban Affairs* 17(2): 107–129.

Williams, Diana. 1996. "A Lukewarm Goodbye to E. 14th Street: International Boulevard Is New Name—Why Not?" *Oakland Tribune*. May. [www.visitron.com] Accessed July 11, 2002.

Wilson, Terry. 1995. "In Uptown, Condo Buyers Find a Friend." *Chicago Tribune*. April 19.

Wilson, Thomas C. 1996. "Prejudice Reduction or Self-Selection: A Test of the Contact Hypothesis." *Sociological Spectrum*. 16:43–60.

Wilson, William Julius. 1997. *When Work Disappears*. New York: Knopf.

Winnick, Louis. 1990. *New People in Old Neighborhoods*. New York: Russell Sage Foundation.

Wolfe, Eleanor. 1963. "The Tipping Point in Racially Changing Neighborhoods." *Journal of the American Institute of Planners*. 29(3): 217–222.

Wong, William. 1996. "Organizing at Its Most Basic Level." *Oakland Tribune*. [www.visitron.com] Accessed May 13, 2002.

Woods, Katherine. 1998. "Park Hill, Denver." *Cityscape: A Journal of Policy Development and Research*. 4(2): 89–103.

Woods, Semion. 1996. "New Oakland Laws Unfair to Youth." *Power*. Oakland: Youth of Oakland United.

Woods-Jones, Dezie. 1996. "Celebrating Our Diversity—Respecting Our Differences." *Oakland Tribune*. April. [www.visitron.com] Accessed June 28, 2002.

Woodson, R. L. 1988. "Integration Maintenance: Noble Intentions, Ignoble Results." Hearings before the Subcommittee on Civil and Constitutional Rights of the Committee on the Judiciary, U.S. House of Representatives, December 12, 151–154. Washington, D.C.: U.S. Government Printing Office.

Woodstock Institute. 1994. *Focusing In: Indicators of Economic Change in Chicago's Neighborhoods*. Chicago: Woodstock Institute. May.

Wyly, Elvin, Thomas Cooke, Daniel Hammel, Steven Holloway, and Margaret Hudson. 2000. "Ten 'Just-Right' Urban Markets for Affordable Homeownership." Washington, D.C.: Fannie Mae Foundation 2000 Annual Housing Conference.

Yancey, William, Eugene Ericksen, and Richard Juliani. 1976. "Emergent Ethnicity: A Review and Reformulation." *American Sociological Review*. 41:461–491.

Yinger, John. 1996. *Closed Doors, Opportunities Lost*. New York: Russell Sage.

———. 1999. "Sustaining the Fair Housing Act." *Cityscape: A Journal of Policy Development and Research*. 4(3): 93–106.

Younis, Mona. 1998. "San Antonio and Fruitvale." *Cityscape: A Journal of Policy Development and Research*. 4(2): 221–244.

Zukin, Sharon. 1995. *The Cultures of Cities*. London: Blackwell.

Index